W9-ABI-642

JONATHAN WORDSWORTH

# Visionary Gleam

Revolution and Romanticism
1789—1834

JONATHAN WORDSWORTH

# Visionary Gleam

*Forty books from the*
*Romantic period*

Woodstock Books
*London and New York*
1993

First published 1993 by
Woodstock Books
Spelsbury House, Spelsbury, Oxford OX7 3JR
and
Fifth Floor, 387 Park Avenue South
New York, NY 10016—8810

ISBN 1 85477 126 4
Copyright © Woodstock Books 1991, 1992, 1993

Reprinted 1994

Typeset by Keyboard Services, Luton
Printed and bound in Great Britain by
Smith Settle, Otley, West Yorkshire LS21 3JP

★

# Contents

# Contents

# Contents

# Contents

★

# Abbreviations

| | |
|---|---|
| Butler | Butler, James, ed.: William Wordsworth, *The ruined cottage*, Cornell 1979 |
| Griggs | Griggs, E.L., ed.: *Collected letters of Samuel Taylor Coleridge*, 6 vols, Oxford 1956–68 |
| Grosart | Grosart, A.B., ed.: *The prose works of William Wordsworth*, 3 vols, London 1876 |
| Howe | Howe, P.P., ed.: *The works of William Hazlitt*, 21 vols, London 1930–4 |
| Kinsley | Kinsley, J.W., ed.: *The poems and songs of Robert Burns*, 3 vols, Oxford 1968 |
| *Lakes tour* | Gilpin, William: *Observations relative chiefly to picturesque beauty made in the year 1772 on several parts of England, especially the mountains and lakes*, London 1786 |
| Masson | Masson, D., ed.: *Collected writings of Thomas De Quincey*, 14 vols, Edinburgh 1889–90 |
| Morley | Morley, Edith J., ed.: *Henry Crabb Robinson on books and their writers*, 3 vols, London 1938 |
| Patton and Mann | Patton, Lewis and Mann, Peter, eds.: *Coleridge: Lectures 1795 on politics and religion*, Princeton and London 1971 |

## Abbreviations

Sandford          Sandford, M.E.P.: *Thomas Poole and his friends*, 2 vols, London 1888

Tibble            Tibble, J.W. and A., eds.: *The prose of John Clare*, London 1951

Ward              Ward, Aileen, ed.: *Thomas De Quincey, Confesssions of an English opium-eater and other writings*, 1966, reissued New York 1985

★

# Preface

The forty books discussed below augment those brought together in *Ancestral Voices* (1991), enhancing our view of the Romantic period, filling out our awareness of trends, making it a little more possible to arrive at definitions and generalizations that will stand. They include a number of major first editions (*The excursion*, 1814; *Christabel*, 1816; *Endymion*, 1818; *Don Juan*, 1819; *Adonais*, 1821; *Essays of Elia*, 1823; *The shepherd's calendar*, 1827); a number of successes of the day, now less regarded, or disregarded (Holcroft's *Road to ruin*, 1792; Southey's *Thalaba*, 1801; Scott's *Lay of the last minstrel*, 1805; Campbell's *Gertrude of Wyoming*, 1809; Maturin's *Bertram*, 1816); and a number of choice works from the byways of Romanticism: Lamb's *Rosamund Gray*, 1798; Mary Tighe's *Psyche*, 2nd ed., 1811; Frere's *Whistlecraft*, 1818; Wordsworth's *Peter Bell* and Shelley's *Cenci*, 1819; Hazlitt's *Liber amoris*, 1823.

Above all, this collection is rich in the sense it conveys of origins and points of departure. Definitions of the picturesque in Gilpin's *Observations on the river Wye* (1782) lead naturally to Romantic modes of imaginative perception; behind the *Lyrical ballads* experiment with simplicity of diction, spontaneity and depth of emotion, lies the Kilmarnock edition of Burns (1786); the sonnets of Charlotte Smith (5th ed., 1789) and Bowles (1789) establish an elegiac voice that will modulate into the tones of *Tintern abbey* and the great Romantic lyrics of regret. Among political writers, Price (*A discourse on the love of our country*, 1789) provokes Burke to his intemperate *Reflections* and in doing so initiates the Revolution debate; with his experience in republican America behind him, Paine (*Rights of Man*, part I, 1791) reaches out to a new working-class audience; Godwin's *Political justice*, meanwhile (1793), gives hope to intellectuals of the day, Wordsworth and Shelley among them; carrying forward Godwin's ideals into the nineteenth century and the science of factory management, Owen's *New view of society* (3rd ed., 1817) is the work of a capitalist utopian, later caught up in the trades union movement, who will be claimed as a founding-father of British socialism.

Books that help us with our placing of Romantic assumptions are no less significant: Goethe's *Sorrows of Werter* (trans. Malthus, new ed., 1789), offering both the prototype Romantic sensibility and a Wordsworthian animated Nature; *The loves of the plants* (*Botanic garden*, part II, 1789) by Charles Darwin's grandfather, Erasmus, who provided for the Romantics a compendium of scientific knowledge, and would have been utterly unsurprised by Victorian findings on evolution; *Peace and union* (1793), which cost Coleridge's Unitarian mentor, William Frend, his fellowship at Jesus, Cambridge, yet is so modest in its wish to reconcile extremes; Coleridge's opportunist *Fall of Robespierre* (written with Southey, 1794), and *Conciones ad populum* (1795) with its brilliant assessment of French revolutionary leaders and English friends of liberty; the sharp tory satire of Canning and Frere in *Poetry of the Anti-jacobin* (1799); Mant's *Simpliciad* (1808), with its reminder of how entrenched the public was that Wordsworth sought to educate; from the 'teens, *The round table*, with Hazlitt's unrivalled sense of period; and Peacock's exquisite caricatures of Shelley, Coleridge, Byron, in *Nightmare abbey* (1818).

Towards the end of the collection, and the period, come a series of works that in their different ways cast forward. Fifty years before the national parks movement, Wordsworth in *Description of the lakes* (1823) sees the Lake District as 'a sort of national property, in which every man has a right and interest, who has an eye to perceive and a heart to enjoy'; as well as printing for the first time *Julian and Maddalo*, *The witch of Atlas* and *Triumph of life*, Mary Shelley begins in *Posthumous poems* (1824) the process of myth−making that will transform her husband from a blasphemer, 'revolting in principle and morality' (*Edinburgh magazine*), to the 'beautiful and ineffectual angel' perceived by Arnold and the Victorians; Felicia Hemans, who vied with Byron in her day, perfects the dramatic monologue while Browning is yet unknown, veiling in *Records of woman* (1828) the dilemma of an artist who gains success at the expense of love; Tennyson in *Poems chiefly lyrical* (1830) offers his compelling redefinition of Romanticism; and De Quincey in *Klosterheim* (1832) his reworking of the gothic. It is the 21-year-old Tennyson who, with Keats in his thoughts, sounds the end of an era in a voice that is unmistakeably new:

> A spirit haunts the year's last hours
> Dwelling amid these yellowing bowers . . .
>     Heavily hangs the broad sunflower
>         Over its grave i' the earth so chilly;
>     Heavily hangs the hollyhock,
>         Heavily hangs the tigerlily . . .

The essays printed below were written originally as introductions to Woodstock facsimile volumes in the third and fourth series of *Revolution and Romanticism 1789–1834*, published in 1990–1 and 1991–2. They have been revised and are offered, like those of *Ancestral voices* (1991), as a chronological survey of the Romantic period viewed in a selection of outstanding books. Scholarly apparatus has again been kept to a minimum. Page and line references are normally to Woodstock facsimiles (with the pagination of the original editions), and to other volumes and editions of the period. A small number of cited modern texts are listed in the table of abbreviations, pp. xi–xii. Letters, reviews and magazine articles are identified by date.

As before I am grateful especially to James Price, whose creation of *Revolution and Romanticism* has given me the pleasure of writing these essays, and who compiled the index, as well as acting as copy editor. Henry Wordsworth has again given generous help with word-processing, and Walter Bruan kindly read a set of page-proofs. I am grateful to Blanford Parker for making me aware of the presence of Rabelais in the background of Frere's *Whistlecraft*, and should like to record the help I derived from Lorna Clarke's *Ambitious heights* when writing about Felicia Hemans's *Records of woman*.

J.W.

# I

## WILLIAM GILPIN

---

# Observations on the river Wye

*and several parts of South Wales, &c. relative to picturesque beauty;
made in the summer of the year 1770*
1782

'The enchanting beauties of the River Wye', John Thelwall comments at
the start of his essay in the *Monthly magazine* for May 1798,

are by this time pretty generally known among the lovers of the picturesque.
They have acquired a due celebrity from the descriptions of GILPIN, and curiosity
has been inflamed by poetry and by prose, by paintings, prints, and drawings, till
they have been rendered a subject of universal conversation; and an excursion on
the Wye has become an essential part of the education, as it were, of all who
aspire to the reputation of elegance, taste, and fashion.

The *Tours* that established the Reverend William Gilpin as theorist of the
picturesque had been composed in the years 1770–6, then circulated in
manuscript. The *Wye tour*, composed 1770, published 1783 (with a 1782
title–page), was at both stages a prototype. When recording his original
journey from Ross-on-Wye to Bristol, via Tintern and Chepstow,
Gilpin devised the method of combining verbal descriptions with ink-
and-wash drawings that was to be the hallmark of his work. Twelve
years later, when new technology opened up a relatively cheap form of
publication, he chose the *Wye* in preference to the longer and more
complex *Lakes tour* as his experiment in the art of printing in aquatint.

The *Wye tour* was read in manuscript by Thomas Gray shortly before
his death in July 1771. Four years later, the King, the Prince of Wales and
Horace Walpole were among Gilpin's admirers. Publication increased
his growing reputation. Coming in the wake of Burke's *Philosophical
enquiry into the origin of our ideas of the sublime and beautiful* (1757), Gilpin's
theory offered practical hints, personal observations, rather than
academic distinctions. Tourists of the day were told what to look for in

5

the countryside, and how to appreciate what they saw. The connoisseur of natural beauty viewed the natural world as if it were art, valuing it for qualities that he associated with Claude, Gaspard Poussin, Salvator Rosa. If he did not actually make a drawing or watercolour on the spot (outdoor oil-painting in England was rare), he transformed the scenery mentally into a 'correct' view. Some tourists of the late eighteenth century used a concave tinted mirror, or Claude-glass, obtaining the image seen through the wide-angle lens of a modern camera, but having to stand with their backs to the landscape as they did so. Gray, who swore by his glass, memorably fell over backwards while taking a view in Keswick. Gilpin could see the point of such mechanical aids, but on the whole was against them. His concern was to train the eye.

Nature was not to be tamed, as by the landscape-gardener; it was to be seen imaginatively with the vision of the painter who recomposes the 'prospect' in front of him, yet in doing so catches that which is essential. 'Nature is always grand in design', Gilpin comments early in the *Wye tour*, 'but unequal in composition':

> She is an admirable colourist; and can harmonize her tints with infinite variety, and inimitable beauty: but is seldom so correct in composition, as to produce an harmonious whole. Either the foreground, or the background, is disproportioned: or some awkward line runs across the piece: or a tree is ill-placed: or a bank is formal: or something, or other is not exactly what it should be.

It is not that Nature has got it wrong, but that she works on too large a scale. Hers is an immensity 'beyond human conception':

> The artist, in the mean time, is confined to a *span*. He lays down his little rules therefore, which he calls the *principles of picturesque beauty*, merely to adapt such diminutive parts of nature's surfaces to his own eye, as come within its scope. (p. 18)

Early readers of the *Wye tour* were surprised how different the aquatints were from the scenes that were named. Gilpin was equally surprised that anyone might think him a mere topographer. The *Wye* plates, he insisted, were '*general ideas, or illustrations*' – anything but 'exact portraits'. The plate of Tintern abbey from the river is an excellent example. On this occasion it is a work of man, rather than Nature, that is refusing to conform. In place of the blockish upright building that is still to be seen, Gilpin shows a long ruin that harmonizes with the landscape and therefore makes a good picture. It is the letterpress that gives the 'exact portrait':

No part of the ruins of Tintern is seen from the river, except the abbey-church. It has been an elegant Gothic-pile; but it does not make that appearance as a *distant* object, which we expected. Though the parts are beautiful, the whole is ill-shaped. No ruins of the tower are left, which might give form, and contrast to the walls . . . Instead of this, a number of gabel-ends hurt the eye with their regularity; and disgust it by the vulgarity of their shape.

Gilpin has his remedy – not one that a conservationist would now apply, but one that makes sense in terms of the picturesque:

A mallet judiciously used . . . might be of service in fracturing some of them, particularly those of the cross isles, which are not only disagreeable in themselves, but confound the perspective. (pp. 32–33)

Whether or not they 'hurt the eye', the gable-ends of Tintern abbey are obstinately complete and obstinately triangular. They resemble the 'disproportioned' foregrounds and 'ill-placed' trees that have to be corrected in the natural scene. 'He who culls from Nature the most beautiful parts', Gilpin writes in the *Lakes tour*,

a *distance* here, and there a *fore-ground* – combines them artificially, and removing everything offensive, admits only such parts as are *congruous* and *beautiful*, will in all probability, make a much better landscape, than he who takes all as it comes . . .

The artist is to achieve his effects by an imaginative process of conflation and remaking. In the words of Coleridge's definition of the secondary imagination in *Biographia literaria*, he 'dissolves, diffuses, dissipates, in order to recreate':

Trees he may generally plant, or remove, at pleasure. If a withered stump suit the form of his landscape better than the spreading oak, which he finds in Nature, he may make the exchange . . . He may pull up a piece of awkward paling – he may throw down a cottage – he may even turn the course of a road, or a river, a few yards on this side, or that. (*The Lakes tour*, xxvi, xxix)

  Gilpin does not make the great claims for imagination that the Romantics will make, but he is an important forerunner nonetheless. Brought up, like Wordsworth, in Cumbria, he tended in his definitions of the picturesque to favour the sublime against the beautiful – the 'withered stump', against the 'spreading oak'. His readers were trained both to appreciate the grand effects of Nature, and to regard Nature as subordinate to the mind's arranging power. Arriving with his sister at Tintern on 11 July 1798, Wordsworth was inspired to take the further

7

step, create the mind as its own true subject. In doing so he was following the Coleridge of *Frost at midnight*, written five months before. Almost certainly, however, it was Thelwall's powerful account that had brought him to the Wye, and almost certainly the guide he carried with him was Gilpin. Before he and Dorothy reached Bristol on 13 July, Wordsworth, it seems, had composed in his mind the entire 160 lines of *Tintern abbey*. His opening is especially significant:

> Five years have passed; five summers, with the length
> Of five long winters! and again I hear
> These waters, rolling from their mountain-springs
> With a sweet inland murmur. Once again
> Do I behold these steep and lofty cliffs,
> Which on a wild secluded scene impress
> Thoughts of more deep seclusion; and connect
> The landscape with the quiet of the sky.
>
> (ll. 1–8)

Gilpin's method had been to create from the details of a natural scene a picture that was more 'correct'; the process had been imaginative, but correctness was achieved at the expense of fluidity. Wordsworth goes the further stage, creating in poetry an idiom that will convey the still fluid interaction of mind and Nature.

In his creation of 'the picture of the mind' Wordsworth is no less selective than Gilpin. From the *Wye tour* (and personal experience too no doubt) he is aware that the 'wild secluded scene' incorporates much that is 'offensive' and incongruous. The ruin itself houses beggars living in wretchedness and squalor, one of whom Gilpin describes in detail. Within half a mile the industrial revolution obtrudes, in the form of 'great iron-works' that 'introduce noise and bustle into these regions of tranquillity'. In *Tintern abbey* the beggars and their suffering play no part; industry, meanwhile is transmuted, rendered harmonious, with the aid of one of Gilpin's most sensitive observations:

Many of the furnaces, on the banks of the river, consume charcoal, which is manufactured on the spot; and the smoke, which is frequently seen issuing from the sides of the hills; and spreading its thin veil over a part of them, beautifully breaks their lines, and unites them with the sky. (p. 12)

In a single sentence Gilpin offers the source both of Wordsworth's numinous 'wreathes of smoke / Sent up, in silence, from among the trees' (ll. 18–19), and of the cliffs that 'connect / The landscape with the quiet of the sky'.

Gilpin's observation is delicate and pleasing, but response in the picturesque tradition is aesthetic. Wordsworth is talking about harmonies that go deeper. Few would doubt that he has created a new way, or a new sense, of experiencing the natural scene. There is no feeling of strain as he does so; yet his lines, in their fusions and transferences, defy any logic but their own. Cliffs impress thoughts not upon the mind, but on the 'wild secluded scene', and in the process connect the landscape not with the sky, but with its quietness. It is the same with the later passage of *Tintern abbey*:

> I cannot paint
> What then I was. The sounding cataract
> Haunted me like a passion: the tall rock,
> The mountain, and the deep and gloomy wood,
> Their colours and their forms, were then to me
> An appetite: a feeling and a love,
> That had no need of a remoter charm,
> By thought supplied, or any interest
> Unborrowed from the eye.
>
> (ll. 76–84)

The cataract, the tall rock, the mountain, the deep and gloomy wood, are stage-props of the picturesque. 'Their colours and their forms' would have been for Gilpin the raw-materials of a painting. Wordsworth is working in quite another realm. A waterfall, that might have been the centrepiece of a picture (or picturesque description), now has broken free, and has the power to haunt. The metaphor is surprising enough, but we are then told in the simile that follows that the cataract does its haunting 'like a passion' – a human emotion. Rock, mountain and wood are experienced not for themselves, or their pictorial qualities, but as a craving for nourishment, a feeling, a form of love. Henceforward it would be Wordsworth's name rather than Gilpin's that gave Tintern and the Wye their 'due celebrity'.

2

ROBERT BURNS

Poems chiefly in the Scottish dialect
1786

*Poems chiefly in the Scottish dialect*, published in July 1786 when Burns was
twenty-seven, has an excellent claim to be the first work of English
Romantic literature. Blake, who was fourteen months older, had come
into print in 1783 with *Poetical sketches*, but had yet to develop the voice
that we associate (however undefinably) with Romanticism. We
respond in the early Blake to hints of what is to come – just as we
respond to them in Collins or Cowper, or, for that matter, in early
publications of the later Romantics (Wordsworth's *Evening walk*, for
instance, of 1793). In Burns there is from the first something new and
powerfully immediate. Lamb on 10 December 1796 refers to him as 'the
god of my idolatry'. Hazlitt in his *Lectures on the English poets* (1818)
sees in him a Shakespearean 'life of mind':

With but little of [Shakespeare's] imagination or inventive power, he had the
same life of mind: within the narrow circle of personal feelings or domestic
incidents, the pulse of his poetry flows as healthily and vigorously. He had an eye
to see; a heart to feel . . .

Burns did not achieve his effects 'by tinkling siren sounds, or piling up
centos of poetic diction':

for the artificial flowers of poetry, he plucked the mountain-daisy under his feet;
and a field-mouse, hurrying from its ruined dwelling, could inspire him with the
sentiments of terror and pity. (Howe, v, 127–8)

   In his allusion to Aristotle and the *catharsis* of pity and terror, Hazlitt
responds to mock-heroic tones in the poetry – 'The best laid schemes o'
*Mice* an' *Men*, / Gang aft agley' – but at the same time he is alive to the
tenderness underlying Burns's comic exaggeration. In his sympathy
Burns takes us into a world not unlike that of Henryson in his medieval

Scottish version of the Town and Country Mouse. Henryson, though, for all his observation of the ways of animals, is using *prosopopeia*. Both comedy and pathos in his fable derive from the fact that his mice are human: 'My fair sister . . . have me excusit. / This rude dyat and I can not accord.' Burns's mouse stays a mouse:

> Wee, sleeket, cowran, tim'rous *beastie*,
> O, what a panic's in thy breastie!
> Thou need na start awa sae hasty,
>     Wi' bickering brattle!
> I wad be laith to rin an' chase thee,
>     Wi' murd'ring *pattle*!
>
> I'm truly sorry Man's dominion
> Has broken Nature's social union,
> An' justifies that ill opinion,
>     Which makes thee startle,
> At me, thy poor, earth-born companion,
>     An' *fellow-mortal*!
>                                    (pp. 138–9)

In the more solemn tones of Wordsworth's *Ruined cottage*, 'Nature's social union' – so rudely broken as the plough crashes into the mouse's nest – will become 'a bond of brotherhood' between Margaret and her natural surroundings. It is appropriate that the epigraph to this first great Wordsworthian poem of country life should be drawn, in the manuscript of 1798, from Burns's *Epistle to J. Lapraik, an old Scotch bard* (present in the Kilmarnock edition):

> Give me a spark of natures fire,
> 'Tis the best learning I desire . . .
> My Muse though homely in attire
> May touch the heart.
>                         (Butler, pp. 134–5)

Wordsworth, it would seem, has anglicized the poem in his mind, and is quoting from memory – as he does in the Pedlar's important allusion to Burns within the text of *The ruined cottage*:

> My best companions now the driving winds
> And now the 'trotting brooks' and whispering trees,
> And now the music of my own sad steps . . .
>                                         (*ibid*. 62)

The passage to which Wordsworth's misquotation draws attention

11

comes from *Epistle to W. Simpson* in the Kilmarnock *Poems*. It could scarcely be more to the point:

> O NATURE! a' thy shews an' forms
> To feeling, pensive hearts have charms!
> Whether the Summer kindly warms,
>     Wi' life an' light,
> Or Winter howls, in gusty storms,
>     The lang, dark night!
>
> The *Muse*, nae *Poet* ever fand her,
> Till by himsel he learn'd to wander,
> Adown some trottin burn's meander . . .
>
> (p. 212)

To judge from his gothic *Vale of Esthwaite* (1786–7), Wordsworth early 'learn'd to wander' alone, seeking the muse 'in gusty storms, / The lang, dark night'. A letter of December 1787 from his sister Dorothy shows that at the age of seventeen he has already read Burns's *Poems*, 'and admired many of the pieces very much' (Dorothy herself likes particularly *To a mountain daisy* and *To a Louse*). We might expect immediate signs of influence, and are in fact encouraged to do so by Wordsworth's elegy, *At the grave of Burns* (1803):

> He was gone
> Whose light I hailed when first it shone,
>     And showed my youth
> How Verse may build a princely throne
>     On humble truth.
>
> (ll. 32–36)

Building a throne 'on humble truth', however, did not come early or easily to Wordsworth. It took time to achieve the 'life of mind' that marked his affinity with Burns, and made it possible to follow his light.

It is significant that looking back in his *Letter to a friend of Robert Burns* (1816), Wordsworth should dwell on creation of the poetic self from inner resources:

Not less successfully does Burns avail himself of his own character and situation in society, to construct out of them a poetic self – introduced as a dramatic personage – for the purpose of inspiriting his incidents, diversifying his pictures, recommending his opinions, and giving point to his sentiments. (p. 24)

Introduced 'as a dramatic personage' to tell the story of Margaret, the

Pedlar of *The ruined cottage* wanders the hills, 'His eye / Flashing poetic fire' as he repeats 'The Songs of Burns'. There can be no doubt that Wordsworth's incidents, pictures, opinions and sentiments, all gain in sharpness by his presence. As the poetic self he has created tells of ' "trotting brooks" and whispering trees', Wordsworth the poet acknowledges an inspiration that has lain dormant for ten years, waiting its time.

In making his selection for Kilmarnock, Burns tends to play down his broader humour for the sake of fastidious readers, but the range of poems and emotions is surprisingly wide – far wider than Hazlitt, for instance, implies. Burns's masterpiece, *Tam O'Shanter*, with its gusto and compulsive rhythms –

> Kings may be blest, but *Tam* was glorious,
> O'er a' the ills o' life victorious . . .
> > (Kinsley, ii, 557)

was to follow in 1790, but already in the Kilmarnock volume there is the flamboyant *Holy fair*:

> There's some are fou o' *love divine*;
> There's some are fou o' *brandy*;
> An' monie jobs that day begin,
> May end in *Houghmagandie*
> Some ither day.
> > (p. 54)

It is interesting that Wordsworth, who delights in the drunken Tam (regarding him as the prince of 'poetic selves'), should see Burns as capable also of being 'energetic, solemn and sublime in sentiment, and profound in feeling'. Writing to Coleridge on 27 February 1799, he cites the Kilmarnock *Despondency, an ode* as a poem he 'can never read without the deepest agitation'. To a modern reader, *Despondency* seems like a half-way point between Gray's *Eton college* ode and Wordsworth's own *Intimations*:

> Oh, enviable, early days,
> When dancing thoughtless Pleasure's maze,
> To Care, to Guilt unknown!
> How ill exchang'd for riper times,
> To feel the follies, or the crimes,
> Of others, or my own!
> Ye tiny elves that guiltless sport,

> Like linnets in the bush,
> Ye little know the ills ye court,
> When Manhood is your wish!
> The losses, the crosses,
> That *active man* engage;
> The fears all, the tears all,
> Of dim declining *Age*!
> (p. 159)

The Burns poem that echoes through Wordsworth's 1798 *Lyrical ballads* (before turning up in 1802 at the outset of *Resolution and Independence*) is *Man was made to mourn*:

> A few seem favourites of Fate,
> In Pleasure's lap carest . . .
> But Oh! what crouds in ev'ry land,
> All wretched and forlorn,
> Thro' weary life this lesson learn,
> That Man was made to mourn!
> (pp. 162–3)

Not only is the bulk of mankind condemned to poverty, the poor are 'made' – created by their Maker – in order to suffer. In its mingling of protest and resignation, satire and subdued bitterness, Burns's poem is a remarkable questioning of divine intentions:

> If I'm design'd yon lordling's slave,
> By Nature's law design'd,
> Why was an independent wish
> E'er planted in my mind?
> If not, why am I subject to
> His cruelty, or scorn?
> Or why has Man the will and pow'r
> To make his fellow mourn?
> (p. 164)

'To her fair works', Wordsworth writes in *Lines written in early spring*,

> did nature link
> The human soul that through me ran;
> And much it griev'd my heart to think
> What man has made of man.
> (1798 *Lyrical ballads*, 115)

Again the theme is 'Nature's social union'. *Man was made to mourn* is clearly in Wordsworth's thoughts, yet beside Burns he seems distanced from cruelty and scorn. He accepts in March 1798 a version of Coleridge's Unitarian pantheism, with its reliance on the 'pure principle of love'. Aware as he is of 'man's inhumanity to man', he is privileged not to feel it with personal intensity. He is not forced, as Burns is, to contrast Nature's instinctive liberality with the ways of 'partial Heaven'. 'Man', Burns had written despairingly, ten years before,

is by no means a happy creature. – I do not speak of the Selected Few, favored by partial Heaven . . . I speak of the neglected Many, whose nerves, whose sinews, whose days, whose thoughts . . . are sacrificed and sold to those few bloated Minions of Heaven! (Kinsley, iii, 1. 1088)

In the words of the *Edinburgh magazine* for October 1786, the Kilmarnock volume is 'a striking example of native genius bursting through the obscurity of poverty and the obstructions of labouring life'. To some extent Burns in his Preface plays up to this image:

Unacquainted with the necessary requisites for commencing Poet by rule, [the Author] sings the sentiments and manners he felt and saw in himself and his rustic compeers around him, in his and their native language. (p. iii)

Yet the Preface shows Burns's skill in writing English, as opposed to his native Scots, and the poems demonstrate a wide knowledge of English poetry. Discerning readers saw in him not so much the uneducated as the genuine. In an age that produced the spurious epics of Ossian and Chatterton's *Rowley poems*, Burns was the real thing – a poet whose occupation as ploughman (or small-holder) guaranteed the freedom from artificiality and sophistication which readers were looking for. Here was primitivism that was up-to-date, natural, from the heart.

Success was immediate. Burns, who in desperation had booked a passage to the West Indies, made £20 and many friends with the Kilmarnock *Poems*, and was able to stay in Scotland. He was taken up by Henry Mackenzie (whose novel, *The man of feeling* (1771) was among Burns's 'bosom favourites') and Hugh Blair, defender of the authenticity of *Ossian* and author of the primitivist *Lectures on rhetoric and belles lettres* (1783), that inspired the Preface to *Lyrical ballads*. For the Edinburgh edition of 1787 there were thirty-eight pages of subscribers; Burns received £450, enough to buy a farm. Dublin, Belfast and London editions followed in 1787, Philadelphia and New York in 1788. None of Burns's fellow Romantics were to achieve such recognition with their first appearance in print.

# 3

## JOHANN WOLFGANG VON GOETHE

---

# The sorrows of Werter

*a German story*
1789 (1779)

'The grenadier Gobain has committed suicide from love; he was in other respects an excellent soldier.' So, according to Hazlitt, begins an order issued by Napoleon to his Guard in 1802. 'This is the second incident of the same nature', the order continues,

that has occurred within a month. The First Consul directs it to be inserted within the order-book of the Guard:- That a soldier ought to know how to vanquish the pangs and melancholy of the passions; that there is as much true courage in bearing up against mental sufferings with constancy as in remaining firm on the wall of a battery. To give ourselves up to grief without resistance, or to kill ourselves to escape affliction, is to abandon the field of battle before the victory is gained. (Howe, xv, 282)

It tells us much about the period following the publication of Goethe's *Sorrows of Werter* (in German, 1774; in French, 1776; in English, 1779), that a commanding officer should concern himself about 'suicide from love' among members of the Guard. We cannot know whether the good soldier Gobain had read *Werter*, but Napoleon did so many times. He took the book with him on his Egyptian campaign of 1798 (four years before Gobain's death), and discussed it with Goethe in 1806. In 1829 Goethe himself told Crabb Robinson that *Werter* had been in the Emperor's library on St Helena.

Werter, it should be said, does not kill himself 'to escape affliction', or 'give [himself] up to grief without resistance'. There must be a sense in which he dies 'for love', but he is drawn to death, as Hamlet is drawn, not least because he is more than usually alive. Everything Werter does is heightened, extreme, yet credible. A touchstone of sensibility is offered early in the novel by Goethe's definition of the 'tranquil being', for whom 'the falling leaves raise no idea, but that of approaching winter' (p. 23). Those who are susceptible of the melancholy of autumn are capable of being raised imaginatively to the extremes of Werter's passion.

Goethe shows us the way in his own heightening of fact into fiction. Werter, as he sheds tears of sentiment in his ruined arbour, muses on 'the divine breath of that all-powerful Being which created us', and falls heedlessly in love with a girl engaged to someone else, is very close to being Goethe himself. As the novel proceeds, however, and the theme of suicide becomes more dominant, Werter merges into the historical figure of Karl Wilhelm Jerusalem, who killed himself in October 1772 in precisely the way that the ending describes. Goethe has imagined himself into the role of Jerusalem, using his own temperament, his own experience, to understand how one could arrive at a state of mind in which it was natural, inevitable, to borrow a pair of pistols from a friend, sit down at one's desk, drink a glass of wine, and shoot oneself in the head.

*Die Leiden des jungen Werthers* was heavily revised by Goethe in 1783. Appearing first in 1779, Daniel Malthus's English version follows the original text, but is in fact based on one of three early French translations. Malthus and his French model have felt free to make small changes (usually in matters concerned with religion), but essentially *The sorrows of Werter* is the novel as completed when Goethe was twenty-four. Malthus's text was many times reprinted, and there were six further English versions by 1810. Like Schiller's *Robbers* (translated 1792), *Werter* plays an important part in the beginnings of English Romanticism. Indeed it could be seen as entwined with them in a single tradition. Kant read Burke on *The sublime and beautiful* and Young's *Conjectures on original composition*; Goethe was aware of Richardson's use of the epistolary form (as well as Rousseau's), responded to the nostalgia of Goldsmith, and – most important – was a passionate reader of *Ossian*. Talking to Crabb Robinson, he played this down:

Something led [Goethe] to speak of *Ossian* with contempt. I remarked: 'The taste for *Ossian* is to be ascribed to you in a great measure. It was *Werter* that set the fashion.' He smiled and said: 'That's partly true! But . . . it was never remarked by the critics that Werter praised Homer while he retained his senses, and *Ossian* when he was going mad.' (Morley, i, 368)

By 1829 it had long been established that *Ossian* was a fake; Goethe had long ago moved away from the Romanticism ('Sturm und Drang', in German terms) of *Werter*. His comments are interesting nonetheless, implying a clear-cut distinction between sanity and madness which the book seems to belie. The Ossianic world inhabited by the young Werter, and the young Goethe, blurred such distinctions. It was a world of sensibility encouraged and heightened into unreality.

it was a gloomy and awful sight! the moon was behind a cloud, but by means of a few scattered rays I could perceive the foaming waves rolling over the fields and meadows, and beating against the bushes; the whole valley was a stormy sea, tossed by furious winds. The moon then appeared again, and rested on a dark cloud; the splendor of her light increased the disorder of nature. The echoes redoubled and repeated the roarings of the wind and the waters. I drew near to the precipice; I wished and shuddered; I stretched out my arms, and leaned over, I sighed, and lost myself in the happy thought of burying all my sufferings, all my torments, in that abyss, and tossing amidst the waves. (p. 176)

'With what delight', Werter adds, 'should I have changed my nature, and have incorporated with the whirlwinds to rend the clouds and disturb the waters.'

The relation of mind and nature here is more strange, powerful, complex, than in anything written in England for the next quarter of a century. Tossed by a stormy sea and furious winds, the landscape (over which he has many times walked with Charlotte in pastoral calm) is an emblem of Werter's consciousness. Suicide is desired as an act of sublime self-immolation. Yet Werter does not wish merely to become passive, an object tossed by the waves, he wishes to 'incorporate' with the whirlwinds, be at one with the forces of power and destruction. Implicit is the possibility of seeing the landscape itself as transformed by the violence of his despair (as the slopes of Snowdon are transformed by the mist-sea of imagination at the end of Wordsworth's *Prelude*). 'My sufferings are great', Werter had complained at an earlier stage, 'I have lost the only charm of my life; the active sacred power, which created worlds around me'.

The tones we hear are those of Coleridge's *Dejection: an ode* (1802) –

> But now afflictions bow me down to earth:
> Nor care I that they rob me of my mirth,
>     But oh! each visitation
> Suspends what nature gave me at my birth,
> My shaping spirit of Imagination.
>     (*Sibylline leaves*, p. 241)

Almost thirty years before Coleridge, Goethe had defined in his 'active sacred power' (itself a very Coleridgean phrase) the outgoing Romantic imagination. And he had done so in a work that assumes the existence of a Platonist life-force closely akin to Coleridge's Unitarian pantheism:

The vivifying heat which animates all nature, was every where displayed before my eyes; it filled and warmed my heart. I was lost in the idea of infinity. (p. 90)

There is no reason why *Werter* should not have influenced Coleridge, but equally there is no evidence that it did. Resemblances should probably be credited to the spirit of the age. Some are very close. 'I can *at times* feel strongly the beauties, you describe', Coleridge writes to Thelwall in a confessional moment,

but more frequently *all things* appear little . . . the universe itself – what but an immense heap of *little* things? – I can contemplate nothing but parts, & parts are all *little* –!– My mind feels as if it ached to behold and know something *great* – something *one & indivisible* . . . (4 October 1797)

*Werter* provides the answer that Coleridge himself would provide in a different mood:

Weak mortal! all things appear little to you, for you are little yourself. Craggy mountains, deserts untrodden by the foot of man, even the unknown confines of the immense ocean, are animated by the breath of the Eternal, and every atom to which he has given existence and life, finds favour in his sight. (p. 90)

Goethe's admiration for Ossian led him in the original German to incorporate a very long extract at the centrepiece of Werter's last visit to Charlotte. This is cut down by the French translator, and by Malthus, but is not the less important. It is through Werter's reading of the lament of the warrior Armin – 'The time of my fading is near, and the blast that shall scatter my leaves' – that Charlotte becomes aware of his decision to kill himself. And it is through the reading that she becomes so wrought as momentarily to give herself up to his passion, thus making the suicide by a crazy logic inevitable:

I am beloved! am beloved by her! the delightful sense of it for the first time penetrated, enflamed my heart. My lips still feel the sacred warmth they received from thine . . . From this moment you are mine – yes, Charlotte, you are mine. I go before you, I go to my father, to thy father; I shall carry my sorrows to the foot of his throne, and he will give me comfort till you arrive . . . I do not dream, I do not rave; drawing near to the grave, my perceptions are more clear. (pp. 204, 205)

Malthus's translation was praised by Goethe in 1783. It has the

Johann Wolfgang von Goethe

flexibility to cope with shifts of mood and extremes of feeling. At the same time it has a *gravitas* that is appropriate, and a sense of period that no modern version (however it might score in point of accuracy) can ever achieve. Reading it we can believe in the extraordinary power that this book originally possessed.

# 4

## CHARLOTTE SMITH

---

# Elegiac sonnets
### 1789 (1784)

When the first edition of *Elegiac sonnets* came out in May 1784, Charlotte Smith was living with her wastrel husband in a London debtors' prison, the King's Bench. She was just 35, and had had eleven children, of whom nine were living. Before she left Benjamin Smith in 1787, she would have a twelfth. All told, she had a good deal to be elegiac about. Her mother died when she was three. When she was fifteen, her father remarried (to restore his finances), and thought it might be best if she were married too. The man he picked was the 21-year-old second son of a director of the East India Company, with remarkably little to recommend him.

From a life spent mainly in beautiful countryside on the Sussex downs, Charlotte was removed to gloomy rooms in Cheapside, where she had two children before she was eighteen, the first dying as the second was born. The marriage is openly described in *Emmeline*, first of her ten frequently autobiographical novels, written immediately after the separation and published in 1788:

Mr Stafford was one of those unfortunate characters, who having neither perseverence and regularity to fit them for business, or taste and genius for more refined pursuits, seek, in every casual occurrence or childish amusement, relief against the tedium of life . . . Married to a woman who was the delight of her friends and the admiration of her acquaintance, surrounded by a lovely and encreasing family, and possessed of every reasonable means of happiness, he dissipated that property, which ought to have secured it's continuance, in vague and absurd projects . . .

Mrs Stafford, who had been married to him at fifteen, had long been unconscious of his weakness: and when time and her own excellent understanding pressed the fatal conviction too forcibly upon her, she still, but fruitlessly, attempted to hide from others what she saw too evidently herself. (ii, 147–8)

*Elegiac sonnets* went through eleven editions, the last appearing in 1851.

# Charlotte Smith

There were many reprints of different kinds, and there were French and Italian translations. To support her family, Smith published a new novel almost every year, 1788–99, also producing translations from French (notably of *Manon Lescaut*), collections of stories and books for children. She never gave up writing poetry, however, adding quietly to her sequence of sonnets, and writing a number of longer poems, including *The emigrants* (1793) and the unfinished *Beachy head* (published after her death in 1807). In 1835 Wordsworth referred to her as 'a lady to whom English verse is under greater obligations than are likely to be either acknowledged or remembered'. 'She wrote little', he added, 'and that little unambitiously, but with true feeling for rural nature' (*Yarrow revisited* 270).

Wordsworth's relationship to Charlotte Smith went back a long way. The *Vale of Estwaite*, written when he was seventeen, suggests that he may well have known her work at Hawkshead Grammar School. As a Cambridge undergraduate, he bought the 1789 fifth edition of *Elegiac sonnets*, adding his own name carefully in pen (with that of Myers, fellow student of St John's) to the supplementary list of subscribers. *En route* for France in November 1791 he took the opportunity of going to visit Smith, while waiting in Brighton for a boat. Despite some uneasy family connections (John Robinson, powerful London lawyer and cousin of Wordsworth's father, acted for Benjamin Smith), he was received 'in the politest manner'. It was a particularly important moment in Wordsworth's life, just before the relationships with Annette Vallon and Michel Beaupuy committed him, respectively, to fatherhood and revolutionary politics. Smith was writing her fourth novel, *Desmond*, set in France and pro-revolutionary. She gave Wordsworth an introduction to Helen Maria Williams (author of *Letters from France*, referred to by Mrs Thrale on 15 October 1791 as 'our little democratic friend'), and quite possibly also to Brissot, the Girondin leader.

'Charlotte Smith and Bowles', Coleridge tells the readers of *Poems* 1797, 'are they who first made the Sonnet popular among the present English'. From them, and not from the Italian Petrarch, he will derive its 'laws':

In a Sonnet . . . we require a developement of some lonely feeling, by whatever cause it may have been excited; but those Sonnets appear to me the most exquisite, in which moral Sentiments, Affections, or Feelings, are deduced from, and associated with, the scenery of Nature. Such compositions generate a habit of thought highly favourable to delicacy of character. They create a sweet and indissoluble union between the intellectual and material world. (p. 72, Introduction to the Sonnets)

Charlotte Smith is named first, as she should be (Bowles's *Fourteen sonnets* coincides with the fifth edition of her poems), but it is Bowles to whom Coleridge's own Sonnets are dedicated.

Moralizing Nature and human response, Bowles creates an idiom, and demonstrates a sensibility, that Coleridge finds especially appealing:

> Ah! soothing are your quiet scenes – the tear
>   Of him who passes weary on his way
> Shall thank you, as he turns to bid adieu . . .
>     (*River Wenbeck, Fourteen sonnets* p. 5)

Turning on from Coleridge's 1797 Introduction, we come with no surprise on the opening words of Sonnet I: 'My heart has thank'd thee, BOWLES! for those soft strains / Whose sadness soothes me'.

Sadness did not soothe Charlotte Smith. When reviewers expressed their anxiety, she said she 'wrote mournfully because [she] was unhappy'. Among her sonnets, Wordsworth singled out in May 1830 her celebration of 'sober-suited night':

> Tho' no repose on thy dark breast I find,
>   I still enjoy thee – cheerless as thou art;
>   For in thy quiet gloom, the exhausted heart
> Is calm, tho' wretched; hopeless, yet resign'd.
>     (p. 39)

There is a plain speaking here, a refusal to exaggerate emotion, that truly points forward. Though tuned to the sonnet's formal requirements, Smith's is a natural lyricism. Adulthood has been far more grievous for her, the childhood she mourns is far less complex, but in her temperament she is as clearly Wordsworth's predecessor as Bowles is Coleridge's. *Elegiac sonnets* gave to the undergraduate Wordsworth (then writing *An evening walk*, his study in the picturesque) the example of one for whom Nature and emotion were truly an 'indissoluble union':

> Ah! hills belov'd! – where once, a happy child,
>   Your beechen shades, 'your turf, your flowers, among',
> I wove your blue-bells into garlands wild,
>   And woke your echoes with my artless song.
> Ah! hills belov'd! – your turf, your flowers remain;
>   But can they peace to this sad breast restore,

For one poor moment soothe the sense of pain,
And teach a breaking heart to throb no more?

(p. 5)

It is not great writing. There is a triteness in some of the adjectives (*artless* song, *sad* breast, *breaking* heart); the final line falls back on pathos just when strength and intuition were most needed. Yet we do not doubt that the hills were indeed beloved. The blue-bells bring a vivid sense of colour and authenticity into the poetry.

The 781 subscribers to *Elegiac sonnets* 1789 represent the nobility and gentry of the day. Dukes and duchesses, earls and countesses; lords, baronets and knights in profusion; an array of the landed and professional classes, amongst whom a Jane Austen heroine could safely look for her man. Charlotte Smith had kind and well-connected friends (Blake's patron, Hayley, above all) who gathered the names for her. No doubt they admired the way she was supporting her enormous family, fighting lawyers for the money they should have inherited, rising above personal unhappiness. There must have been a number, though, who, like Wordsworth and Myers, added their names because they were aware of a new voice in English poetry:

The dark and pillowy cloud; the fallow trees,
Seem o'er the ruins of the year to mourn;
And cold and hollow, the inconstant breeze
Sobs thro' the falling leaves and wither'd fern.

(p. 42)

The melancholy of Gray and Goldsmith has given place to a more personal mingling of mood and observation. The movement of the verse is the movement of early Romantic poetry. By way of a footnote one might add that Charlotte's use of the adjective, 'pillowy', predates the first example in the *NED* (Sotheby's *Oberon*, 1798). It is picked up by Wordsworth in his wonderful image of the Cambridge undergraduates amongst whom he read the *Elegiac sonnets* of 1789: 'unthinking natures, easy minds, / And pillowy' (1805 *Prelude*, iii, 519–20).

# 5
## WILLIAM LISLE BOWLES

## Fourteen sonnets
*elegiac and descriptive. Written during a tour*
1789

Bowles was the poet of a single moment and a single mood. He was a sort of John the Baptist to Coleridge – except that Coleridge started by worshipping him. Wordsworth, late in his life, recalled buying *Fourteen sonnets* (at Christmas 1789), and annoying his brother John by pausing to read it in a niche of London Bridge. The occasion seems to have been remembered as much for John, drowned at sea in 1805, as for the poetry. Bowles certainly had an influence on Wordsworth's few surviving early sonnets, but in the building up of his style and sensibility Charlotte Smith was probably more important. Coleridge, by contrast, made Bowles his hero. *Fourteen sonnets* appeared at the time of his love for Mary Evans, daughter of the family that befriended him in his half-orphaned city life at Christ's Hospital. He was, as he makes clear in *Biographia literaria*, waiting to be carried away 'by a style of poetry, so tender, and yet so manly, so natural and real, and yet so dignified and harmonious, as the sonnets . . . of Mr. Bowles'.

'My earliest acquaintance', Coleridge writes,

will not have forgotten the undisciplined eagerness and impetuous zeal, with which I laboured to make proselytes, not only of my companions, but of all with whom I conversed, of whatever rank, and in whatever place. As my school finances did not permit me to purchase copies, I made, within less than a year and a half, more than forty transcriptions, as the best presents I could offer to those, who had in any way won my regard. (*Biographia literaria*, i, 14–15)

Even if Coleridge made only half the copies he claimed, it is not surprising that he knew the *Sonnets* rather well, assimilating from them the tender melancholy that Bowles himself had inherited from his Oxford tutor, Thomas Warton, Fellow of Trinity and Poet Laureate. Warton's sonnet *To the river Loden* (1777) is the inspiration for Bowles's *To the river Itchin, near Winton* (1789), just as Bowles inspires Coleridge's *To the river Otter* (1796). Warton had started a fashion:

> AH! what a weary race my feet have run,
> Since first I trod thy banks with alders crown'd,
> And thought my way was all through fairy ground,
> Beneath thy azure sky, and golden sun:
> Where first my muse to lisp her notes begun!
> While pensive memory traces back the round,
> Which fills the varied interval between;
> Much pleasure, more of sorrow, marks the scene.
> Sweet native stream! those skies and suns so pure
> No more return, to chear my evening road!
> Yet still one joy remains, that not obscure,
> Nor useless, all my vacant days have flow'd,
> From youth's gay dawn to manhood's prime mature;
> Nor with the Muse's laurel unbestow'd.
>
> (Warton, *Poems* 1777, p. 83)

There are touches of Gray and Goldsmith ('While pensive memory traces back the round' would fit unchanged into *The deserted village*), but Warton's nostalgia is more personal, more wistful. The sonnet form – rare since Milton, and used with distinction perhaps only by Gray at the end of the *Elegy* – has found a new voice. Bowles takes up where his old tutor leaves off, investing the poetry with an aura of sensibility, emotion enjoyed for its own sake. Warton would not have spoken of a 'shiv'ring sense of pain' – let alone, taken pleasure in it:

> Itchin, when I behold thy banks again,
>     Thy crumbling margin, and thy silver breast,
>     On which the self-same tints still seem to rest,
> Why feels my heart the shiv'ring sense of pain?
>     Is it, that many a summer's day has past
> Since, in life's morn, I carol'd on thy side?
> Is it, that oft, since then, my heart has sigh'd,
>     As Youth, and Hope's delusive gleams, flew fast?
> Is it that those, who circled on thy shore,
> Companions of my youth, now meet no more?
>     Whate'er the cause, upon thy banks I bend
> Sorrowing, yet feel such solace at my heart,
>     As at the meeting of some long-lost friend,
>     From whom, in happier hours, we wept to part.
>
> (Sonnet viii)

## Fourteen sonnets

'My heart has thanked thee, BOWLES!' Coleridge writes in *Effusion I* of *Poems on various subjects* (1796), 'for those soft strains / Whose sadness soothes me, like the murmuring / Of wild-bees in the sunny showers of spring'. Bowles licensed the self-indulgence and soothing sadness that are so limiting to Coleridge's early verse. Yet without him, *To the river Otter* would never have achieved its sharper sense of loss and its moment of near transcendence:

> Dear native Brook! wild Streamlet of the West!
>    How many various-fated years have past,
>      What blissful and what anguish'd hours, since last
> I skimm'd the smooth thin stone along thy breast,
> Numbering its light leaps! yet so deep impresst
> Sink the sweet scenes of childhood, that mine eyes
>    I never shut amid the sunny blaze,
> But strait with all their tints thy waters rise,
>    Thy crossing plank, thy margin's willowy maze,
> And bedded sand that vein'd with various dyes
> Gleam'd through thy bright transparence to the gaze.
>    Visions of Childhood! oft have ye beguil'd
> Lone manhood's cares, yet waking fondest sighs:
>    Ah! that I were once more a careless child!
>
>                    *(Poems* 1797, p. 78)

The 'various-fated years', the 'mournful hours', 'Lone manhood's cares' and 'fondest sighs', stay in the moralizing, generalizing, world of Bowles. But the poetry is in transition. A new particularity shows itself in the 'smooth thin stone' and the 'crossing plank'. For a moment, as the colours of the sand gleam through the 'bright transparence' of the Otter, the physical world becomes symbolic of the 'Visions of Childhood' and the workings of the mind.

*Fourteen sonnets* (a 'sonnet' of sonnets) claims to be 'Elegiac and Descriptive. Written During a Tour'. The second edition (also of 1789, but entitled merely *Sonnets*) raises the number of poems to twenty-one, describing them as 'Written Chiefly on Picturesque Spots, During a Tour'. West and Gilpin had made this the hey-day of the picturesque, but few can have had less interest than Bowles in pictorial effects. His opening poem, *Written at Tinemouth*, has a single Gilpinesque detail (imitated at once in an early Wordsworth sonnet): 'The lifted oar far off with silver gleam / is touched'. But description is perfunctory in his visits to Bamborough Castle, to the rivers Wenbeck, Tweed and Itchin, to

# William Lisle Bowles

Dover and Ostend. We have little sense of a tour, little feeling that the interspersed poems addressed to abstractions (Philosophy, Evening, Poverty, Time) are different in kind from those attached to specific locations. Bowles has replaced the picturesque with a ruminative poetry. In the words of *Biographia*, he and Cowper are 'the first who combined natural thoughts with natural diction; the first who reconciled the heart with the head' (*Biographia literaria*, i, 25). The sonnets are a pointing of the way. Augmented by *Monody at Matlock* (1791), they lead on, through minor Coleridge, into the great imaginative revisitings of *Frost at midnight*, *Tintern abbey* and *The prelude*.

Lamb it is who best evokes for us both the appeal and the weakness of the *Sonnets*. 'I love you for dedicating your poetry to Bowles', he writes to Coleridge on 14 November 1796. His tones are affectionate, but the mockery that follows could be one reason why the dedication of Coleridge's 1797 poems was switched to his brother George:

Genius of the sacred fountain of tears, it was [Bowles] who led you gently by the hand through all this valley of weeping, showed you the dark green yew trees and the willow shades where, by the fall of waters, you might indulge an uncomplaining melancholy, a delicious regret for the past . . .

Byron was more brutal. Bowles in *English bards and Scotch reviewers* (1809) is 'The maudlin prince of mournful sonneteers'. Coleridge's own most discerning comments come in his letter to Sotheby of 10 September 1802. Bowles has, he complains, a

perpetual trick of *moralizing* every thing – which is very well, occasionally – but never to see or describe any interesting appearance in nature, without connecting it by dim analogies with the moral world, proves faintness of Impression.

Tacitly, Bowles, Coleridge's hero of the early 1790s, is being compared to 'the God Wordsworth', hero since 1797 (and never really deposed). In the process, a highly important definition of the Romantic imagination emerges:

A Poet's *Heart & Intellect* should be *combined*, *intimately* combined & *unified*, with the great appearances in Nature – & not merely held in solution & loose mixture with them, in the shape of formal Similes . . .

# 6

## ERASMUS DARWIN

---

# The loves of the plants

*The botanic garden, Part II.*
*Containing The loves of the plants, a poem*
1789

Nothing that Charles Darwin worked out in the 1850s would have surprised his grandfather, Erasmus. It is not so much that he knew it all already, as that he had asked the questions, and asked them in the right terms. While Christian orthodoxy held that the world had been created in 4004 BC (and would last for six thousand years), he was prepared to think in terms of 'millions of ages', and evolution from an original 'living filament'. 'Would it be too bold', he asks in volume one of *Zoonomia, or the laws of organic life* (1794):

to imagine, that in the great length of time since the earth began to exist, perhaps millions of ages before the commencement of the history of mankind . . . all warm-blooded animals have arisen from one living filament, which THE GREAT FIRST CAUSE endued with animality . . . possessing the faculty of continuing to improve by its own inherent activity, and of delivering down these improvements by generation to its posterity, world without end!

Darwin understood (as indeed did a number of his contemporaries) that fossils represented extinct earlier species. He saw the oceans as the ultimate source of life. His grandson's research into natural selection would have seemed to him the logical way forward.

Though written when he was in his fifties, *The loves of the Plants* (published as *Botanic garden*, part two, in 1789) ranks as early Darwin. Part one, the longer and more ambitious *Economy of vegetation*, appeared in June 1792 (with a 1791 titlepage), to be followed by *Zoonomia* (1794–7), *A plan for the conduct of female education* (1797), *Phytologia; or the philosophy of agriculture and gardening* (1800) and *The temple of nature* (1803). Deriving its couplets from the Pope of *Rape of the lock* (1717), *Loves of the plants* has a

29

Erasmus Darwin

playfulness and fantasy that is all its own. Darwin seems to have written
it on the side while working on his weighty translations of Linnaeus,
*System of vegetables* (1783) and *Families of plants* (1787). His intention is 'to
inlist Imagination under the banner of Science', transmit the Linnaean
classification in a form that has charm. In tuning his reed to the 'Gay
hopes, and amorous sorrows of the mead', he is offering a strange
version of pastoral:

> From giant Oaks, that wave their branches dark,
> To the dwarf Moss, that clings upon their bark,
> What Beaux and Beauties croud the gaudy groves,
> And woo and win their vegetable Loves . . .
>
> (I, 7–10)

Darwin's readers were to enjoy botany through poetry, and enjoy the
poetry through nostalgia for the lost world of beaux and belles at the
court of Queen Anne. As in Pope –

> The *Knave of Diamonds* tries his wily Arts,
> And wins (oh shameful Chance!) the *Queen of Hearts*.
>
> (1717 *The Rape of the Lock*, iii, 87–88)

– they were to be amused by innuendo; but in place of the earlier
decorous battles of the sexes, Darwin presents Linnaeus's world of
thriving and ingenious vegetable sexuality. Sex within the individual
flower offers the basis both for Linnaean classification, and for poetic
enjoyment. Pistils are female, stamens (anthers), male. The fact that
they come in different numbers, and behave in different idiosyncratic
ways, permits a basic division of plants into twenty-four 'classes'
(thence, in Darwin's day, into 120 'orders', 2,000 'families', 20,000
'species' – plus the countless 'varieties'). The American Cowslip,
Meadia, has one pistil, five stamens. In terms of the poetry, she wantons
with five admirers:

> MEADIA's soft chains *five* suppliant beaux confess,
> And hand in hand the laughing belle address;
> Alike to all, she bows with wanton air,
> Rolls her dark eye, and waves her golden hair.
>
> (i, 61–64)

Darwin's footnote fills in the detail, but scientific fact is far from dry in
this world of 'fecundating dust':

Five males and one female. The males, or anthers, touch each other . . . The pistil

30

is much longer than the stamens, hence the flower-stalks have their elegant bend, that the stigma may hang downwards to receive the fecundating dust of the anthers.

Reading the poem is a sharing in the author's enjoyment – pleasure in the fantasy of 'suppliant beaux' (who are really stamens), pleasure in the fact of the flower-stalks' 'elegant bend', pleasure in countless other details noted by a scientific mind that is excited by ideas and experience, and charmed by incongruity.

Darwin conceives of his book as a Poetic Exhibition, a magic-lantern show 'in which are lights and shades dancing on a whited canvas, and magnified into apparent life'. Readers are invited to step in and 'view the wonders of his INCHANTED GARDEN'. Ovid turned men and women to flowers and trees, Darwin will reverse the metamorphosis, release the human forms that have been so long prisoners 'in their respective vegetable mansions'. Classification, though, is a serious business. In Canto One thirty-seven successive plants perform their courtship rituals before us on the whited canvas, each with a note to make sure we take the botanical point. Mimosa, the Sensitive Plant, belongs to class xxi, 'Male flowers and female flowers separate, but on the same plant'. Darwin sees her beautifully as 'an eastern bride', 'Queen of the bright seraglio of her Lord':

> Veil'd, with gay decency and modest pride,
> Slow to the mosque she moves, an eastern bride;
> There her soft vows unceasing love record,
> Queen of the bright seraglio of her Lord –
> So sinks or rises with the changeful hour
> The liquid silver in its glassy tower.
> So turns the needle to the pole it loves,
> With fine vibrations quivering, as it moves.
>
> (i, 255–62)

Not content with conferring on a plant the gentleness of human love, Darwin has animated first a thermometer, then a compass (both of course instruments noted for sensitivity). Pope's imagination has at times the same visually enchanting Metaphysical quality –

> The Tortoise here and Elephant unite,
> Transformed to *Combs*, the speckled and the white
>
> (1717 *The Rape of the Lock*, i, 135–6)

– but Darwin's tenderness ('So turns the needle to the pole it loves') takes us back to Donne (and compasses of the other sort):

31

If they be two, they are two so
   As stiff twin compasses are two;
Thy soul, the fixed foot, makes no show
   To move, but doth, if th'other do.
And though it in the center sit,
   Yet when the other far doth roam,
It leans and hearkens after it,
   And grows erect, as that comes home.
     (*A valediction: forbidding mourning*, 25–32)

Cantos II–IV of Darwin's Inchanted Garden offer a new diversity in their exhibits. Montgolfier ascends (like thistle-down) in his 'silken castle'. For a moment we join the spectators as man's first flying-machine passes overhead:

Silent with upturn'd eyes unbreathing crouds
Pursue the floating wonder to the clouds . . .
     (ii, 31–32)

The nymph Gossypia (cotton) permits a digression on Arkwright's 'curious and magnificent machinery . . . in vain attempted by many ingenious artists before him':

Then fly the spoles, the rapid axles glow;
And slowly circumvolves the labouring wheel below.
     (ii, 103–4)

We learn of Howard's prison-visits, Fuseli's *Nightmare*, the making of paper, the evils of slavery, the workings of warm springs, and mining of salt:

So, cavern'd round in vast Polandish mines,
With crystal walls a gorgeous city shines . . .
     (iv, 309–10)

The writing is endlessly inventive, full of intellectual curiosity and excitement. Wordsworth may reflect on the 'sad incompetence of human speech', Darwin notes in wonderment how much is achieved with how little: 'About twenty letters, ten cyphers, and seven crochets, represent by their numerous combinations all our ideas and sensations.'

*The loves of the plants* was published anonymously because Darwin – by common consent the greatest doctor of his day – thought his practice might suffer if he was known to be a poet. In the event, patients, friends, reviewers, the reading public, were all delighted. No one knew that there was about to be a Romantic period, that Wordsworth would soon be denouncing Augustan poetic diction, or Coleridge proclaiming imagination at the expense of fancy. Since the 1790s Darwin has found few sensitive readers. Like the Shelley of *Queen Mab*, he is praised for his learning, and his notes, by critics who contentedly disparage the poetry. It is their loss. Horace Walpole, who couldn't understand the botany and resented the notes, sent *The loves of the plants* to Hannah More on 22 April 1789, with the words, 'I flatter myself you will agree that the author is a great poet'. Six days later a copy went off to Mary and Agnes Berry, with whom Walpole felt more relaxed:

I send you the most delicious poem upon earth. If you don't know what it is all about, or why, at least you will find glorious similes about everything in the world . . . all, all, all, is the most lovely poetry.

It was left to the *Anti-Jacobin* parodists to suggest that plant sexuality was not very acceptable – that young ladies should be protected from knowing what it is all about:

> ALAS! that partial Science should approve
> The sly RECTANGLE's too licentious love!
> *(Loves of the triangles, 75–76)*

# 7
## RICHARD PRICE

---

# A discourse on the love
# of our country
## 1789

G. Washington presents his most respectful compliments to Dr Price. With much thankfulness he has received, and with the highest gratification he has read, the doctor's excellent observations on the importance of the American revolution, and the means of making it a benefit to the world.

Washington's letter belongs to November 1785, midway between the end of the American War of Independence in 1782 and the Fall of the Bastille in July 1789. From an early stage Price had been in touch with the American leaders. He was not merely a political theorist and dissenting theologian, but a mathematician, and expert on insurance and finance. In October 1778, he had been offered American citizenship, Congress resolving:

That the Honourable Benjamin Franklin, Arthur Lee and John Adams, Esqrs or any one of them, be directed forthwith to apply to Dr Price, and inform him that it is the desire of Congress to consider him as a citizen of the United States, and to receive his assistance in regulating their Finances.

At 55, Price felt too old to emigrate, but he continued to offer support and advice. Recognizing his services, Yale in April 1781 awarded him an honorary doctorate alongside Washington; three years later he published his *Observations on the importance of the American Revolution*, editions appearing, 1784–6, in London, Dublin, Amsterdam, Boston, New Haven, Trenton, Philadelphia and Charleston.

Known to twentieth-century readers only through Burke's satirical portrait in *Reflections on the Revolution in France*, Price was in his day a figure of international importance. In the *Observations* he makes available to his wide audience the ideals and assumptions that lie behind *A discourse on the love of our country*, preached originally as a sermon on 4 November 1789. Despite the title of the *Discourse*, Price is not concerned with patriotism as such: he is a millenarian thinker, who discerns in recent events the hope of general future happiness. 'Next to the introduction of Christianity among mankind', he tells his readers in *Observations*, 'the American revolution may prove the most important step in the progressive course of human improvement' (p. 6). The United States will, he trusts, become 'the seat of liberty, science and virtue . . . whence there is reason to hope these sacred blessings will spread, till they become universal' (p. 3). The reasons he gives for this optimism are surprisingly close to those that supported the early Wordsworth. In place of the Lake District 'statesmen' (small independent farmers), living their life of integrity, family love, and closeness to the soil, Price sees:

an independent and hardy [American] YEOMANRY, all nearly on a level – trained to arms, instructed in their rights – cloathed in homespun – of simple manners – strangers to luxury – drawing plenty from the ground – and that plenty, gathered easily by the hand of industry . . . giving rise to early marriages, a numerous progeny, length of days, and a rapid increase – the rich and the poor, the haughty grandee and the creeping sychophant, equally unknown – protected by laws, which (being their own will) cannot oppress; and by an equal government, which, wanting lucrative places, cannot create corrupt canvassings and ambitious intrigue. (*Observations*, p. 69)

Like his fellow dissenter, Priestley, and Priestley's disciple, Coleridge, Price sees the 'course of human improvement' as not only 'progressive', but ordained. Letters to Franklin, Adams and Jefferson, in the period leading up to July 1789, show that he predicted a revolution in France that would embody the American spirit. When it came, he welcomed it in terms that laid him open to the sarcasm of Burke, but which were nonetheless consistent with the political situation as it stood four months after the Bastille was sacked. 'What an eventful period is this!' he exclaims at the end of the *Discourse*,

I am thankful that I have lived to it; and I could almost say, *Lord, now lettest thou thy servant depart in peace, for mine eyes have seen thy salvation.* I have lived to see a diffusion of knowledge, which has undermined superstition and error – I have lived to see the rights of men better understood than ever; and nations panting for liberty, which seemed to have lost the idea of it. I have lived to see THIRTY MILLIONS of people, indignant and resolute, spurning at slavery, and demanding liberty with an irresistible voice; their king led in triumph, and an arbitrary monarch surrendering himself to his subjects. (p. 49)

# Richard Price

'After sharing in the benefits of one Revolution', Price continues,

I have been spared to witness two other Revolutions, both glorious. And now, methinks, I see the ardor for liberty catching and spreading; a general amendment beginning in human affairs; the dominion of kings changed for the dominion of laws, and the dominion of priests giving way to the dominion of reason and conscience.

Price was a radical dissenter, but also a constitutionalist. First of the three Revolutions to which he refers – the one from which he himself derived (rather slender) benefits – was the officially 'glorious' Revolution of 1688, which had ousted the catholic James II, bringing the protestant William of Orange to the English throne. According to the argument accepted by Price and his audience (and vehemently disputed by Burke), the people had conferred kingship upon a monarch of their choice, who thus held it at their will. Monarchy had become subject to 'the dominion of laws'. From a dissenter's point of view in 1789 this might be a little theoretical: the same laws excluded him from the universities and public office, and failed to guarantee freedom of worship. From a constitutionalist's point of view, the people (whether or not the king was ultimately responsible to them) were still without adequate representation; there was appalling abuse both of the electoral system and of taxation. Yet, for all this, the settlement of 1688 had established a parliamentary democracy that was more advanced than any in Europe. It had formed the basis of radical American thinking, and America had in turn inspired the French. The 'ardor for liberty' was 'catching and spreading'.

The original audience of Price's *Discourse* had reason to hope that the spirit (rather than the political fact) of revolution would spread back to England. They had met at the Old Jewry in London, under the auspices of the Society for Commemorating the Revolution in Great Britain, a group, mainly of dissenters, that existed to celebrate the more positive aspects of 1688 and work for constitutional reform. At a dinner that followed Price's sermon, the Society passed a series of resolutions that showed the radicalism of its members, and led directly to Burke's attack in *Reflections*. First, it affirmed three fundamental principles, all following from the spirit of the 1688 settlement, but unacceptable to the government of the day:

1. That all civil and political authority is derived from the people.
2. That the abuse of power justifies resistance.
3. That the right of private judgment, liberty of conscience, trial by jury, the

freedom of the press, and the freedom of election, ought ever to be held sacred and inviolable.

(*Discourse*, Appendix 12)

Then it resolved on two measures to spread, or share, these evidently seditious views: the setting up of corresponding societies 'to form that grand concentrated union of the true friends of public liberty, which may be necessary to maintain its existence', and the sending of congratulations to the National Assembly of France.

In moving the Society's address to the French, Price rejoiced in the prospect of Britain and France, 'the two first Kingdoms in the World', sharing in 'the blessings of Civil and Religious Liberty'. Making no compromises, he noted

the tendency of the glorious example given in France to encourage other nations to assert the unalienable rights of mankind, and thereby to introduce a general reformation in the governments of Europe, and to make the world free and happy. (*Discourse*, Appendix 13)

The stage was set not merely for Burke's reply, denying the validity of these 'unalienable rights', but for the replies to Burke, of Wollstonecraft, Priestley, Paine, Mackintosh and Godwin. Intemperate as he was, Burke was not wrong to see in Price and the Revolution Society principles that would undermine existing social structures. 'General reformation in the governments of Europe' was unlikely to be a peaceful process; those who proposed it, however idealistically, as a vision of future happiness, were a danger to society.

That said, Burke's methods seem fairly unscrupulous. At a time when there had been little bloodshed in France, and reformers were trying earnestly to work within the structure of a constitutional monarchy, he indulges in crude distortions, lampooning Price as a lover of violence, and misrepresenting the political situation:

Plots, massacres, assassinations, seem to some people a trivial price for obtaining a revolution. A cheap, bloodless reformation, a guiltless liberty, appear flat and vapid to their taste. There must be a great change of scene; there must be a magnificent stage effect; there must be a grand spectacle to rouze the imagination, grown torpid with the lazy enjoyment of sixty years security, and the still unanimating repose of public prosperity. The Preacher found them all in the French revolution. This inspires a juvenile warmth through his whole frame. His enthusiasm kindles as he advances; and when he arrives at his peroration, it is in a full blaze. Then, viewing from the Pisgah of his pulpit, the free, moral,

Richard Price

happy, flourishing, and glorious state of France, as in a bird–eye landscape of a
promised land, he breaks out into the following rapture:
  'What an eventful period is this! . . .

(*Reflections*, pp. 96–7)

Burke's voice will always be louder than Price's. Coming two years
after *Reflections*, the Reign of Terror gave to it a somewhat spurious air
of prophecy; rhetoric and sarcasm give to it a pleasurable edge. Price,
though, survives the ridicule. He speaks for a moment when the
well-intentioned leaders of America and France (many of them known
to him personally) truly represented the hope of a world free and happy.
He was not unaware of deficiencies and problems (denouncing
American acceptance of slavery, for instance), but believed in the
inevitability of human progress. Dying in 1791, he was never forced, as
were Priestley, Wordsworth and others, to redefine his expectations.

# 8

## THOMAS PAINE

---

# The rights of man [Part I]

*being an answer to Mr Burke's attack
on the French Revolution*
1791

It was Paine's nature to go straight to the point. His prose, his principles and his practical suggestions, were all strong and simple. He was more optimistic than we can be about human progress – 'It is an age of Revolutions, in which every thing can be looked for' (*Rights of man* i, 162) – but his observations are shrewd, and his arguments rarely fail to convince. Paine's background was unpromising. Leaving school at the age of twelve he was apprenticed to his father's business of stay-making. Later he became a customs officer and was dismissed for writing his first political pamphlet, *The case of the officers of excise* (1772), protesting against low pay. Two years later he left for America, aged 37, with a brief letter of recommendation from Franklin, whom he had met in London. There, after little more than a year, he published the immensely influential pamphlet, *Common sense*, setting out the grounds for a break with Great Britain. He then joined the army in the fight for independence. Though he never dropped out of political journalism, in the early 1780s Paine turned his practical talents to designing a bridge. It was to be made of iron, and cross the Schuylkill River in a single span.

Returning to Europe in 1787 in order to find backing for his project, Paine was in France during the early stages of the Revolution, when connections with America were at their closest. In Paris he was in touch with Ambassador Jefferson, and was entrusted with the key of the Bastille by Lafayette (French hero of the American War) to be presented as a symbolic gift to Washington. In London, supposedly *en route* for the States, Paine read Burke's *Reflections on the Revolution in France* (1 November 1790), with its two-fold attack: on Richard Price, as representative of

English radicalism, and on the French National Assembly. On 22 February 1791 he published *Rights of man*, Part One.

Wollstonecraft's *Vindication of the rights of men*, first and most indignant of the replies to Burke, had come out before the end of November '91, to be followed by Priestley's *Letters to the Right Honourable Edmund Burke*, stating the Unitarian view. Defending his fellow dissenter, Price, against Burke's sarcasm, Priestley interprets the American and French Revolutions in terms of the bible. They are, he suggests, a beginning to the reign of peace, 'distinctly and repeatedly foretold in many prophecies, delivered more than two thousand years ago'. Paine, by contrast, writes as first-hand observer of political realities. His tones are confident and calm:

As I used sometimes to correspond with Mr Burke, believing him then to be a man of sounder principles than his book shews him to be, I wrote to him last winter from Paris, and gave him an account of how prosperously matters were going on. Among other subjects in that letter, I referred to the happy situation the National Assembly were placed in; that they had taken a ground on which their moral duty and their political interest were united. They have not to hold out a language which they do not themselves believe, for the fraudulent purpose of making others believe it . . . They are not in the case of a ministerial or an opposition party in England, who, though they are opposed, are still united to keep up the common mystery. (p. 83)

Burke, Paine notes, has '*voluntarily* declined going into a comparison of the English and French constitutions':

He apologizes (in page 241) for not doing it, by saying he had not time. Mr Burke's book was upwards of eight months in hand, and is extended to a volume of three hundred and fifty-six pages. As his omission does injury to his cause, his apology makes it worse; and men on the English side of the water will begin to consider, whether there is not some radical defect in what is called the English constitution, that made it necessary for Mr Burke to suppress the comparison, to avoid bringing it into view. (p. 84)

The 'radical defect' of the British Constitution is non-existence. The radical defect of Burke's thinking is that he fudges the issue, depending upon the concept of tradition, but asserting and denying historical precedent as he chooses.

Writing as a citizen of America, the one country in the world that does have a constitution, Paine sees all government as arbitrary unless it conforms to the will of the people. Monarchy, with its lavish expenditure and worthless aristocratic entourage, he sees as particularly unacceptable.

Price in his Old Jewry sermon of November 1789 (*Discourse on the love of our country*) had not gone so far. He was not a republican, and would have been content to see quite modest reforms in the British parliamentary system. Burke was nonetheless infuriated by the *Discourse*, with its claims for the rights and powers of the people. According to Price's view (widely held among radicals) the British people had shown the ability in 1688 to create a king, and must therefore have the ability to dismiss one if the need arose. To counter this argument Burke is forced to construe with an absurd literalness the language of abnegation used by Parliament in the 1688 Declaration of Rights: 'The lords spiritual and temporal, and commons, do, in the name of the people . . . most humbly and faithfully submit *themselves, their heirs and posterities for ever.*'

For Burke there is no more to be said. The agreement is binding for all time. Its terms, in effect, constitute a Constitution. For Paine the idea is preposterous, appalling:

There never did, there never will, and there never can exist a parliament, or any description of men, or any generation of men, in any country, possessed of the right or the power of binding and controuling posterity to the '*end of time*', or of commanding how the world shall be governed, or who shall govern it . . . Every age and generation must be as free to act for itself, *in all cases*, as the ages and generations which preceded it. (p. 9)

'I am contending for the rights of the *living*', Paine adds impressively, 'and Mr Burke is contending for the authority of the dead' (p. 10). One cannot, as Hazlitt remarks in *Table talk*, open a page of Paine's 'best and earlier works without meeting with some maxim, some antithetical and memorable saying, which is a sort of starting-point for the argument, and the goal to which it returns' (Howe, viii, 51).

Paine's antithesis between the rights of the living and the authority of the dead returns again and again. The French have asserted the principle of natural rights not only as the basis for a new Constitution, but as justification for the Revolution itself. It is as important to Paine to uphold the principle as it is to Burke to denounce it. Burke has referred to the French *Declaration of the Rights of Man* (published by the National Assembly as the basis of a constitution) as 'paltry and blurred sheets of paper about the rights of man'. 'Does Mr Burke', Paine demands,

mean to deny that *man* has any rights? If he does, then he must mean that there are no such things as rights anywhere, and that he has none himself; for who is there in the world but man? But if Mr Burke means to admit that man has rights, the question then will be, What are those rights and how came man by them originally? (p. 44)

At the centre of Paine's thinking is a distinction that we now take for granted, between natural rights ('those which appertain to man in right of his existence'), and civil rights ('those which appertain to man in right of his being a member of society'). Insofar as the individual is a member of society, he voluntarily accepts civil rights in exchange for natural. Natural rights, however, can never be forfeited or removed:

every civil right grows out of a natural right; or, in other words, is a natural right exchanged . . . this is the only mode in which governments have a right to arise, and the only principle on which they have a right to exist. (pp. 50, 52)

Save the American republic, and the new French constitutional monarchy, all governments in the Christian world have in practice been based on conquest. The sword has 'assumed the name of sceptre', and, 'in contradiction to the Founder of the Christian religion', the Church has supported the temporal power. In a metaphor appropriately drawn from aristocratic coats of arms, Paine concludes 'the key of St Peter and the key of the Treasury, [have been] quartered on one another' (p. 51).

If Burke is unwilling to compare the French and British modes of government, Paine is happy to do so. Burke is taunted with the incongruities and unfairnesses of the English electoral system, unreformed despite shifting population and the coming of the Industrial Revolution:

The constitution of France says, that every man who pays a tax of sixty sous *per annum* (2s. and 6d. English) is an elector. What article will Mr Burke place against this? Can any thing be more limited, and at the same time more capricious, than the qualifications of electors are in England? . . . not one man in an hundred (I speak much within compass) is admitted to vote . . . (p. 56)

The French constitution says, that the number of representatives for any place shall be in a ratio to the number of taxable inhabitants or electors. What article will Mr Burke place against this? . . . The town of old Sarum, which contains not three houses, sends two members; and the town of Manchester, which contains upwards of sixty thousand souls, is not admitted to send any. Is there any principle in these things? Is there any thing by which you can trace the marks of freedom, or discover those of wisdom? No wonder . . . Mr Burke has declined the comparison, and endeavoured to lead his readers from the point by a wild unsystematical display of paradoxical rhapsodies. (pp. 57–8)

For Paine the rights of man are synonymous with human dignity. He is not an egalitarian – the iron-bridge was a capitalist venture – but affectations of rank he detests. Titles irritate him especially, marking 'a sort of foppery in the human character which degrades it'. In England the aristocracy, by virtue of the accident of birth, holds power in both political parties, and in the Commons as well as the Lords. In France, '*nobility* is done away, and the *peer* is exalted into MAN'. The law of primogeniture has gone, and with it the aristocratic temper:

> They begin life by trampling on all their younger brothers and sisters, and relations of every kind, and are taught and educated so to do . . . a body of men holding themselves accountable to nobody, ought not to be trusted by any body. (pp. 70, 71)

The argument, of course, is truer still of kings. 'What is monarchy?', Paine demands. 'Is it a thing, or is it a name, or is it a fraud . . . what services does it perform, what is its business, and what are its merits? . . . What are those men kept for?' (pp. 130, 131).

It is the voice of American republicanism that we hear. Urging the states towards a break with England in 1775, Paine had announced, 'in America THE LAW IS KING' (*Common sense*). His language in the *Rights of man* is no less confident. Like Price, he believes that a chain reaction has been set in motion by the examples of America and France. And like him he assumes that monarchs owe their position to the people. He assumes, as Price doesn't, however, that their days are numbered:

> Sovereignty, as a matter of right, appertains to the Nation only, and not to any individual . . . The romantic and barbarous distinction of men into Kings and subjects, though it may suit the condition of courtiers, cannot that of citizens; and is exploded by the principle upon which Governments are now founded. (p. 157)

Republics, Paine believes, have a natural tendency to promote peace, because no distinction exists in them between the will of the individual and the interest of the nation. As 'hereditary governments are verging to their decline', he suggests mildly, 'it would be an act of wisdom' to produce revolutions by reason and agreement, rather than waiting for them to emerge from political upheaval. In a backward glance at Henry IV of France, he even envisages a European Congress for the prevention of war. No wonder *Rights of man*, Part One, sold a record-breaking 200,000 copies, largely to working-men's clubs. And no wonder that Paine, after publication of the still more successful Part Two, was condemned (*in absentia*) for sedition.

# 9

## THOMAS HOLCROFT

---

# The road to ruin
*a comedy*
1792

To his biographer Hazlitt (who chose his words carefully), Holcroft was a 'great and good man'. It was he who converted Godwin, author of *Political justice* (1793), to his faith in universal benevolence. Though working as actor, manager, dramatist, jack of all theatrical trades, Holcroft was a political idealist. He believed in the human race. Hearing from the newspapers in September 1794 that he was among those indicted by the Government for high treason (the others had been arrested, and were mostly in the Tower), he presented himself in court, on the grounds that 'the virtuous man has no need to fear accusation'. As a writer, he was (in his own words) prepared to 'sacrifice ease, peace, health, and life' in order to accomplish works that would 'promote the general good'. The results now sometimes seem incongruous. Lucy Peckham in *The school for arrogance* (1791) lectures her well-bred Count for basing his self-esteem on family and wealth. The heroine of *Anna St. Ives* (1792), goes further. 'Dare you think', she demands of Coke Clifton, in what he hopes will be a love-scene,

the servant that cleans your shoes is your equal, unless not so wise or good a man; and your superior, if wiser and better? Dare you suppose mind has no sex, and that woman is not by nature the inferior of man?–

'Madam', Clifton interposes, but Anna is not to be stopped:

Nay, nay, no compliments; I will not be interrupted – Dare you think that riches, rank, and power, are usurpations . . . Dare you make it the business of your whole life to overturn these prejudices, and to promote among mankind the spirit of universal benevolence which shall render them all equals, all brothers . . . (ed. Faulkner, p. 192)

*The road to ruin* has no harangues. Sandwiched between *The school for arrogance* and *Anna St Ives*, the play is immensely funny and (except for some cumbrous jesting in the Prologue) wholly unpolitical. According to Hazlitt, it carried Holcroft's fame 'into every corner of the kingdom':

Nothing could exceed the effect produced by this play at its first appearance, nor its subsequent popularity. It not only became a universal favourite, but it deserved to be so . . . It had a run greater than almost any other piece was ever known to have, and there is scarcely a theatre in the kingdom, except Drury Lane, and the Haymarket, in which it has not been acted numberless times. (Howe, iii, 121–2)

At the centre of *The road to ruin* is the great comic creation of Goldfinch, the gambling, horse-fancying, hard-driving, improbable suitor of Widow Warren, who speaks a language all his own, of brilliant disconnection:

*Widow*. Pardon me, Mr Goldfinch; if a certain event were by the wise disposition of Providence to take place, I should think proper to drive.
*Goldfinch*. You drive!– If you do, damn me!
*Widow*. Sir!
*Goldfinch*. I'm christened and called Charles – Charles Goldfinch – The knowing Lad that's not to be had – Winter and Summer – Fair weather and foul – Low ruts or no ruts – Never take a false quarter – No, no, Widow – I drive – Hayait!– Ah!– Ah! Get on !– St – St– Touch Whitefoot in the flank – Tickle Snarler in the ear – Cut up the Yelper – Take out a fly's eye – Smack, crack – That's your sort!

The exuberance, the bursting into rhyme, the frenzied encouragements to himself and his horses, create for us a sense of Goldfinch taking to the road, four-in-hand and whip in hand, in front of our eyes. The opening solemnity ('I'm christened and called Charles – Charles Goldfinch') in which he tells his name over as a sort of charm, a guarantee that only he can drive, has a Dickensian rightness. 'Totherest Governor', Riderhood says to Bradley Headstone in *Our mutual friend*,

I know wot it is to be loud, and I know wot it is to be soft. Nat'rally I do. It would be a wonder if I did not, being by the Cris'en name of Roger . . .

The last strange utterance of Goldfinch's speech – 'That's your sort!' – appears again and again throughout the play, meaningless and compulsive, till it seems on its own to evoke his whole chaotic state of mind. Hazlitt points to the pleasure in its repetition, for both character and audience:

*That's your sort* comes in at least fifty times, and is just as unexpected and lively

45

# Thomas Holcroft

the last time as the first, for no other reason than because Goldfinch has just the same pleasure in repeating it. This mechanical humour was so much the more striking in its effect, because every person could make it his own. It was very transferable . . . (Howe, iii, 122–3)

Goldfinch, and the strange gaiety of the play as a whole, seem to have been a relief to the author. It is with the honest old banker, Dornton, that *The road to ruin* opens. We witness from the first the loving but desperate confusion that he feels over his ne'er-do-well son, Harry. Harry is profligate, he is ruining the firm, he must be cut off without a penny. It was all very near the bone. Holcroft's sixteen-year-old son William had shot himself in 1789, having run away from home many times, and on the last occasion stolen £40 to get him to the West Indies. It was his father's following him onto the ship that caused him to fire. The play is a coming to terms with pain. In place of Holcroft's usual preoccupation with politics there is an urgent personal need to make things right. Though muttering terrible threats, the elder Dornton is unfailingly kind. Harry, though squandering his father's money, rallies to him at once when he hears that the firm is in trouble:

My father! Sir! [*Turning away*] Is it possible? – Disgraced? – Ruined? – In reality ruined? – By me? . . .
*Dornton.*   Calm yourself, Harry!
*Harry.*   I am calm! Very calm! – It shall be done! – Don't be dejected – You are my father – You were the first of men in the first of cities – Revered by the good and respected by the great – You flourished prosperously! – But you had a son! – I remember it!
*Dornton.*   Why do you roll your eyes, Harry?
*Harry.*   I won't be long away!
*Dornton.*   Stay where you are, Harry! [*Catching his hand*] All will be well! I am very happy! Do not leave me! – I am very happy! – Indeed I am, Harry! – Very happy!

The William who would have reformed, who loved his father and did not need to die, is brought to life. The father's wish-fulfilment is acted out. To have handled such material within the framework of a comedy may seem at first extraordinary. Yet on second thoughts *The road to ruin* resembles much great art of this period that draws its strength from the need to assuage, to atone, to understand.

10

# WILLIAM FREND

# Peace and union

*recommended to the associated bodies
of republicans and anti-republicans*
1793

'At this moment perhaps the decree is gone forth for war' – William Frend, Unitarian minister and Fellow of Jesus College, Cambridge, was writing the final paragraph of *Peace and union* in the last days of January 1793. Louis XVI (styled by the French and their sympathisers, Louis Capet, since the declaration of the Republic in September) had been executed on the 21st; France would declare war on 1 February, and England follow suit on the 11th. There can seldom have been less prospect of harmony and union between the British groups of republicans and anti-republicans to whom Frend addressed himself. Rumours of 'civil commotions' had led in December to the calling out of local militias and the recall of Parliament. In the Commons on 13 December, and again in his published *Letter* to the Westminster Electors, the Whig leader, Charles James Fox, had warned against over-reaction:

Those who differ from us in their ideas of the constitution, in this paroxysm of alarm we consider as confederated to destroy it.

Frend's is a case in point. Though his brief appendices, 'On the Execution of Louis Capet' and 'The Effect of War on the Poor', were more contentious, he made in *Peace and union* a sincere attempt to reason the extremes of British politics towards a middle ground. As a result he was publicly tried by the University and deprived of his Fellowship. 'Were not the times', the Vice Chancellor demanded in his closing speech,

most critical? Did the authour inculcate the necessity of peace and good order? When the national convention of France had filled up the measure of their crimes, by murdering the king, and destroying all lawful government, and their

47

# William Frend

deliberations breathed nothing but atheism and anarchy, did he inculcate a respect for the king and parliament of this country, and for the reformed religion, and the functions of the clergy as established by law? (*Proceedings*, 181–2)

About the functions of the clergy, Frend, as a Unitarian, had strong views – 'The established church of England can be considered only as a political institution', 'There are few congregations which worship only the one true god' – but even in this area he is seldom provocative. In general, he does indeed 'inculcate the necessity for peace and good order'. It is his primary concern.

Frend's view, stated at the outset of *Peace and union*, is that 'the utmost vigour of government, aided by the exertions of every lover of his country, is necessary to preserve us from all the horrours attendant on civil commotions'. The situation in France he sees as 'an awful example, which providence holds out to an astonished world'. The September Massacres have been shocking, but so was the misery that existed under the *ancien régime*. It must be possible to learn from both:

The assassinations, murders, massacres, burning of houses, plundering of property, open violations of justice, which have marked the progress of the French revolution, must stagger the boldest republican in his wishes to overthrow any constitution: and on the other hand he must be a weak or a wicked man, who lost in admiration of the beauties of a voluptuous and effeminate court, forgets the misery of the poor subjects, whose bodies were bowed down to the grindstone for its support, and brands with every mark of aristocratick insolence the efforts of those patriots, who put an end to the despotism of the antient government. (p. 1)

The original readers of Frend's pamphlet would have seen him as steering a path between the 'aristocratick insolence' of Burke and the 'bold republicanism' of Paine (now a French deputy, but condemned by a British court for seditious libel on 18 December).

Frend is a reformer, by most standards a moderate. The lesson to be learned from France is above all of failure to act in time:

From neglecting to examine and correct the abuses, prevailing through length of time in an extensive empire, we have seen a monarch hurled from his throne, the most powerful nobility in Europe driven from their castles, and the richest [clerical] hierarchy expelled from their altars.

The different orders of French society, even the affluent priesthood, could all have survived had they accepted the need to modify existing institutions:

Had the monarch seasonably given up some useless prerogatives, he might still

48

have worn the crown; had the nobility consented to relinquish those feudal privileges, which were designed only for barbarous ages, they might have retained their titles; could the clergy have submitted to be citizens, they might still have been in possession of wealth and influence. (p.43)

'The proper time', Frend adds, 'to correct any abuse, and remedy any grievance, is the instant, they are known'.

From an English point of view, the words contained a threat. Was it already too late to examine peaceably 'the abuses, prevailing through length of time in [Britain's] extensive empire'? Frend does not think so. He has practical, humanitarian suggestions to put forward for modifying the constitution, increasing representation (so that 'all laws relating to the conduct of an individual would not only be known to him, but receive his approbation or censure'), assisting the not–quite–so–poor (the class that is Wordsworth's concern in *The last of the flock*), disestablishing the Church: what could prevent George III (who, as King of England and Scotland and Elector of Hanover, is a member of three different churches himself) from saying to all, 'Be peaceable citizens, and worship god as you please'? Anxious as he is for peace, Frend is not without a sharp side to his tongue. Representation is to exclude those 'obstinately attached to vicious and bad customs'; the priest, 'whether he celebrates the orgies of Bacchus, or solemnizes the rites of the Eucharist' will oppose every truth that threatens his authority; to secure the repeal of the Test Act, presbyterians, baptists and independents, might band together, but they

would on the obtaining of that point, retire to their different camps, and be separated from each other by the usual marks of theological hatred. (pp. 31–2)

Frend had been an Anglican parson himself until, learning Hebrew and becoming a translator of the bible (his work was burned by the mob that destroyed Priestley's house in July 1791), he decided that scriptural evidence was against the doctrine of the Trinity. Conversion to Unitarianism in 1787 cut him off both from the 'men in black' of the established Church (he alone wore blue in the Common Room at Jesus) and from dissenters who believed 'idolatrously' in the divinity of Christ. As he made clear at the trial, however, his creed is love:

if we neglect the principle of universal benevolence, our faith is vain, our religion is an empty parade of useless and insignificant sounds . . . every christian is bound to entertain sentiments of universal benevolence, to love his fellow creatures of every sect, colour or description . . . (*Proceedings*, 89)

Coleridge, who was a member of Frend's college, and by this stage a disciple, applauded him so vigorously from the gallery that he barely escaped arrest by the Proctor. Intellectually Coleridge's Unitarianism of the mid 1790s derives from Priestley (and Hartley). But it was Frend's more emotional faith that inspired his vision of 'the vast family of Love / Rais'd from the common earth by common toil' (*Religious musings*). It also supported for a time the hopes he placed in a smaller, emigrant 'family of love' (Pantisocracy) on the banks of the Susquehanna.

The change of tone as Frend brings *Peace and union* to an end and moves into his appendices could hardly be more abrupt. One moment we are reading a plea that 'republicans be moderate in their demands, the anti-republicans not pertinacious in opposing every reform', the next we hear that 'Louis Capet has provided an excellent topic for parliamentary declamation':

The supreme power in the nation declared, that France should be a republick: from that moment Louis Capet lost his titles. He was accused of enormous crimes, confined as a state prisoner, tried by the national convention, found guilty, condemned, and executed. What is there wonderful in all this? . . . If Louis Capet did, when king, encourage the invasion of his country, however we may be inclined to pity the unfortunate man for the errour of his conduct, we have no right to proclaim him innocent in point of law. (pp. 45–6)

'It is in short no business of ours', Frend adds, 'and if all the crowned heads on the continent are taken off, it is no business of ours.' Perhaps it was a little provocative.

Like the Wordsworth whose *Letter to the bishop of Llandaff* (February 1793) dismisses mourning for Louis as an 'idle cry of modish lamentation', Frend reserves his sympathy for the poor who will suffer especially from the war that is starting. Walking from Cambridge to St Ives to see his pamphlet through the press, he overhears the conversation of market-women who have had their wages for spinning wool reduced by a quarter: 'We are to be sconced three-pence in the shilling . . . We are to be sconced a fourth part of our labour. What is all this for?' In Wordsworth's phrase, the women and their families are 'about to smart under the scourge of labour, of cold, and of hunger', in 'a war from which not a single ray of consolation can visit them'. It is from their uncomprehending complaints that Frend creates his vehement concluding paragraph:

At this moment perhaps the decree is gone forth for war. Let others talk of glory, let others celebrate the heroes, who are to deluge the world with blood, the words of the poor market women will still resound in my ears, we are sconced three-pence in the shilling, one fourth of our labour. For what! (p. 49)

## II

# WILLIAM GODWIN

_____

# An enquiry
# concerning political justice

1793


> This was the time when, all things tending fast
> To depravation, the philosophy
> That promised to abstract the hopes of man
> Out of his feelings, to be fixed henceforth
> For ever in a purer element
> Found ready welcome.

At work on the *Prelude* in autumn 1804, Wordsworth looks back ten years to the period when the influence of *Political justice* was at its height. 'Tempting region that', he adds, with the ironic detachment of the one-time disciple,

> Where passions had the privilege to work,
> And never hear the sound of their own names . . .
> $\qquad$ (1805 *Prelude*, x, 805–12)

From a slightly different viewpoint, Hazlitt would describe the fault of Godwin's system as 'too much ambition', conceiving 'too nobly of his fellows':

The author of the *Political justice* took abstract reason for the rule of conduct, and abstract good for its end. He places the human mind on an elevation, from which it commands a view of the whole line of moral consequences; and requires it to conform its acts to the larger and more enlightened conscience which it has thus acquired. He absolves man from the gross and narrow ties of sense, custom, authority, private and local attachment, in order that he may devote himself to the boundless pursuit of universal benevolence. (*Spirit of the age*, p. 36)

For Hazlitt, Godwin is a prime example of the spirit of the age at work – one who 'blazed as a sun in the firmament of reputation', and is now, in 1825, 'sunk below the horizon', living on 'a sort of posthumous fame'.

For Wordsworth (eight important years older than Hazlitt, and a first-hand witness of the Revolution), Godwin is a hope that failed, a way of life that should have worked, a philosophy that ought to have been unassailable.

No book ever came out at a more opportune moment than *Political justice*. On 21 January 1793, Louis XVI was guillotined. On 1 February the French National Assembly declared war on Britain. Britain entered the war on the 11th. *Political justice*, with its reassuring creed of human rationality, was out three days later. Louis had been guilty of the charges brought against him (conspiring against the constitution to which he had sworn allegiance), but that did not lessen the shock of his death. In his immediate recantation of French sympathies, the Bishop of Llandaff spoke for all but the most determined British radicals, when he wrote on 25 January:

I fly with terror and abhorrence, even from the altar of Liberty, when I see it stained with the blood of the aged, of the innocent, of the defenceless sex, of the ministers of religion . . . My heart sinks within me when I see it streaming with the blood of the monarch himself. (*Westminster dispensary sermon*, Appendix p. 19)

War turned those who remained loyal to the Revolution into traitors, isolating them still further. 'I only', Wordsworth writes of hearing prayers sent up in church for British victory,

> like an uninvited guest
> Whom no one owned, sate silent – shall I add,
> Fed on the day of vengeance yet to come!
> (1805 *Prelude*, x, 272–4)

Amid this confusion of sympathies, Godwin offered 'to abstract the hopes of man / Out of his feelings'. Justice would come as the result, not of politics, but of dispassionate reason. There would be no need for conflict or violence. The man

who regards all things past, present and to come as links of an indissoluble chain, will, as often as he recollects this comprehensive view, be superior to the tumult of passion; and will reflect upon the moral concerns of mankind with the same clearness of perception, the same unalterable firmness of judgement, and the same tranquillity as we are accustomed to do upon the truths of geometry.
(1793 *Political justice*, i, 316–17)

It was this sense of the inevitability of progress that so attracted Godwin's contemporaries. He had been brought up a Calvinist, and trained in the dissenting academy at Hoxton. From 1779–83 he had worked as minister with two successive congregations, but found difficulty in adjusting his views to theirs. Moving away from a Calvinist belief in the elect and the damned, he had briefly accepted a Priestleyan Unitarianism, before losing his faith in the late 1780s. At the time of *Political justice* he was considered to be an atheist, yet his work continued to reflect assumptions from his earlier Christian thinking. Though different in almost every way, Priestley and Calvin had it in common that they were determinists. And behind Priestley was Hartley, whose *Observations on man* (reprinted by Joseph Johnson in 1791) spoke of 'the necessity of human actions, and the ultimate happiness of mankind' (Preface, p. v).

For Hartley, God is not merely 'the source of all good', but 'consequently must at last appear to be so'. Man is led towards the Deity by a constant refining within the mind of the power of association. Godwin puts his emphasis upon reason rather than associationism, and is no longer a theologian, but he too sees the mind as equipped in itself for the achievement of ultimate happiness. Hartley looks forward (both within the individual and within the species) to the moment when the idea of God 'shall absorb' all other ideas, permitting God to become, 'according to the language of the scriptures, *all in all*' (1791 *Observations*, i, 114). *Political justice* too rests upon the concept of perfectibility: 'The legitimate instrument of effecting political reformation is truth. Let truth be incessantly studied, illustrated and propagated, and the effect is inevitable' (ii, 593). The rational mind will achieve its fulfilment in a recognition of truth, that will be followed, of necessity, by a 'just' relation to society.

In practice, Godwin's thinking in *Political justice* relies upon indoctrination: 'Infuse just views of society into a certain number of the liberally educated and reflecting members; give to the people guides and instructors; and the business is done' (i. 69). Book One, chapter four, present only in the first edition, considers 'Three Principal Causes of Moral Improvement': i. Literature, ii. Education, iii. Political Justice. Literature is defined, rather surprisingly, as 'the diffusion of knowledge through the medium of discussion, whether written or oral', education, as 'a scheme for the early impression of right principles upon the hitherto unprejudiced mind', and political justice, as the 'adoption' of principles of morality and truth 'into the practice of a community' (i, 19).

Defined as intellectual discussion, literature takes on immense significance. It is not Shakespeare or Milton to whom Godwin turns (well-read though he is), but Locke and Newton, predecessors in the quest for truth, and evidence in their own right of the march of human progress:

> Literature has reconciled the whole thinking world respecting the great principles of the system of the universe, and extirpated . . . the dogmas of superstition. Literature has unfolded the nature of the human mind . . . Locke and others have established certain maxims respecting man, as Newton has done respecting matter, that are generally admitted for unquestionable. (i, 20)

Education, in the sense of schooling, could not fail to be of importance to Godwin. He regards it, however, as wasteful of resources ('an immense combination of powers' being necessary for the shaping of a single individual), and 'exceedingly incompetent to the great business of reforming mankind'. Until society is reformed, the teacher is at the disadvantage of having to protect his student from outside influence: 'No task . . . can easily be supposed more difficult, than that of counteracting universal error, and arming the youthful mind against the contagion of general example'. 'Where', Godwin demands,

> can a remedy be found for this fundamental disadvantage? where but in political justice, that all comprehensive scheme, that . . . embraces millions in its grasp, and that educates in one school the preceptor and the pupil? (i, 27)

Like the rest of this highly important section, Godwin's reference to the 'all comprehensive scheme' of political justice is found only in the text of 1793. De Quincey commented in 1845 that 'The second edition [of *Political justice*], as regards principles, is not a re-cast, but absolutely a travesty of the first' (Masson, xi, 328). They are strong words, but Godwin's own statement in the Preface of 1796 is that five of the eight original books (the first four and the last) 'may, without impropriety, be said to be rewritten' (1796, i, xvi). Times changed, and Godwin changed with them. As perhaps one should expect, it is the most important sections of the 1793 first edition – those that had been responsible for its fame, or notoriety – that are left out, or timidly revised. Yet the 1793 text has never been reprinted, and is read by almost nobody. Scholars typically base their views of *Political justice* on the text of the third edition (1798), noting perhaps the 1793 readings in passing, but gaining at best a poor idea of the power and clarity of Godwin's original position.

*Political justice*, as the original Preface makes clear, was inspired by the French Revolution. Planned in May 1791, and finished in January '93, it preserves in its changes of mind and mood the record of a period of transition. Against the background of increasing violence in France and increasing repression in England, Godwin strove to convey an optimistic philosophy, dependent on the assumption of human progress. Consistency was not helped by the fact that type for early parts of the book was set up before the rest had been written. Readers were warned in the circumstances to expect an 'occasional inaccuracy of language, particularly in the first book, respecting the word government' (p. x). There were other problems too. Signing his Preface on 7 January 1793, with the French king on trial for his life (and Paine recently condemned in England for sedition), Godwin felt a justifiable anxiety. The tory Government might decide to prosecute. In his respect for truth he had been unguarded throughout. One section in Book Four (not, of course, present in later editions) looked forward to a chain-reaction of political revolutions that must certainly involve his own country:

only six years elapsed between the completion of American liberty and the commencement of the French revolution. Will a term longer than this be necessary, before France, the most refined and considerable nation in the world, will lead other nations to imitate and improve upon her plan? Let the true friend of man be incessant in the propagation of truth . . . and he will have every reason to hope an early and a favourable event. (i, 224–5)

Viewed as improvements in the science of government, revolutions were examples of human progress to put beside the discoveries of Newton and Locke. In practical terms, they came step by step nearer to creating a system of political justice within which the individual could lead a fully rational existence. How far Godwin (at any stage) believed that government would one day be dispensed with, it is difficult to say. There could be no doubt that it was an intrusion on personal freedom. In a rational society it shouldn't be needed. Book Two in 1793 quotes with approval Paine's definitions from the opening page of *Common sense* (1775): 'Society is produced by our wants, and government by our wickedness. Society is in every state a blessing; government even in its best state but a necessary evil' (i, 79). During an interim period, government has a part to play in the establishing of political justice; at a later stage, it should dwindle to the minimum implied by a society of rational, and therefore self-governing, people. In Book Three Godwin takes the view that because 'Truth is in reality single and uniform',

There must in the nature of things be one best form of government, which all intellects, sufficiently roused from the slumber of savage ignorance, will be irresistibly incited to approve. (i, 181–2)

By the end of Book Five, after a more detailed look at the failings of government – monarchy, aristocracy, democracy – he is prepared to write with a flourish:

> With what delight must every well informed friend of mankind look forward to the auspicious period, the dissolution of political government, of that brute engine, which has been the only perennial cause of the vices of mankind, and which, as has abundantly appeared in the progress of the present work, has mischiefs of various sorts incorporated with its substance, and no otherwise to be removed than by its utter annihilation. (ii, 578–9)

Whatever Godwin's insistence on reason, we respond to his pronouncements as embodying an emotional need. We watch him making statements of faith, and though we draw back, we do so knowing the need to be one that we share. We are not likely to look on truth, reason, benevolence, with his expectations, but any hope we may have for the future depends on human beings to some extent embodying these qualities. *Political justice* takes everything to extremes. Truth for Godwin is not merely 'single and uniform', it is omnipotent. Yet it has to be taken on trust. In the supposedly atheist world of *Political justice* it functions as a quasi-religious concept. The point is taken by Coleridge in the *Lectures on revealed religion* of May 1795. Dismissing *Political justice* with evident pleasure, he proclaims: 'Whatever is just in it, is more forcibly recommended in the Gospel and whatever is new is absurd' (Patton and Mann, 164).

The tones have a marvellous finality. And that, says Coleridge, is that! Yet Pantisocracy – the scheme in which he had so passionately believed the previous summer – had been designed as an experiment in political justice. Coleridge had no doubt seen the planned American commune in terms of Priestley's recent emigration, but the ideals of Pantisocracy had come in the first place, *via* Southey, from Godwin. There was much in *Political justice* to which Coleridge would inevitably be drawn. It is clear from his letter to Southey of 21 October 1794 that at this stage he accepted some even of Godwin's more convoluted views: it is the 'Individual's *duty* to be Just, because it is in his *Interest*'. 'All that is good in Godwin' is to go into Coleridge's projected 'Book of Pantisocracy'. That there was 'bad' in him too went without saying. Godwin's atheism had been denounced by Coleridge as early as 11 September ('I set him at Defiance').

To a believer in Hartley's Christian determinism, there could be no basis for Godwinian optimism. The system, however attractive, was flawed at its centre. As Pantisocracy became a less immediate prospect, Coleridge's distrust hardened into antagonism. By the time of the political lectures of February 1795 (revised as *Conciones ad populum* in December), Godwin had become the enemy against whom Coleridge defined his own Unitarian views of society.

Wordsworth's relation to Godwin went deeper, but is less well documented. To judge from his *Letter to the Bishop of Llandaff*, he was in English terms a Painite (in French, a Girondin) when *Political justice* came out. But Paine, for all his rightness about rights and practicality about political detail, offered no hope in the face of repression. Wordsworth's dependence on Godwin emerges in letters to William Matthews, of 23 May and 8 June 1794, announcing himself a member of 'that odious class of men called democrats' and projecting a magazine to 'diffuse' the 'rules of political justice'. In France the Great Terror was at its height, in England habeas corpus had been suspended and the leading radicals (with the surprising exception of Godwin) sent to the Tower. Wordsworth's magazine never got started, but it is clear that he turned to *Political justice*, and political theory, at a moment when the confidence generated during his visit to France during 1792 could no longer be sustained. Godwin's diary shows that in the period February – August 1795 he and Wordsworth met on nine separate occasions. Conversations are not recorded, but neither of them had much small talk. Godwin, his reputation augmented by the publication of *Caleb Williams* (May 1794), was 'blazing as a sun in the firmament', and rewriting *Political justice*. Wordsworth, fourteen years younger, with no career and no successes to speak of, was surely a disciple.

Like Coleridge, Wordsworth came to define himself against Godwin, but the affinities were greater, and the outcome had more bearing on his own creativity. Straightforward Godwinian influence is seen briefly in *Adventures on Salisbury plain* (November 1795), where the central figure is a good-hearted murderer on the run, performing acts of benevolence though driven by society to crime. *The borderers*, written a year later, is more complex. Wordsworth, it seems, has set out to write a cautionary-tale showing that Godwinian reason may be put to bad uses, and that intuition is the surer guide. As the play develops, and the poetry develops, however, we see instead a Wordsworthian version of the aspiring human mind, dependent not on rationality, but on powers released by the intensity of emotional experience:

> I had within me
> A salient spring of energy, a fire
> Of unextinguishable thought – I mounted
> From action up to action with a mind
> That never rested . . .
> I seemed a being who had passed alone
> Beyond the visible barriers of the world,
> And travelled into things to come.
>
> (1799 *Borderers*, IV, ii, 119–22, 143–5)

Godwin had had his vision of the man of the future, freed from social restraints and Blakean 'mind-forged manacles':

The genuine and wholesome state of mind is, to be unloosed from shackles, and to expand every fibre of its frame according to the individual and independent impressions of truth upon that mind. (ii, 569)

Wordsworth's vision, by contrast, is of the fully imaginative human being.

Godwin, it seems, is held back. In the name of reason he makes an act of faith in the future, and in the power of the human mind. In this sense he might himself be described as a Romantic. In their poetry others would pass 'Beyond the visible barriers of the world', and in so doing, pass him by. He is tied, as they are not, to a particular moment of history and way of thinking. Yet he came very close to high Romanticism. As Wordsworth satirizes him in the *Prelude*, it is a thin dividing line between philosopher of reason and the poet whose theme is 'the mind of man':

> What delight!–
> How glorious! – in self-knowledge and self-rule
> To look through all the frailties of the world,
> And, with a resolute mastery shaking off
> The accidents of nature, time, and place,
> That make up the weak being of the past,
> Build social freedom on its only base:
> The freedom of the individual mind,
> Which, to the blind restraint of general laws
> Superior, magisterially adopts
> One guide – the light of circumstances, flashed
> Upon an independent intellect.
>
> (1805 *Prelude*, x, 818–29)

The guide, we are being told, should have been intuition, not the mere 'light of circumstances'. Nature, time and place, should not have been shaken off as 'accidents', they are the forces that for good ends 'build up this our intellectual being'. By the same token, the restraint exercised by 'general laws' is not to be seen as blind. Yet Wordsworth himself places an absolute trust in self-knowledge, self-rule, the freedom of the individual mind, independence of intellect. He had learned much from Godwin. And the central tenets he never turned his back on.

Godwin, of course, did turn his back. De Quincey for one sees the eclipse of his reputation as directly related to his failure, in later editions, to stand by the great attack on authority and affirmation of human potential made in 1793:

In the *quarto* (that is, the original) edition of his *Political justice*, Mr Godwin advanced against thrones and dominations, powers and principalities, with the air of some Titan slinger . . . from Thebes or Troy, saying – 'Come hither, ye wretches, that I may give your flesh to the fowls of the air.' But in the second, or *octavo* edition – and under what motive has never been explained – he recoiled absolutely from the sound himself had made: everybody else was appalled by the fury of the challenge, and, through the strangest of accidents, Mr Godwin also was appalled. The second edition, as regards principles, is not a re-cast, but absolutely a travesty of the first; nay, it is all but a palinode. In this collapse of a tense excitement I myself find the true reason for the utter extinction of the *Political justice*, and of its author considered as a philosopher. (Masson, xi, 328)

## 12

## COLERIDGE AND SOUTHEY

---

# The fall of Robespierre
*an historic drama*
1794

Coleridge was twenty-one, and an undergraduate at Jesus College, Cambridge, when he and Southey met in Oxford in early June 1794. With a friend named Hucks, he had walked the ninety miles between the two Universities on the first leg of a pedestrian tour (of 629 miles, as it turned out). Southey was two years younger. He was talented, ambitious, and had no prospects save to go into the Church, which he didn't wish to do. Tom Poole, who met the two of them in August, noted first that Coleridge was a Unitarian, and 'in Politics a Democrat, to the utmost extent of the word', then added:

Southey, who was with him, is of the University of Oxford, a younger man, without the splendid abilities of Coldridge, though possessing much information . . . and is more violent in his [political] principles than even Coldridge himself. In Religion, shocking to say in a mere boy as he is, I fear he wavers between Deism and Atheism. (Sandford, i, 97)

It was in Southey's rooms at Balliol that the scheme to found an egalitarian commune – Pantisocracy, 'the rule of all' – was evolved. Land would be purchased in America. There would be twelve men and their wives. Property would be held in common. Pantisocrats would be selected for the correctness of their views, and their reliability as educators of a pristine new generation. Children born within the commune would have to be protected from European sophistication and degeneracy. The scheme had soon to be modified, but its principles were similar to those set out by Godwin in *Political justice* (1793) – except that, for Coleridge, at least, they had the Christian basis of Priestleyan Unitarianism. 'Could they realize [their aims]', Poole commented, they would indeed, realize the age of reason; but, however perfectible human nature may be, I fear it is not perfect enough to exist long under the regulations of such a system, particularly when the Executors of the plan are taken from a society in a high degree civilized and corrupted. (Sandford, i, 98)

In August 1794 more immediate problems confronted the scheme. Suitable Pantisocrats had to be found, equipped with suitable partners. And money had to be raised. The Fricker family at Bristol, genteel but impoverished, offered at least four potential wives. The eldest daughter, Mary, was already married to Lovell (minor poet, and in on the scheme), Edith was to marry Southey, Sara was being courted by Coleridge (still in love with Mary Evans, but swayed by pantisocratic convenience), Martha had the spirit to turn down Burnett. As regards money, it was estimated that the scheme would cost a total of £2,000. All would contribute, but Coleridge and Southey could do so only by writing. The events of 8–10 Thermidor (26–8 July) provided the chance for a quick publication. Coleridge wrote Act I of *The fall of Robespierre*, and very possibly mapped out the rest. Southey wrote Acts II and III (though it seems that Lovell had been intended to write the third).

Southey's letter of 3 September, famous for its vision of the settler's life–

When Coleridge and I are sawing down a tree we shall discuss metaphysics; criticise poetry when hunting a buffalo, and write sonnets whilst following the plough

– makes the interesting further comment, 'Poor Robespierre! Coleridge and I wrote a tragedy upon his death in the space of two days!'. Coleridge makes the same claim (in Latin), while writing to Wrangham on 24 October: '*Biduo* effusus est'. It is hard to take literally (to assimilate the complex situation, and plan the work, would have taken time, and there are 771 lines of respectable blank verse), but the play was certainly written fast. It took over two weeks for reports of Robespierre's death to reach London – the first one, *via* military sources in Frankfurt. On 14 August *The Times* printed rumours that he had been murdered; on the 15th he was said to have committed suicide; on the 16th it seemed not only that he had been despatched by members of the National Convention 'with their poniards', but that '10,000 to 14,000 men' had been killed in three days of fighting in the streets of Paris. Two days later, on 18 August 1794, *The Times* had copies of the *Moniteur* for 26–31 July, and was able to give the long and detailed account of Robespierre's final hours on which Coleridge and Southey's play was probably based. No more was heard of the carnage in the streets.

Wordsworth in Cumbria greeted the news of Robespierre's death (given him by a passer-by on Levens Sands) with 'joy / In vengeance, and eternal justice', hoping fervently that the Revolution would revert to its original ideals. Southey, who lacked both his experience of French politics and his genuine commitment, decided to strike an attitude: 'I had rather have heard of the death of my own father' (his own father, be it said, had died the previous year, broken-hearted after the failure of his business, bankruptcy, and spell in prison). Coleridge's reactions are not recorded, but he tended, as Poole observed, to be less extreme. *The fall of Robespierre* is not, in any case, a jacobin play. It presents the facts as they are known, and, in Acts II and III especially, is often very close to *The Times* narrative. Neither Southey, nor Coleridge, however, is guilty of merely versifing the prose. Events that were dramatic on the day, and deadened in the telling, are given a new vividness. We get a genuine sense of the connivance and fear, the uneasy alliances, the in-fighting, the rhetoric, of the Convention. Robespierre's ally St Just makes his ill-judged entrance on the afternoon of 9 Thermidor:

St. Just observed that he was of no faction, but would contend against them all. 'Your Committees of General Surety and Public Safety (said he) have charged me to make a just report on the causes of the evident perversion of opinion: but I mean to address myself to you, and only in my own name.' (*The Times*)

*Enter* St. Just, *and mounts the Tribune.*

St. Just
I come from the committee – charged to speak
Of matters of high import. I omit
Their orders. Representatives of France,
Boldly in his own person speaks St. Just
What his own heart shall dictate.

Tallien seizes the opportunity for an indignant speech, reported verbatim by *The Times*:

Yesterday a Member of the Government (Robespierre) presented to you a report upon his own authority. Today, another Member comes to speak to you in his own name. No good citizen can refrain from lamenting, with tears, the abject and calamitous state to which the Republic is reduced, when individuals pretend thus to dictate to you in their own name, and upon their own authority.

Unable at first to get away from the prose wording, Southey gathers strength, ending with a flourish that lifts the speech, yet remains true to Tallien and the rhetoric of the Revolution:

> TALLIEN
> Robespierre on yester morn pronounced
> Upon his own authority a report.
> Today St. Just comes down. St. Just neglects
> What the Committee orders, and harangues
> From his own will. O citizens of France
> I weep for you – I weep for my poor country –
> I tremble for the cause of Liberty,
> When individuals shall assume the sway,
> And with more insolence than kingly pride
> Rule the Republic.

It is Coleridge who in Act I sets the scene for us. His verse is more powerful than Southey's. He is writing with no obvious source, but handles the conspirators, and Robespierre himself, with considerable dramatic instinct:

> ROBESPIERRE
> What? did La Fayette fall before my power?
> And did I conquer Roland's spotless virtues?
> The fervent eloquence of Vergniaud's tongue?
> And Brissot's thoughtful soul unbribed and bold?
> Did zealot armies haste in vain to save them?
> What! did th' assassin's dagger aim its point
> Vain, as a *dream* of murder, at my bosom?
> And shall I dread the soft luxurious Tallien?
> Th' Adonis Tallien? banquet-hunting Tallien?
> Him, whose heart flutters at the dice-box? Him,
> Who ever on the harlots' downy pillow
> Resigns his head impure to feverish slumbers!

> ST. JUST
> I cannot fear him – yet we must not scorn him.
> Was it not Antony that conquer'd Brutus,
> Th' Adonis, banquet-hunting Antony?
> The state is not yet purified . . .

'The last two Acts', Coleridge wrote to Southey from London on 11 September, 'want a few alterations – which Dyer pointed out'. 'Of course', he goes on, cheerfully adding injury to insult, 'I have your permission to be "plenipo-emendator" '. Eight days later he had taken the play over:

The Tragedy will be printed in less than a week – I shall put my Name – because it will sell at least an hundred Copies at Cambridge. It would appear ridiculous to put two names to *such* a Work. – But if you choose it, mention it – and it shall be done – To every man who *praises* it, of course I give the *true* biography . . .

Just how full Coleridge's emendation was we do not know, but it seems very likely that at this stage he pulled the play together. His stated aim was 'to imitate the empassioned and highly figurative language of the French orators, and to develope the characters of the chief actors on a vast stage of horrors.' French oratory was certainly impassioned. Tallien (a Girondin who had escaped the purge) is quoted by *The Times* as 'invok[ing] the shade of the virtuous Brutus', his eyes fixed on the bust: 'Like him I have a poniard to rid my country of the tyrant.' It was a style that suited Coleridge better than Southey, and which licensed the extravagance, for instance, of the opening of Act III:

> COLLOT D'HERBOIS
> Caesar is fallen! The baneful tree of Java,
> Whose death-distilling boughs dropt poisonous dew,
> Is rooted from its base.

But the play is surprisingly effective. It lacks a considered view of character and motive among the leaders of the Revolution, but perhaps no one in England was in a position to arrive at one. Instead it offers a credible rhetoric and a credible atmosphere:

> Sublime amid the storm shall France arise,
> And like the rock amid surrounding waves
> Repel the rushing ocean.– She shall wield
> The thunder-bolt of vengeance – she shall blast
> The despot's pride, and liberate the world!

# 13

## SAMUEL TAYLOR COLERIDGE

---

# Conciones ad populum
*or addresses to the people*
1795


Coleridge at twenty-two showed remarkable assurance. His political lectures, delivered to a Bristol audience in February 1795 and reworked in November as *Conciones ad populum* (Addresses to the People), are authoritative and uncompromising. Robespierre had been executed the previous year, Louis XVI the year before that; the French Revolution had had no time to become part of history. Yet Coleridge analyses its progress with a confident sense of detachment. 'Revolutions', we are told, 'are sudden to the unthinking only.' 'It is not the character of the possessor which directs the power, but the power which shapes and depraves the character of the possessor.' France is a warning,

recorded in Letters of Blood, that the Knowledge of the Few cannot counteract the Ignorance of the Many; that the Light of Philosophy, when it is confined to a small Minority, points out the Possessors as the Victims, rather than the Illuminators of the Multitude. (p. 9)

In *Conciones* we see for the first time both Coleridge the political journalist, and Coleridge the accomplished Unitarian philosopher, follower of David Hartley (*Observations on man*, reissued 1791), but also thinker-for-himself. He is concerned with principles and motives, ideals of the good leader and the good life. Brissot, leader of the moderate Girondins, and Robespierre, his Jacobin counterpart (who sent him to the guillotine), are compared with extraordinary insight. Juxtapositions of Robespierre and Pitt, French atrocities and British imperialism, show up the hypocrisies of Government and the horrors of unnecessary war. British 'Friends of Liberty' are categorized, and disparaged, as Coleridge presents his picture of the true seeker after truth. Godwin (*Political justice* 1793) is confronted, and his system of rational benevolence replaced by

65

# Samuel Taylor Coleridge

New Testament values of equality and love, such as would have obtained in Coleridge's vision of Pantisocracy.

The French Revolution was for Wordsworth a matter of personal experience. He had seen its achievements on the spot. He knew 'How bright a face is worn when joy of one / Is joy of tens of millions' (1805 *Prelude*, vi, 359–60). 'Looking back, he could write unaffectedly, 'My heart was all / Given to the people, and my love was theirs' (ix, 124–5). Coleridge's position was very different. He was two years younger than Wordsworth, and had never been abroad. The Revolution's hopeful opening phase (July 1789–August 1792) was over before he became politically active. There is no reason to doubt his sympathy with the French, but his thinking was more abstract. Wordsworth was stirred by the sight of a 'hunger-bitten girl' encountered on the Loire, Coleridge by the ideal of egalitarianism. In September 1794, at the beginning of what proved to be his last term at Cambridge, he had rushed into print *The fall of Robespierre*. Letters show him in the next two months defending the principles of Pantisocracy against Southey's pragmatism; suffering over the loss of his early sweetheart and companion, Mary Evans; regretting his engagement to Sara Fricker, made in the name of pantisocratic convenience (each of the twelve male emigrants needed a partner). Events in France do not appear to be uppermost in his mind, but the poetry he writes is increasingly political. At the end of the year, as he leaves Cambridge for London without a degree, the *Morning chronicle* publishes in turn his eleven Sonnets on *Eminent characters*. Names of the chosen take us to the allegiances that we should expect of Coleridge as radical dissenter. We are directed to the murder of Kosciusko, the exile of Priestley, the tergiversation of Burke:

> Great Son of Genius! sweet to me thy Name,
> Ere in an evil Hour with alter'd Voice
> Thou bad'st oppression's hireling Crew rejoice . . .

It is nominally Freedom who speaks.

Retrieved from London by Southey ('a man of *perpendicular* virtue', and engaged to Sara Fricker's elder sister), Coleridge went back to Bristol, and his duty, and Sara, whom he did not love. Pantisocracy had dwindled to a pilot-scheme in Wales, but money had still to be raised. Coleridge and Southey took lodgings in College Street, and turned to lecturing. In late February Coleridge writes to Dyer, fellow Unitarian and author of *Complaints of the poor people of England* (1793):

# Conciones ad populum

Since I have been in Bristol I have endeavored to disseminate Truth by three political Lectures – I believe I shall give a fourth – But the opposition of the Aristocrats is so furious and determined, that I begin to fear, that the Good I do is not proportionate to the Evil I occasion – Mobs and Mayors, Blockheads and Brickbats, Placards and Press gangs have leagued in horrible Conspiracy against me.

Coleridge was not one to play down the drama of his situation, but the threats are credible. The letter to Dyer claims that Coleridge has been 'obliged' to publish the first of his lectures to show that the content was not treasonable. *A moral and political lecture* appeared in February, and in April was flatteringly reviewed by the *Critical*: 'This little composition is the production of a young man who possesses a poetic imagination. It is spirited, and often brilliant; and the sentiments manly and generous.' Despite this success, Coleridge published nothing more till *Conciones ad populum* in November. At this stage, *A moral and political lecture* was augmented (perhaps with material from the second February lecture) to form the *Introductory address*. *On the present war*, the second Address in *Conciones*, does not survive in an earlier text, but is likely to be a conflation of Coleridge's original second and third lectures, minus any sections already realigned.

Coleridge's signing of the Preface to *Conciones* on 16 November 1795 is the first indication of his return to political activity. The events of the summer are of considerable importance. In May-June the political lectures are followed by a series on Revealed Religion (not so different a subject for Coleridge, for whom there could be no political thinking without a religious implication). Verse is stockpiled for *Poems on various subjects*, 1796, and highly important contributions are made to Southey's *Joan of Arc* (extracted as *The Destiny of nations* in *Sibylline leaves*, 1817). In August Coleridge rents a cottage at Clevedon and drafts the *Eolian harp*, with its posturing of love and its great philosophical showpiece:

> And what if all of animated nature
> Be but organic Harps diversely fram'd . . .
> (*Poems* 1796, p. 98)

On 4 October Coleridge marries Sara Fricker. And on 13 November, in a massive roll-call of Southey's faults, he breaks with the man whose moral stance has prevailed on him to go through with the marriage: 'O Selfish money-loving Man! what Principles have you not given up?' Southey had decided that within a pantisocratic scheme he would wish to keep his personal property.

# Samuel Taylor Coleridge

*Conciones* proclaims at the outset a concern with '*bottoming* on fixed Principles' (p. 8). In difficult times we should acquire the habit of referring 'in all our doubts to some grand and comprehensive Truth'. France stands as a warning, not because of its atrocities, but because 'French Freedom is a Beacon, which while it guides to Equality, should shew us the Dangers that throng the road' (p. 9). In a passage not present in *A moral and political lecture*, Coleridge at this point turns surprisingly to a comparison of the French leaders, Brissot and Robespierre. With Brissot and the Girondins he identifies. They are 'men of enlarged views and great literary attainments', but 'deficient in that vigour and daring activity, which circumstances made necessary'. Brissot, seen as 'rather a sublime visionary, than a quick-eyed politician', appeals to Coleridge especially. One might expect that Robespierre would therefore be denounced, but in Coleridge's inspired view he too is a man of principle:

Robespierre, who displaced him, possessed a glowing ardor that still remembered the *end*, and a cool ferocity that never either overlooked, or scrupled, the *means*.

'What that *end* was', Coleridge adds, with a sort of ruminative sympathy, 'is not known':

that it was a wicked one, has by no means been proved. I rather think, that the distant prospect, to which he was travelling, appeared to him grand and beautiful; but that he fixed his eye on it with such intense eagerness as to neglect the foulness of the road. (pp. 10–11)

By contrast, Pitt, who emerges as the central focus of Coleridge's second Address, has undoubtedly wicked ends, travels towards no distant beautiful prospect, and is perfectly aware of the foulness of the road he takes. Added to which, he is a hypocrite, as Robespierre never was. Supporting Fox's motion for peace with America (12 June 1781), Pitt had referred to the war as 'iniquitous and unjust'. 'Our expences were enormous', Coleridge continues, using reported speech, but following Pitt almost verbatim,

while our victories were indecisive, and our defeats fatal – victories celebrated with short-lived triumph over men struggling in the holy cause of Freedom, and defeats which filled the Land with mourning.

'All this', Coleridge adds, 'O calumniated Judas Iscariot! all this WILLIAM PITT said!' (p. 54). Not only is Pitt now in 1795 sustaining another war against 'the holy cause of Freedom', he has as Prime Minister consolidated the crimes of his predecessors. The English are a nation 'professing to believe a God, yet acting as if there were none':

In Europe the smoking Villages of Flanders, and the putrified Fields of La Vendee – from Africa the unnumbered Victims of a detestable Slave-trade – in Asia the desolated plains of Indostan . . . in America the recent enormities of their Scalp-Merchants – the four Quarters of the Globe groan beneath the intolerable iniquity of this nation! (p. 46)

Coleridge's tones are vehement, but the details he draws attention to can all be substantiated. Retreating across Flanders, the Duke of York's troops did indeed burn the villages in spring 1795. Bounties of up to $100 were paid for enemy scalps (by both sides) during the American War.

One might think that this denouncing of Pitt, and of war-mongering imperialist Britain, would be accompanied by praise for the radical opposition. In fact, however, three-fourths of the Friends of Liberty are discounted. One group depends 'with weathercock uncertainty on the winds of rumour, that blow from France' (p. 15). Another, 'stimulated to a lust of revenge, by aggravated wrongs . . . would make the Altar of Freedom stream with blood' (p. 16). A third pursues 'the interests of Freedom steadily, but with narrow and self-centering views':

Whatever is above them they are most willing to drag down; but every proposed alteration, that would elevate the ranks of our poorer brethren, they regard with suspicious jealousy, as the dreams of the visionary . . . (p. 19)

(One recalls that Southey had wished Shad to come to America as servant, not as brother.) Only the 'small but glorious band . . . of thinking and disinterested Patriots' lives up to the Coleridgean ideal. The terms of praise are significant. 'Thinking' (but not activated solely by the mind), 'disinterested' (but not dispassionate), the true patriot 'looks forward with gladdened heart to that glorious period when Justice shall have established the universal fraternity of Love' (p. 21). Coleridge's original audience would have heard in his words a clear distinction between this Justice, leading the heart to universal love, and Godwinian political justice, leading via dispassionate reason to universal benevolence. 'These soul-ennobling views', Coleridge concludes,

bestow the virtues which they anticipate. He whose mind is habitually imprest with them soars above the present state of humanity, and may be justly said to dwell in the presence of the Most High. (p. 21)

69

# Samuel Taylor Coleridge

No work of the 1790s – not even the *Ancient mariner* – tells us more about the essential Coleridge than *Conciones*. He is seen placing in perspective the great events of his day, and in the process defining what is for him the relation of politics and religious truth. Hartley inspires his thinking; opposition to the 'proud Philosophy' of Godwin pushes him to sharper and sharper definitions. '*Bottoming* on fixed principles', as perhaps one should expect, has a great deal to with loving one's neighbour:

> The searcher after Truth must love and be beloved; for general Benevolence is a necessary motive to constancy of pursuit; and this general Benevolence is begotten and rendered permanent by social and domestic affections. Let us beware of that proud Philosophy, which affects to inculcate Philanthropy while it denounces every home-born feeling, by which it is produced and nurtured. The paternal and filial duties discipline the Heart and prepare it for the love of all Mankind. The intensity of private attachments encourages, not prevents, universal Benevolence. (pp. 29–30)

Those who have found truth, Coleridge tells us, and dwell already 'in the presence of the Most High', are 'men who have encouraged the sympathetic passions till they become irresistible habits'. Going now well beyond Hartley, he adds: 'Accustomed to regard all the affairs of man as a process, they never hurry and they never pause.' (p. 20)

Not till we discover that Coleridge later quoted this sentence as a definition of patience are we likely to see its importance. Even then, it may come as a surprise that he should remark: 'In his not possessing *this* virtue, all the horrible excesses of Robespierre did, I believe, originate' (to Thelwall, 17 December 1796). Patience is a knowledge of belonging, of being part of a larger process; a knowledge that one will get there without hurrying or taking exceptional steps. In effect it is a submission to the will of God. Robespierre travels towards a distant prospect that appears grand and beautiful, but cannot see his true relation to the world that is around him. The chosen, by contrast, move on in calmness through stage after stage of an unfolding landscape:

> as they advance the scene still opens upon them, and they press right onward with a vast and various landscape of existence around them. Calmness and energy mark all their actions. (p. 20)

Energy Robespierre has, calmness he lacks. Brissot is his opposite, fatally lacking in energy, but possessed of a philosophical calm that is in its own right admirable. Coleridge brings him back at the end of the

# Conciones ad populum

*Introductory address* in the form of an extended quotation from his 1788 *Travels in America*. Called upon to lead, Brissot was ineffective, but his life was blameless, giving no scope for smears such as Burke had used in his *Letter to a member of the National Assembly* to degrade the arguments of Rousseau. In his writing, Brissot embodies Coleridge's own egalitarian faith and rejection of hypocrisy:

Would you prove to me your Patriotism? Let me penetrate into the interior of your House. What! I see your antechamber full of insolent Lackies . . . I penetrate a little further; your Cielings are gilded – magnificent Vases adorn your Chimney-Pieces – I walk upon the richest Carpets – the most costly Wines, the most exquisite Dishes, cover your Table – a crowd of Servants surround it – you treat them with haughtiness; No! you are not a Patriot. The most consummate pride reigns in your heart, the pride of Birth, of Riches, and of Talents. With this triple pride, a man never sincerely believes the doctrine of Equality: he may repeat its dogmas, but efficient Faith is not in him. (pp. 31–2)

# 14

## CHARLES LAMB

---

# Rosamund Gray

*The tale of Rosamund Gray and
old blind Margaret*
1798


Where are they gone, the old familiar faces?

I had a mother, but she died, and left me,
Died prematurely in a day of horrors –
All, all are gone, the old familiar faces.

I have had playmates, I have had companions,
In my days of childhood, in my joyful school days –
All, all are gone, the old familiar faces.

I have been laughing, I have been carousing,
Drinking late, sitting late, with my bosom cronies –
All, all are gone, the old familiar faces.

I lov'd a love once, fairest among women.
Clos'd are her doors on me, I must not see her –
All, all are gone, the old familiar faces.

I have a friend, a kinder friend has no man.
Like an ingrate, I left my friend abruptly;
Left him, to muse on the old familiar faces.

Ghost-like I pac'd round the haunts of my childhood.
Earth seem'd a desert I was bound to traverse,
Seeking to find the old familiar faces.

Friend of my bosom, thou more than a brother!
Why wert thou not born in my father's dwelling?
So might we talk of the old familiar faces.

# Rosamund Gray

> For some they have died, and some they have left me,
> *And some are taken from me*; all are departed;
> All, all are gone, the old familiar faces.
>
> (*Blank verse* 1798, 89–91)

Lamb was 22 when he composed this best known of his poems. It was January 1798; links to Wordsworth's *Ruined cottage* suggest that *Rosamund Gray* was begun in March, or soon after.

Eighteen months before, on 22 September 1796, Lamb's much loved older sister, Mary, had killed their mother with a kitchen-knife in a moment of insane violence. Lamb had come on the scene too late to do more than 'snatch the knife out of her grasp'. Writing to Coleridge five days later, he asks him to send 'as religious a letter as possible'. Mary he describes as, 'My poor dear dearest sister, the unconscious instrument of the Almighty's judgments to our house'. On 3 October he lists his own resolves:

I hope that *I* shall thro' life never have less recollection nor a fainter impression of what has happened than I have now; tis not a light thing, nor meant by the Almighty to be received lightly; I must be serious, circumspect, & deeply religious thro' life; & by such means may both of us escape madness in future if it so pleases the Almighty . . .

Lamb was indeed to be 'deeply religious thro' life'. He did himself 'escape madness' (despite having started the year 1796 'in a mad house at Hoxton'). Mary was not so fortunate: she spent part, or parts, of almost every year in an asylum. But each time – until his death in 1834 – her brother brought her lovingly home again. 'Circumspect', Lamb could not always be ('drunken dog' was one of the epithets he applied to himself); 'serious' he was, but with a seriousness that is beautifully complemented and qualified by humour. In answer to his plea for a religious letter, Coleridge had written:

I look upon you as a man called by sorrow and anguish and a strange desolation of hopes into quietness, and a soul set apart and made peculiar to God!

Every verse of *Old familiar faces* speaks of an underlying pain: the 'day of horrors' (stanza one); the loss of childhood friends and boon companions (2–3); the loss of Ann Simmons, still regretted though she had been his sweetheart at the age of fifteen (4); Mary's relapse the previous month, on Christmas Eve 1797 – '*And some are taken from me*' (8). Less easy to construe in Lamb's poem is the role of the 'friends' of stanzas five and seven. In November Coleridge had published his 'Nehemiah Higginbottom' sonnets in the *Monthly magazine*, parodying himself and Southey along-side his two recent collaborators, Lamb and Charles Lloyd (both two years younger than him, and both disciples, though Lamb of much longer standing). The poems were funny:

> Pensive at eve on the *hard* world I mus'd,
> And *my poor* heart was sad: so at the Moon
> I gazed – and sigh'd, and sigh'd – for, ah! how soon
> Eve darkens into night.

But the joke misfired. Southey, for one, took offence. No reactions are preserved from Lamb and Lloyd, but soon would come Lamb's sad two-year estrangement from Coleridge. Lloyd, who had been Coleridge's pupil at Nether Stowey in 1796, had a hand in bringing it about. He too was mentally unstable. Presumably he was also jealous of Lamb's dependence on Coleridge. On the night when *Old familiar faces* was written, Lamb and Lloyd were together, in company. 'Lloyd had been playing on a pianoforte', Lamb recalls, 'till my feelings were wrought too high not to require Vent.' 'I left 'em suddenly', he adds, 'and rushed into ye Temple, where I was born'. 'Ghost-like' he paces the Inns of Court, seeking a past that cannot be recaptured.

For a moment the poetry at this point breaks out of its enclosed circle:

> Earth seem'd a desert I was bound to traverse,
> Seeking to find the old familiar faces.

Confronted by the desert stretching before him, Lamb calls to mind, not the new friend, Lloyd ('kinder friend has no man'), but Coleridge, who had so long been his support:

> Friend of my bosom, thou more than a brother!
> Why wert not thou born in my father's dwelling?
> So we might talk of the old familiar faces.

More than a brother, and yet less. Had Coleridge been of the family, Lamb might have talked to him of Mary (in her asylum), of their mother (deeply loved, but dead by Mary's hand), of their father (wounded on the 'day of horrors', living now in a limbo of senility and cards), of Aunt Hetty (devoted to Lamb, and source of the Unitarianism that he shared with Coleridge), whose gloomy life had come to an end within months of the horrors. Maybe Lamb might also have been able to talk of the strangest emotion that we feel in *Old familiar faces*: the sense that in her death he had been deserted by – of all people – his mother. It is scarcely possible to read the second line, 'I had a mother, but she died, and left

me', without an implication of betrayal. The tones are those of Wordsworth who, as unwarrantably, reproached his mother for dying when
he was a child: 'She left us destitute, and as we might/Trooping together'
(1805 *Prelude*, v, 259–60).

*Rosamund Gray* too is about loss. Familiar faces once again are scattered
by violence. Old blind Margaret Gray dies at once. Rosamund, her
grandchild, follows: she is loved and valued by Allan Clare, tenderly
nursed by Elinor, his sister, but as the embodiment of innocence she is
not permitted to survive. Elinor dies too, an unrelated death that is
felt nevertheless to be part of a pattern. Nothing it seems is left of the
idyllic past, as the story-teller (now himself an orphan) decides to revisit
ten years later 'the scenes of [his] native village':

Our old house was vacant, and to be sold. I entered, unmolested, into the room
that had been my bedchamber. I kneeled down on the spot where my little bed
had stood – I felt like a child – I prayed like one – it seemed as though old times
were to return again – I looked round involuntarily, expecting to see some face I
knew – but all was naked and mute.

Again the quest for the familiar face. 'The bed was gone', Lamb
continues,

My little pane of painted window, through which I loved to look at the sun,
when I awoke in a fine summer's morning, was taken out, and had been replaced
by one of common glass. (p. 109)

Childhood's coloured vision is replaced by the light of common day.
It should be no surprise that the symbol is purely Wordsworthian. At
one point in Lamb's story Rosamund is reading *Julia de Roubigné*, and
Henry Mackenzie, with his sentimental tales, half fable, half novel, is
certainly an influence. Far more important, though, is Wordsworth's
*Ruined cottage*, read to Lamb in July 1797 when he visited Coleridge
and the Wordsworths at Alfoxden, but clearly known to him in the
extended version of March 1798. From the beginning of chapter one – 'It
was noontide. The sun was very hot' (recalling Wordsworth's opening
line, ''Twas summer and the sun was mounted high') – *Rosamund Gray* is
shot through with reminiscences. Old blind Margaret is named after
Wordsworth's central figure. She spins 'in a little arbour at the door of
her cottage', as the earlier Margaret spins in her final years. 'Allan and his
Sister, Margaret and her Grandaughter' appear at times to Lamb's
narrator 'like personages of a dream – an idle dream' (p. 106). Passing
Margaret's cottage after her death, Wordsworth's Pedlar had been so

# Charles Lamb

struck by the 'image of tranquillity' that grief 'Appeared an *idle dream* that could not live / Where meditation was' (Butler, p. 279).

Exploring his old home, Lamb's unnamed story-teller finds just one piece of furniture – a harpsichord:

I played some old Scottish tunes, which had delighted me when a child. Past associations revived with the music – blended with a sense of *unreality*, which at last became too powerful – I rushed out of the room to give vent to my feelings. (p. 110)

The scene behind *Old familiar faces* is being reenacted. The wood he rushes into, he had named as a child, the *Wilderness* ('Earth seem'd a *desert* I was bound to traverse'). 'Softened' that the wood should seem unchanged, he reflects:

My parents were both dead – I had no counsellor left, no experience of age to direct me, no sweet voice of reproof. The LORD had taken away my *friends*, and I knew not where he had laid them. (pp. 112–13)

Once more there is the sense of betrayal. In the background we hear, 'I had a mother, but she died, and left me'. Lamb's seeking to understand, seeking of assuagement, has taken a strange form. Though it has the appearance of a sentimental tale, *Rosamund Gray* is akin to Romantic autobiography. Leaving the *Wilderness*, round which he has 'paced . . . seeking a comforter', the narrator prostrates himself upon the grave of his parents, and rises from it to greet Alan Clare, lost friend of former years, miraculously retored to him. In an obvious sense Clare suggests Coleridge (with whom Lamb made up his quarrel in 1799, and of whom he permitted himself in 1834 to write: 'He was my fifty years old friend without a dissention'). But Clare, dressed in black and transformed by his loss to a visitor of hospitals, is also Lamb himself, tender, attentive, loving, the 'soul set apart':

to stay by a bedside the whole day, when something disgusting in a patient's distemper has kept the very nurses at a distance – to sit by, while the poor wretch got a little sleep – and be there to smile upon him when he awoke – to slip a guinea, now and then, into the hands of a nurse or attendant – these things have been to Allan as *privileges*, for which he was content to live, choice marks, and circumstances, of his Maker's goodness to him. (pp. 128–9)

'What a lovely thing is [Lamb's] *Rosamund Gray*', Shelley commented to Hunt c. 20 August 1819, 'how much knowledge of the sweetest and deepest part of our nature is in it!'

# 15

## CANNING AND FRERE

─────────

# Poetry of the Anti-jacobin

## 1799

*A subterraneous Vault in the Abbey of Quedlinburgh . . . Toads, and other loathsome Reptiles are seen traversing the remoter parts of the Stage – Rogero appears, in chains, in a Suit of rusty Armour . . .*

*Rog.*  Eleven years! it is now eleven years since I was first immured in this living sepulchre – the cruelty of a Minister – the perfidy of a Monk . . . Hah! the twenty-eighth of August! How does the recollection of it vibrate on my heart! It was on this day that I took my last leave of Matilda . . . I stood gazing on the hated vehicle which was conveying her away for ever. – The tears were petrified under my eyelids. – My heart was crystalized with agony . . .

The writer at this stage in *The rovers* – spoof German tragedy, published in the *Anti-jacobin*, June 1798 – is probably John Hookham Frere (schoolfriend of Canning and fellow tory MP, working at the Foreign Office). Rogero concludes his soliloquy, surprising the reader with the words, 'Let me see whether the damps of this dungeon have not yet injured my guitar.' Parody becomes still more outrageous, as Canning (aged twenty-seven, Under Secretary of State for Foreign Affairs) takes up the pen:

*[Rogero] begins the following Air with a full accompaniment of Violins from the Orchestra:*

> Whene'er with haggard eyes I view
>   This dungeon that I'm rotting in,
> I think of those companions true
>   Who studied with me at the U –
>     -niversity of Gottingen,
>     -niversity of Gottingen.

*[Weeps, and pulls out a blue kerchief, with which he wipes his eyes; gazing tenderly at it, he proceeds –*

# Canning and Frere

> Sweet kerchief, check'd with heav'nly blue,
>> Which once my love sat knotting in! –
> Alas! Matilda *then* was true! –
>> At least I thought so at the U –
>>> -niversity of Gottingen,
>>> -niversity of Gottingen.

[*At the repetition of this Line Rogero clanks his Chains in cadence.* (pp. 175–8)

It is all very light-hearted. The writers, it seems, share Wordsworth's view of 'sickly and frantic German tragedies' (Preface to *Lyrical ballads*, 1800), but are not going to be earnest about it. German extravagance of every kind is sent up: plot, character, emotion, language, even the incongruous use of stage-directions. As its name suggests, however, the *Anti-jacobin* is a political newspaper. Even in its lightest moods the satire has a purpose. *The rovers* is subtitled *The double arrangement*, drawing attention to Schiller's *Robbers* (translated 1792), but also to Goethe's newly translated *Stella*. Anarchy and misguided idealism are paired with sexual license. The *Anti-jacobin* is Burkean in its standards, attacking all that can be labelled radical or French, defending all that is decent and established within the fabric of English society. The paper appeared weekly during the parliamentary session, 18 November 1797–9 July 1798, coming to an end after thirty-six issues with the boast: 'the SPELL of *Jacobin invulnerability* is now broken'.

Canning was founder of the *Anti-jacobin*, but Pitt (Prime Minister since 1783) involved himself to surprising extent, writing articles on finance and a proportion of the leaders. Secrecy was maintained. Contributions were unsigned; copy was transcribed for the printer by an amanuensis so that handwriting should not be recognized. Frere had worked with Canning on the satirical *Microcosm* at Eton, and was a Foreign Office colleague. George Ellis, their main collaborator, was an older man, who had published *Specimens of early English poets* in 1790, and recently taken part in failed peace negotiations with the French. In July Canning had written to him in France: 'There is but one event, but that is an event for the world – Burke is dead.' William Gifford, chosen by Canning as editor, was author of the *Baviad* and *Maeviad* (1791 and '94), and later to edit the *Quarterly*. He was at once methodical and belligerent, setting the tone for the paper with his weekly refutations of the left-wing press (notably the *Morning chronicle*, *Post* and *Courier*), divided conveniently into LIES, MISREPRESENTATIONS and MISTAKES.

It was the satirical poetry that gave the *Anti-jacobin* distinction, but some of the prose has a similar flair. Writing seems to have been a team effort. It was surely Canning and/or Frere who produced the brilliant account of a Meeting of the Friends of Freedom, billed on 30 November 1797 as 'an Authentic Copy of a part of a future *Morning chronicle*, which a Correspondent of ours has had the good fortune to anticipate'. *Mr Fox's birthday* (29 January 1798) has the same satirical edge, as does the best of the spoof correspondence. Letitia Sourby tells us on 18 December that her father, 'a respectable Manufacturer in the Calico line', has been seduced from his patriotic principles by 'hearing a Lecturer who went about the Country, reading History and Philosophy, and . . . "kindling a holy enthusiasm of Freedom"' (Thelwall, clearly). Miss Sourby's mother, meanwhile, has been 'sadly vexed' by her spouse's new 'French' attitudes to marriage:

It was but the other day that he told her, that if he were to choose again, by the New Law in the only Free Country in the world, he would prefer Concubinage – so he said in my hearing.

The satirical poetry of the *Anti-jacobin* begins as clever but limited parody, rising in the longer poems to a more imaginative, more general, evoking of the spirit of jacobinism. It is Southey who comes first under attack, travestied for his republicanism (*Inscription for the door of a cell in Newgate*), parodied in his use of classical metres, taunted with the stinginess of doctrinaire socialism. The true jacobin, we should recall, 'refrains from *relieving* the object of his compassionate observation . . . well knowing, that every diminution from the general mass of human misery, must proportionately diminish the force of his argument'. The *Widow* from Southey's *Poems* 1797 ('Cold was the night wind, drifting fast the snow fell') is scarcely more than an exercise in sapphics. It strikes a jacobin pose, however, and is duly overwhelmed by *The friend of humanity*:

'Tell me, Knife-grinder, how you came to grind knives?
Did some rich man tyrannically use you?
Was it the squire? or parson of the parish?
           Or the attorney? . . .

*I* give thee sixpence! I will see thee damn'd first –
Wretch! whom no sense of wrongs can rouse to vengeance . . .'

[*Kicks the Knife-grinder, overturns his wheel, and exit in a transport of Republican enthusiasm and universal philanthropy.*] (pp. 10–11)

Canning and Frere

Southey is brilliantly, but rather too easily, despatched. The great achievement of the *Anti-Jacobin* poets is the creation of Mr Higgins, author not merely of *The rovers*, but of *The progress of man* and *The loves of the triangles*. Higgins is the composite all-purpose jacobin poet, who writes to the editors 'from his study in St Mary Axe, the window of which looks upon the parish pump'. *The rovers*, he believes, will

do much to unhinge the present notions of men with regard to the obligations of Civil Society; and to substitute in lieu of sober contentment, and regular discharge of the duties incident to each man's particular situation, a wild desire of undefinable latitude and extravagance – an aspiration after shapeless somethings, that can neither be described, nor understood – a contemptuous disgust of all that is, and a persuasion that nothing is as it ought to be . . . (p. 162)

An earlier dig at Coleridge ('My good friend, the Bellman', too busy to supply a promised stanza of dactyllics) confirms that St Mary Axe, with its bucolic pump, is his Devonshire birthplace, Ottery St Mary. On this occasion, however, the satire is mainly directed at Godwin. 'Disgust of all that *is*' had been expressed in *Caleb Williams* (1794), correctly titled *Things as they are*. In its portrayal of the 'shapeless somethings' that would guarantee a rational future, *Political justice* (reissued in 1796) was openly subversive of God and King and law.

Higgins's brilliantly funny *Progress of man* is dedicated to Richard Payne Knight as author of *The progress of civil society* (1796), a didactic poem in six books which does not at first sight look jacobin at all. Though writing in Pope's couplets, Knight is close to Thomson in his celebration of

> Almighty Love! whose unresisted sway
> Earth, air, and sea, with one accord, obey . . .

Book I of *The progess* tells of Hunting, II of Pasturage, III of Agriculture, IV of Arts, Manufactures, and Commerce, V of Climate and Soil; Book VI, of Government and Conquest, is more evidently controversial. While deploring the excesses of the Revolution, Knight sees the Terror as parallel to the cruelties of the *ancien régime*. Britain he sees, not as particularly vicious, but as waiting for revolution or dictatorship –

> For come it will – the inevitable day,
> When Britain must corruption's forfeit pay,
> Beneath a despot's, or a rabble's sway.

Higgins's parody is presented in three fragments. From the first there are hints that Knight's mild liberalism is being crossed with the dangerous radical views of Erasmus Darwin's *Loves of the plants*:

ANIMATED BEINGS – Birds – Fish – Beasts – the Influence of the Sexual Appetite – on Tigers – on Whales – on Crimpt Cod – on Perch – on Shrimps – on Oysters. Various Stations assigned to different Animals – Birds – Bears – Mackarel – Bears remarkable for their fur – Mackarel cried on a Sunday – Birds do not graze – nor Fishes fly . . . (p. 72)

Canning's annotated copy of *Poetry of the Anti-jacobin* claims sole authorship of *The progress*. He has a marvellous ear, and the true humorist's sense of the incongruous:

> First – to each living thing, whate'er its kind,
> Some lot, some part, some station is assign'd.
> The feather'd race with pinions skim the *air* –
> Not so the mackarel, and still less the bear . . .
>
> (p. 75)

The notes sustain, and develop, the humour, but underneath it all there is the serious purpose. God's 'assigning' of lots, parts and stations, had been questioned on many sides. Some had even dared to ask

> Whether the joys of earth, the hopes of heaven,
> By Man to God, or God to Man, were given?
>
> (p. 74)

Canning's note at this point is important: 'See Godwin's *Enquirer*; Darwin's *Zoonomia*; Paine; Priestley, &c. &c. &c.; also all the French Encyclopedists.'

An immediate context for the *Anti-jacobin* emerges. *The Enquirer* had come out in 1797, *Zoonomia* in 1794–7, Paine's *Age of reason* was 1795; Priestley had emigrated in '94 (leaving Coleridge to propagate his views in *Religious musings*, 1796). Godwin was an atheist, Paine a deist, Priestley a radical dissenter; the French Encyclopedists were guilty of asking the questions that led to the Revolution. Darwin was a still greater threat. His theory of evolution (often ascribed to his grandson) undermines the moral basis of society by denying the biblical account of Creation and the God-given pre-eminence of man.

Outlining his principles as he submits *The loves of the triangles* for publication, Higgins (in this case, Frere) refers enigmatically to '*the eternal and absolute Perfectibility of Man*'. Darwin saw man as the result of improvement, but not as perfectible; Godwin saw him as perfectible,

81

but not in a sense that was eternal or absolute; Coleridge (with the aid of Hartley) did see the human mind as potentially eternal, capable of merging with the divine. Frere has devised an elegant jacobin mélange:

if, as is demonstrable, we have risen from a level with the *cabbages of the field* to our present comparatively intelligent and dignified state of existence, by the mere exertion of our own *energies*; we should, if these *energies* were not repressed and subdued by the operation of prejudice, and folly, by KING-CRAFT and PRIEST-CRAFT . . . in time raise Man from his present biped state, to a rank more worthy of his endowments and aspirations; to a rank in which he would be, as it were, *all* MIND . . . (p. 110)

'There is one Mind, one omnipresent Mind / Omnific', Coleridge had written in *Religious musings*, and ''Tis the sublime of man . . . to know ourselves / Parts and proportions of one won'drous whole'.

There may be some justice in the claim to have broken the spell of jacobin invulnerability. Certainly the paper had a major impact. Darwin's reputation was lastingly injured (the fact that he was right didn't matter), Godwin's would decline steeply from now on, Southey would write no more radical poetry. Political events, meanwhile, made pro-French sympathies more and more difficult to sustain. The take-over by the Directory in Paris in September 1797 was followed by the invasion of republican Switzerland in March, the threatened invasion of England, and the rise of Napoleon. In April 1798 Coleridge's recantation, *France, an ode*, was published in the *Morning post*. In so far as literary jacobinism had a future, it lay with the poet whom the *Anti-jacobin* nearly names, but doesn't quite:

> And ye five other wandering Bards, that move
> In sweet accord of harmony and love,
> Coleridge and Southey, Lloyd and Lambe and Co.
> Tune all your mystic harps . . .
>
> (p. 235, *New morality*)

Someone on the staff must have known that Southey, Lloyd and Lamb, were all on bad terms with Coleridge. Just possibly they knew too that Coleridge and Co. (Wordsworth) would be wandering soon to Germany. They could not know that *Lyrical ballads* – to be published in September – would establish Co. as the truly 'levelling muse'.

# 16

## ROBERT SOUTHEY

---

# Thalaba the destroyer

### *a metrical romance*
### 1801

There must be fifty people who know that Francis Jeffrey attacked *Thalaba* in the *Edinburgh review* (October 1802), for every one who has glanced at the poem. Yet Jeffrey was not entirely hostile. In fact he was attacking Southey almost by mistake. It was the first number of the *Edinburgh*. As joint-editor he wished to make clear the values of the new journal, and he wished especially for an excuse to examine the principles of the Lake School, 'the most formidable conspiracy that [had] lately been formed against sound judgment in matters poetical'. On the strength of his *English eclogues* (*Poems* 1797), Southey was correctly named as one of 'the chief champions and apostles' of this sect of '*dissenters* from the established system on poetry and criticism'. Jeffrey was aware, however, that *Thalaba* (stressed on the first syllable) was something different. He could persuade himself that the poem was 'written in a very vicious taste', but not that its vices were the same as those of the writer of the preface to *Lyrical ballads*. His excuses are somewhat lame:

As Mr Southey is the first author, of this persuasion, that has yet been brought before us for judgment, we cannot discharge our inquisitorial office conscientiously, without premising a few words upon the nature and tendency of the tenets he has helped to promulgate.

The diction and metre of *Thalaba* offended Jeffrey, very much as the diction and metre of *Lycidas* had offended Dr Johnson twenty years before in his *Life of Milton* (1781). In a Johnsonian spirit he was critical too of the improbabilities of Southey's narrative, and the handling of supernatural beings. Yet he goes out of his way to say that *Thalaba* 'contains passages of very singular beauty and force'. To which he adds: 'We do not remember any poem, indeed, that presents, throughout, a greater number of lively

Robert Southey

images, or could afford so many subjects for the pencil.' Among the
passages he quotes as breathing 'the true spirit of Oriental poetry' – all of
them well chosen – is Thalaba's approach to the garden of Laila in Book
Ten:

> a little, lowly dwelling place,
> Amid a garden, whose delightful air
> Felt mild and fragrant, as the evening wind
> Passing in summer o'er the coffee-groves
> Of Yemen and its blessed bowers of balm.
> A Fount of Fire that in the centre played,
> Rolled all around its wonderous rivulets,
> And fed the garden with the heat of life.
>
> (ii, 223–4)

The poetry has a sensuous – almost a numinous – quality about it,
never felt in the jacobin Southey of the 1790s. We recognize in it without
hesitation a major Romantic talent. Laila will die to save Thalaba from
her father Okba's dagger, then, in the form of a green bird, guide him
towards the fulfilment of his quest. Though its hero is human, the poem
is supernatural throughout. Everything is destined, a conflict between
forces of good and evil in which the outcome is known (though
prophecy is, of course, not always understood). Sorcerers line the route,
but divine helpers turn up too at appropriate moments; heavenly voices
intervene to encourage the hero as he passes test after test. Before
dismissing the quest as fanciful, however, it is worth noting that *Thalaba*
was admired not only by the Shelley of *Alastor* and *Queen Mab*, but by
Newman. Looking back in chapter one of his *Apologia* to the early
1830s, Newman reflected, 'Now it was . . . that Southey's beautiful
poem of *Thalaba*, for which I had an immense liking, came forcibly to
my mind. I began to think that I had a mission.' '*Thalaba*', he
commented in a letter of 22 March 1850,

has ever been to my feelings the most sublime of English poems – I don't know
Spenser – I mean *morally* sublime . . . [Southey's] poems generally end, not with
marriage, but with death and future glory. The verse of *Thalaba* is most
melodious too . . . ⸱

Thalaba the Destroyer is dedicated as a child to vengeance on his
father's murderer: in the end, not only does he spare him, he asks on
his behalf divine forgiveness. The framework of this eastern tale
is Mahommedan, but the virtues, and quite often the language, are

84

*Thalaba the destroyer*

Christian. In the vaults of Domdaniel, before the living idol of Eblis, Thalaba faces the final test:

> Sure of his stroke, and therefore in pursuit
> Following, nor blind, nor hasty on his foe,
> Moved the Destroyer. Okba met his way,
> > Of all that brotherhood
> He only fearless, miserable man,
> > The one that had no hope.

Singled out in his courage and misery, Laila's father, murderer and arch magician, has a strange resemblance to the staunch angel Abdiel of *Paradise Lost*: 'Among the faithless, faithful only he!' His guilt is in no way mitigated, but evil as he is, inhuman as he is, he is to be the recipient of divine mercy:

> 'On me, on me', the childless Sorcerer cried,
> 'Let fall the weapon! I am he who stole
> Upon the midnight of thy Father's tent,
> This is the hand that pierced Hodeirah's heart,
> That felt thy brethren's and thy sister's blood
> Gush round the dagger-hilt. Let fall on me
> The fated sword! the vengeance hour is come!
> > Destroyer, do thy work!'
> Nor wile, nor weapon, had the desperate wretch,
> > He spread his bosom to the stroke.
> 'Old man, I strike thee not!' said Thalaba,
> 'The evil thou hast done to me and mine
> > Brought its own bitter punishment.
> For thy dear Daughter's sake I pardon thee . . .'
> > (ii, 322–3)

The verse has dignity and power, but also a telling simplicity: 'Old man, I strike thee not!' There is real drama, real conviction.

Southey's most sympathetic reviewer was his friend and mentor, William Taylor of Norwich, responsible for the introduction of Bürger to the British public in 1796, and a force behind the new poetry of *Lyrical ballads*. Writing in the *Critical* in December 1803, Taylor has many criticisms to make ('The adventures do not enough grow out of one another'; as a 'child of destiny, miraculously reared', Thalaba does not engage the imagination), but he knows too why the poem is finally so impressive. Where Jeffrey regards the metre as 'a jumble of all the measures that are known in English poetry (and a few more), without

85

# Robert Southey

rhyme, and without any sort any sort of regularity', he writes of 'a plasticity and variety, of which epic poetry offers no other example':

In turn, the ballad lends its affecting simplicity, the heroic poem its learned solemnity, the drama its dialogue form, and the ode its versatility of metre.

*Thalaba* is for Taylor 'a gallery of successive pictures'. The 'personages, like the figures of landscape-painters, are often almost lost in the scene', but

the imagery suggested to the mind is always sensible [perspicuous], vivid, distinct. Thomson and Cowper are among the best of our describers; but they are surely left behind by the descriptions in *Thalaba*.

If one asks where Southey gets the inspiration for this new, vivid, eastern, descriptive poetry, the answer is clearly books. 'He had read every thing which could inform him upon the subject', the *Monthly mirror* comments in October 1801, adding with surprise, 'his notes are not only illustrations – they were the *materials* of the poem.' Jeffrey is more dismissive:

It is impossible to peruse this poem, with the notes, without feeling that it is the fruit of much reading, undertaken for the express purpose of fabricating some such performance.

The implication, curiously, seems to be that writers should not be inspired by literature. Yet Ariosto, Spenser, Milton, patently were – and Coleridge, too, to a considerable extent. Southey's bookishness is a strength. It releases the imagination that is felt to be lacking in his early humanitarian poetry:

> Behold this vine, I found it a wild tree
> >Whose wanton strength had swoln into
> Irregular twigs, and bold excrescencies,
> And spent itself in leaves and little rings,
> In the vain flourish of its outwardness
> >>Wasting the sap and strength
> >>That should have given forth fruit.
> >>But when I pruned the Tree,
> Then it grew temperate in its vain expence
> Of useless leaves, and knotted, as thou seest,
> Into these full, clear, clusters, to repay
> >The hand whose foresight wounded it.
> >>>>(ii, 123)

'In these lines', the note reads, 'I have versified a passage in Bishop Taylor's Sermons, altering as little as possible his unimproveable language.' There follows an excerpt from Taylor which shows that Southey has done just as he said. The source is excellent prose, the verse is excellent poetry. Changes that have been made are in the spirit of the original. Are we therefore to think that *Thalaba* is unoriginal? To labour the pun, does originality consist in the lack, or concealment, of origins? Response to Southey is confused not just by his open display of source-material, but by our continuing to judge him alongside Wordsworth and Coleridge. If *Thalaba* does indeed have links with a Lake School, they consist not in a doctrinaire preference for 'humble and rustic life', or in personal experience of sublimity among the mountains, but in the strong simple traditional values that underlie its beauty and eastern exoticism. Newman may not have felt the 'immense liking' for Wordsworth's *Michael* that he felt for *Thalaba*, but he would have recognized in the integrity of the Cumbrian shepherd a kindred form of the 'morally sublime'.

# 17

# WALTER SCOTT

---

# The lay of the last minstrel
*a poem*
1805

Among writers of Romantic poetry Scott's *Lay of the last minstrel* set a new fashion for romance. It was also a best-seller. Appearing in January 1805, it sold over 20,000 copies by 1812. As Scott's son-in-law Lockhart comments in 1837, nothing 'in the history of British Poetry' had ever equalled this demand. As it turned out, *Marmion* (1808), sold even better, and *The lady of the lake* (1810), with almost 30,000 copies by 1819, proved to be the high point of Scott's career as a poet. The *Lay*, though, established his reputation, creating the demand for the next two poems. It is also decidedly the most imaginative of the three. Scott has found a way to distil into a single work his unique combination of talents, as poet, fanciful story-teller, collector and writer of ballads, bringer-alive of a romantic Scottish landscape and romantic Scottish past.

Since his Bürger translations, *William and Helen* and *The chase* (1796), he had published a play based on Goethe and written a group of supernatural ballads for Monk Lewis's *Tales of wonder* (1801). More important, he had gathered together the three-volume *Minstrelsy of the Scottish border* (1803), collecting, editing and reworking the traditional ballad of the Lowlands, and adding his own skilful imitations. As he began work on the *Lay* in summer 1803 it was his post as quartermaster of the Edinburgh troop of volunteer cavalry that had most of his attention. Coming after ten years of war with France, the Peace of Amiens (1802–3) had proved to be a temporary truce. Now there were new threats of invasion. South of the Border, Wordsworth was drilling as a foot-soldier with the Westmorland Volunteers; Scott's role was more gratifying, and no less patriotic. A letter to Anna Seward, quoted by Lockhart, makes clear his pleasure in the 'sport of swords':

# The lay of the last minstrel

The Edinburgh troop, to which I have the honour to be quartermaster, consists entirely of young gentlemen of family, and is, of course, admirably well mounted and armed . . . I must own that to one who has, like myself, *la tête un peu exaltée*, the pomp and circumstance of war gives, for a time, a very poignant and pleasing sensation. The imposing appearance of cavalry, in particular, and the rush which marks their onset, appear to me to partake highly of the sublime. (*Memoirs of Scott*, 1837, i, 385)

Like most – perhaps all – writers of long poems, Scott began work without being able to see the form his poem would take. His 'lovely chieftainess', Lady Dalkieth, had suggested he tell the story of the goblin-page of Scottish folk-tale, Gilpin Horner. Scott seems to have made a start on his task, but found himself before long writing chivalric romance instead. The cavalry manoeuvres were doubtless a factor. Wheeling in formation, with sabre drawn, helmet and plume and polished breastplate, Scott could not fail to be reminded of the 'pomp and circumstance' of earlier warfare. The horses and armour were lighter, the guns to be faced were deadlier, but much of the experience was the same as it had been at the end of the middle ages. Gilpin Horner, Scott felt obliged to include, but goblins could hardly be said to 'partake highly of the sublime'. Border feuds, fought over the landscape he knew so well, offered more scope.

'I wrote', he commented in March 1805, 'knowing no more than the man in the moon how I was to end. At length the story appeared so uncouth, that I was fain to put it in the mouth of my old minstrel' (*Memoirs* ii, 28). The tone is characteristic. As Scott works on his sequel to the *Lay* three years later, he tells Lady Louisa Stewart:

Marmion is, at this instant, gasping upon Flodden field, and there I have been obliged to leave him for these few days in the death pangs. I hope I shall find time enough this morning to knock him on the head with two or three thumping stanzas. (*Memoirs* ii, 136)

Behind this public refusal to take his work too seriously, Scott was a dedicated writer. Afterthought the Minstrel may have been, but it is his presence above all that shapes and controls the *Lay*, enabling the poet to bring together his disparate material.

Sympathy within the poem for the old man –

> He tried to tune his harp in vain.
> The pitying Duchess praised its chime,
> And gave him heart, and gave him time . . .
>
> (p. 7)

Walter Scott

– goes far towards guaranteeing sympathy for the writer himself. Each
of the six Cantos is introduced and concluded by the Minstrel, and often
we are conscious of his voice elsewhere, making a personal and
emotional response to his story:

> 'Tis done, 'tis done! that fatal blow
>   Has stretched him on the bloody plain;
> He strives to rise – Brave Musgrave, no!
>   Thence never shalt thou rise again!
> He chokes in blood – some friendly hand
> Undo the visor's barred band,
> Undo the gorget's iron clasp,
> And give him room for life to gasp! –
> In vain, in vain – haste, holy friar . . .
>
> (pp. 145–6)

To the Minstrel, singing in old age to the wife of the Duke of
Monmouth (executed 1686, but kin to Scott's 'chieftainess'), events of
the mid–sixteenth century have the immediacy almost of personal
experience. Scott, who in *Waverley* ten years later was to emerge as the
great historical novelist, has taken his story back in two leaps instead of
one, placing the Minstrel's audience in the same relation to the events of
1550 as his own is to those of the 1680s. In each case the story that is told
is beyond memory, but not out of hearsay. Immediacy is gained that
would have been impossible had the narrative merely been dated back
two hundred and fifty years. The technique is interestingly different
from Coleridge's creation of pseudo-medieval settings for the *Ancient
mariner* and *Christabel*. Coleridge requires a certain distancing for his
stories, but has no more concern for the middle ages than Shakespeare
has in *Lear* for ancient Britons. Scott, for all his willingness to
incorporate folk-tale, deals in the imaginative recreation of history.

It is for reasons of a different kind that Scott is drawn to *Christabel*.
John Stoddart, as is well known, recited parts of Coleridge's
unpublished poem to him after hearing it at Grasmere in October 1800.
'The singularly irregular structure of the stanzas', Scott recalled in his
1830 Introduction to the *Lay*,

and the liberty which it allowed the author to adapt the sound to the sense,
seemed to be exactly suited to such an extravaganza as I meditated on the subject
of Gilpin Horner.

Scott seized at once on the principles of Coleridge's verse: four stresses to the line, whatever its length or rhythm. Being untroubled by thoughts of plagiarism (as the author of *Christabel* could never be), he offers in the opening lines of Canto First an imitation that catches beautifully his delight in the metre:

> The feast was over in Branksome tower,
> And the Ladye had gone to her secret bower;
> Her bower, that was guarded by word and by spell,
> Deadly to hear, and deadly to tell –
> Jesu Maria, shield us well!
> No living wight, save the Ladye alone,
> Had dared to cross the threshold stone.
>
> (p. 9)

It is to be some while before we meet the Goblin Page; magic, though, is present from the first. The Lady of Branksome has 'learned the art, that none may name' from her father, who learned it in distant Padua, and was in league with the wizard, Michael Scott. Though dead and buried, Scott's magician forbear presides over the poem, providing through his 'mighty book' a source of supernatural power, and even on occasion taking an active part. The Monk of Melrose tells us of his burial in verse that is typical of Scott's exuberant narrative:

> I swore to bury his mighty book,
> That never mortal might therein look;
> And never to tell where it was hid,
> Save at his chief of Branksome's need;
> And when that need was past and o'er,
> Again the volume to restore.
> I buried him on St Michael's night,
> When the bell tolled one, and the moon was bright;
> And I dug his chamber among the dead,
> Where the floor of the chancel was stained red,
> That his patron's cross might over him wave,
> And scare the fiends from the wizard's grave.
>
> (p. 45)

Scott's is the world of medieval romance, in which magic arts, though illicit and unblessed, seem almost to be within the scheme of Christianity. It is not just that they may be white as well as black, but that the black is wicked rather than evil. We are permitted to enjoy it, because we know from the first that things will come right. Borrowing from the *Ancient mariner* the device of spirit voices that represent an overseeing power (a River Spirit and a Mountain Spirit in this case), Scott tells his readers that Teviot and Branksome cannot thrive 'Till pride be quelled and love be free'. Insofar as there is a plot, it shows the pride of the Lady of Branksome humbled and the love of Cranstoun and Margaret freed. But there isn't very much. Byron summed it all up to his satisfaction in *English bards and Scotch reviewers*:

> Thus Lays of Minstrels – may they be the last! –
> On half-strung harps, whine mournful to the blast.
> While mountain spirits prate to river sprites,
> That dames may listen to the sound at nights;
> And goblin brats of Gilpin Horner's brood
> Decoy young Border-nobles through the wood,
> And skip at every step, Lord knows how high,
> And frighten foolish babes, the Lord knows why,
> While high-born ladies, in their magic cell,
> Forbidding Knights to read who cannot spell,
> Dispatch a courier to a wizard's grave,
> And fight with honest men to shield a knave.
>
> (ll. 153–64)

The scorn is compounded by a prose note: 'See the "Lay of the Last Minstrel", *passim*. Never was any plan so incongruous and absurd as the ground-work of this production.' Like Jeffrey, chief of the 'Scotch reviewers', Byron condemns an improbability which the public did not mind. The *Lay* was designed to be marvellous, and they were happy to read it as such.

Scott's poem was a new departure, but within a context that is now forgotten. The supernatural was so common in narrative poetry at the turn of the eighteenth century that it was almost the norm. Wordsworth famously renounced it in the joint scheme for *Lyrical ballads* 1798, leaving 'the hemisphere / Of magic fiction' to be exploited by Coleridge in the *Ancient mariner* (and *Christabel*). Southey, meanwhile, was exploiting it in *Rudiger, Donica*, the *Old Woman of Berkeley*, *Thalaba*, and Landor in *Gebir*. A glance at Lewis's two-volume *Tales of wonder*, and the three volumes of Scott's *Border minstrelsy*, will show just how common it had become. The problem was how to use it with originality or power. It was usually so pat, so full of stage-tricks and retributions. Blending the supernatural with personal obsession and guilt, Coleridge achieved new intensities. With an eye on the Burns of *Tam O'Shanter*, Scott, by contrast, found a means of being pleasurably unreal – encouraging us not to suspend disbelief, but to enjoy it.

As the Goblin Page pries open the clasps of Michael Scott's magic book (found on the wounded Deloraine), they shut behind him one by one:

> For when the first he had undone,
> It closed as he the next begun.
> Those iron clasps, that iron band,
> Would not yield to uncristened hand . . .
>
> (p. 71)

Finally getting the book to open (with the help of Deloraine's Christian blood), he is able to read just one useful spell before a buffet from an unseen hand stretches him on the plain:

> From the ground he rose dismayed,
> And shook his huge and matted head;
> One word he muttered, and no more –
> 'Man of age, thou smitest sore!'
>
> (p. 72)

Byron disdains this 'invisible but by no means sparing box on the ear'; but the Page, with his unexplained recurrent cry of 'Lost, lost, lost!' belongs to a world that is bound by no rules. Scott cares little for motivation, nothing for character. Even his antiquarianism, so stressed by Hazlitt in the *Spirit of the age*, never obtrudes fact or reality. He offers not a reconstruction of the middle ages, but a confessedly romantic version. The folk-tale element, necessarily maverick, exists alongside the reassuring structures of chivalry. The Goblin Page, for all his alleged malignancy, does no lasting damage, and has his loyalty to Lord Cranstoun. There is enmity, but not cruelty or pain. Such bloodshed as there is takes place among Scottish and English brother knights, or within the anarchic, but still in its way formalized, context of the Border feud. Scott's enjoyment in the 'sport of swords' is an enjoyment of ritual, not death-dealing.

For the most part the poetry is at its best in the portrayal of action (Deloraine's ride in Canto Two, for instance, from Branksome to Melrose), but Scott's eye for detail when he allows himself to pause can be a delight:

> The moon on the east oriel shone,
> Through slender shafts of shapely stone,
>     By foliaged tracery combined;
> Thou would'st have thought some fairy's hand,

'Twixt poplars straight the osier wand,
  In many a freakish knot, had twined;
Then framed a spell, when the work was done,
And changed the willow wreaths to stone.

That this tenderly fanciful description lies behind the *Eve of St Agnes*, with its 'casement high . . . All garlanded with carven imageries' (ll. 208–9), is confirmed by the detail that follows:

The silver light, so pale and faint,
Shewed many a prophet and many a saint,
  Whose image on the glass was dyed;
Full in the midst, his cross of red
Triumphant Michael brandished,
  And trampled the apostate's pride.
The moon-beam kissed the holy pane,
And threw on the pavement a bloody stain.
                                    (pp. 42–3)

Scott's playfulness persists even in the final couplet, but the discordance is shocking. Keats's reworking of the lines –

Full on this casement shone the wintry moon,
And threw warm gules on Madelaine's fair breast . . .
                        (*Eve of St Agnes*, 217–18)

– introduces a new opposition between the wintry moon and warm 'gules' (heraldic red), but removes the clash of kiss and stain. Where Madelaine is hallowed: 'Rose-bloom fell on her hands . . . And on her hair a glory, like a saint' (ll. 220–2), the resting-place of the magician is marked with a cross of blood.

It is not perhaps a touch that we should ascribe to the Minstrel. Scott uses his old story-teller above all to inject humanity into the poem. In his letter to Miss Seward of March 1805 he remarks that the *Lay* 'is deficient in that sort of continuity which a story ought to have' (*Memoirs* ii, 28). It is precisely the discontinuity, however, that gives the poem its special character. Kept at arm's length by the artifice of romance, we welcome the intrusions of the Minstrel, and the sense of his relationship both to the story and to the audience:

Dejectedly, and low, he bowed,
And, gazing timid on the crowd,
He seemed to seek, in every eye,
If they approved his minstrelsy;

## The lay of the last minstrel

And, diffident of present praise,
Somewhat he spoke of former days . . .
(p. 30)

Invited to recall the Minstrel's presence as each canto comes to an end, we reestablish in him our confidence in the handling of the story as a whole. His age and courage are important to us; we respond to the quality of his performance. Scott worried that the tying up of ends in Canto Six had been forced to continue beyond the poem's natural conclusion in the wedding of Cranstoun and Margaret. For his readers the true ending is with the performer whose lay it has been: 'Hushed is the harp – the Minstrel gone . . .'

# 18

## RICHARD MANT

___

# The simpliciad
*a satirico-didactic poem*
1808

The Reverend William Mant, anonymous author of the *Simpliciad* (1808), was not given to self-doubt. *Lyrical ballads* had gone through four editions, 1798–1805, winning (sometimes grumpy) praise from a wide variety of critics, but he was not a man to take note of changing attitudes, changing poetic decorum. Mant is the conservative reader of his day, well informed, not untalented, no more prejudiced than most. To read him is to understand the weariness in Wordsworth's voice as he speaks of a great poet having to create the taste by which he is enjoyed. In 1802 Mant had edited Thomas Warton, and in 1806 he had published a volume of somewhat innocuous poems himself. The *Simpliciad* was prompted by honest indignation on the appearance of Wordsworth's *Poems in two volumes* the following year. Such triviality could not go unpunished! With Jeffrey's 1802 review of *Thalaba* in mind, Mant purports to attack the Lakers in general:

> Poets, who fix their visionary sight
> On Sparrow's eggs in prospect of delight,
> With fervent welcome greet the glow-worm's flame,
> Put it to bed and bless it by its name;
> Hunt waterfalls, that gallop down the hills:
> And dance with dancing laughing daffodills;
> Or measure ponds from side to side,
> And find them three feet long and two feet wide:
> Poets, with brother donkey in the dell
> Of mild equality who fain would dwell,
> With brother lark or brother robin fly,
> Or flutter with half-brother butterfly . . .
>
> (pp. 13–15)

Nine Wordsworth poems are mocked in succession, with an intermission for Coleridge's political allegory, *Address to a young ass*. In each case Mant has quoted in his footnote the passage that gives him 'authority'. 'The school is incapable of caricature', he comments in the Dedication, 'if a smile be raised by my illustrations, it will be heightened by a perusal of the originals whence they are drawn.' Times have changed. It comes as a shock to find under the heading of the evidently ridiculous:

> *And dance with dancing laughing daffodils, &c.*
> I wander'd lonely as a cloud
> That floats on high o'er vales and hills,
> When all at once I saw a crowd,
> A host of *dancing daffodils*.
>
> ★  ★  ★  ★  ★  ★
> A Poet could not but be gay
> In such a *laughing* company.
>
> ★  ★  ★  ★  ★  ★
> And then my heart with pleasure fills,
> And *dances with the daffodils*.

Jeffrey had singled out 'an affectation of great simplicity and familiarity of language' as the 'most distinguishing symbol' of the Lake School. In his view, the origins of the School lay in a combination of Rousseau's primitivism, 'the simplicity and energy . . . of Kotzebue and Schiller' and the 'homeliness' of Cowper. Cowper was politically neutral, but Rousseau had been among the fathers of the Revolution; Schiller and Kotzebue (represented by *The robbers* and *Lovers' vows*) had put their simplicity and energy to the purpose of undermining social order. With such a pedigree the Lakers' affectation could not be seen as apolitical. Jeffrey was aware of the originality of *Lyrical ballads*, but saw the volume as a 'flagrant act of hostility', a betrayal at once of poetic and social decorum:

The language of the higher and more cultivated orders may fairly be presumed to be better than that of their inferiors . . . But the mischief of this new system is not confined to the depravation of language only; it extends to the sentiments and emotions, and leads to the debasement of all those feelings which poetry is designed to communicate . . . Next after great familiarity of language, there is nothing that appears to them so meritorious as perpetual exaggeration of thought.

Mant is less affronted than Jeffrey, less inclined to see things in political terms, but many of his assumptions are the same. The Lakers do not merely let themselves down by their simplicity, they trivialize poetry by making exaggerated claims for commonplace experience. With *Daffodils* we have no doubt that he is wrong, but what of *The sparrow's nest?* Mant's reference to

> Poets, who fix their visionary sight
> On Sparrow's eggs in prospect of delight . . .

is footnoted by lines that carry for most of us a childish sense of wonderment:

> Look, five blue eggs are gleaming there!
> Few *visions* have I seen more fair,
> Nor many *prospects of delight*,
> More pleasing than that simple sight!

Are the italicized words not an 'exaggeration of thought'? If not, what of *The daisy*, introduced by Mant with the uncharitable comment, 'I know not whether a more perfect instance of silliness is to be detected in the whole farrago of the school, than the following stanza':

> Thou wander'st the wide world about,
> Uncheck'd by pride or scrupulous doubt,
> With friends to greet thee, or without,
>     Yet pleased and willing;
> Meek, yielding to occasion's call,
> And all things suffering from all,
> THY FUNCTION APOSTOLICAL
>     IN PEACE FULfiLLING.

> (pp. 17–18)

Mant's capitalization forces us either to side with him, or to explain Wordsworth's extraordinary language. Already human to the point of wandering the wide world, meek and suffering, the daisy (etymologically the 'eye of day') is finally a witness, or messenger, of God. As so often with the 1802 lyrics published in *Poems in two volumes*, we are uncertain on what level the claims are being made. Wordsworth's later distinction of imagination and fancy doesn't really help. He has at this period a fanciful imagination. To Mant both his wonderment and his playfulness are silly – 'simple' in the unflattering sense of the word applied to those who are 'not all there'.

The *Simpliciad* is not a subtle or discriminating satire. It has neither the brilliance of the *Anti-Jacobin* parodists (1797–8), nor the intuitive sympathy of Hogg's *Poetic mirror* (1816). The lyrical ballads are condemned without exception. After quoting (in derisive italics) beautiful excerpts from *Resolution and independence*,

> *Motionless as a cloud the old man stood,*
> *That heareth not the loud winds when they call* . . .

Mant takes leave of the author, 'with an apology for attempting to give anything like a fair specimen of [his] solemn buffoonery' (pp. 46–47). Bringing together numinous lines from the *Ode* and *Personal Talk*, in a way that nearly approaches genius, he seems unaware that his own verse has been amazingly enhanced:

> The cataracts blow their trumpets from the steep,
> Awaken'd echoes through the mountains throng,
> And kettles whisper their faint undersong.
>
> (p. 38)

For Wordsworth simplicity was a stripping away of the inessential. He did not, as Jeffrey assumed (on a rather frontal reading of the Preface), wish either to write in the language of Cumbrian shepherds, or to express the actual pattern of their thoughts. He wished, in his quest for the essential and abiding, to learn from those whose way of life seemed to him 'more sane, pure and permanent'. The tendency to 'exaggerated thought', disliked by Jeffrey and mocked in the *Simpliciad*, was the clearest sign of a new poetic decorum. 'The feeling therein developed', Wordsworth wrote succinctly of the lyrical ballads, 'gives importance to the action and situation, and not the action and situation to the feeling.' It was a reversal of traditional standards that Mant, for one, could not accept. To him a daisy was a daisy. He was a sort of intellectual Peter Bell:

> A primrose by a river's brim
> A yellow primrose was to him,
>        And it was nothing more.

# 19

## THOMAS CAMPBELL

## Gertrude of Wyoming
### *a Pennsylvanian tale. And other poems*
### 1809

Though he had disparaged *Gertrude of Wyoming* seven years earlier in the *Lectures on British poets* (1818), classing it oddly as 'a kind of historical paraphrase' of Wordsworth's *Ruth*, Hazlitt in the *Spirit of the age* praises the poem in terms that go a long way to explaining the impression it created on his contemporaries:

A great outcry, we know, has prevailed for some time past against poetic diction and affected conceits, and, to a certain degree, we go along with it; but this must not prevent us from feeling the thrill of pleasure when we see beauty linked to beauty, like kindred flame to flame, or from applauding the voluptuous fancy that raises and adorns the fairy fabric of thought, that nature has begun!

Tacitly the appeal is to Shakespeare, who has raised from nature the 'fairy fabric' of Prospero's vision – 'The cloud-capp'd tow'rs, the gorgeous palaces'. To Hazlitt, looking back on his age in 1825, claims made by Wordsworth (Appendix on Poetic Diction, *Lyrical ballads* 1802) and Hunt (Preface to *Rimini*, 1816) for the language of 'real life' appear to have been too sweeping. If the poet of 'voluptuous fancy' can link beauty in art to the beauty that exists in Nature, 'no idle theories or cold indifference should hinder us from greeting it with rapture'.

The passage that Hazlitt has chiefly in mind records Gertrude's early years, brought up by her father in the paradisal valley of Wyoming, Pennsylvania. To read it warmly, admiringly, as he did is no longer easy:

> I may not paint those thousand infant charms;
> (Unconscious fascination, undesign'd!)
> The orison repeated in his arms,
> For God to bless her sire and all mankind;
> The book, the bosom on his knee reclin'd,

Or how sweet fairy-lore he heard her con
(The playmate ere the teacher of her mind):
All uncompanion'd else her years had gone
Till now in Gertrude's eyes their ninth blue summer shone.

And summer was the tide, and sweet the hour,
When sire and daughter saw, with fleet descent,
An Indian from his bark approach their bow'r,
Of buskin'd limb, and swarthy lineament;
The red wild feathers on his brow were blent,
And bracelets bound the arm that help'd to light
A boy, who seem'd, as he beside him went,
Of Christian vesture, and complexion bright,
Led by his dusky guide like morning brought by night.

(pp. 12–13)

'In the foregoing stanzas', Hazlitt writes,

we particularly admire the line –

Till now in Gertrude's eyes their ninth blue summer shone.

It appears to us like the ecstatic union of natural beauty and poetic fancy, and in its playful sublimity resembles the azure canopy mirrored in the smiling waters, bright, liquid, serene, heavenly!

There is indeed a beauty in Campbell's line. But so dominant has the Wordsworthian claim for naturalness become, that we have to be reminded of the power that all periods, including his own, have found in artifice. Wordsworth himself, of course, was perfectly aware of this power. The echo that we should be hearing in Campbell's line is 'The suns of twenty summers danced along', from the the idyllic early section of the *Female vagrant* (*Lyrical ballads* 1798), a poem also centering on a daughter-father relationship at the time of the American War, and also written in spenserians. Campbell's line is more resonant, more personal, more tender, but it is clear where he has taken his cue.

*Gertrude of Wyoming* tells of an Indian massacre of white settlers in 1778, led by a Mohawk chief named Brandt, who was half-European, and held to be especially bloodthirsty. 'Transatlantic Liberty', as Campbell puts it,

arose

Not in the sunshine, and smile of heav'n . . .
Her birth star was the light of burning plains;
Her baptism is the weight of blood that flows
From kindred hearts . . .

(pp. 50–51)

# Thomas Campbell

Among contemporary accounts of the massacre the most indignant is offered by Coleridge in *Conciones ad populum* (1795). Colonists in the Wyoming Valley had neither riches nor poverty:

their climate was soft and salubrious, and their fertile soil asked of these blissful Settlers as much labor only for their sustenance, as would have been otherwise convenient for their health. The Fiend, whose crime was Ambition, leapt over this Paradise – Hell-hounds laid it waste. *English* Generals invited the Indians 'to banquet on blood': the savage Indians headed by an Englishman attacked it. Universal massacre ensued. The Houses were destroyed: the Corn Fields burnt: and where under the broad Maple trees innocent Children used to play at noontide, there the Drinkers of human Blood, and the Feasters on human Flesh were seen in horrid circles, counting their scalps and anticipating their gains. The English Court bought Scalps at a fixed price! SCALPING this *pious* Court deemed a fit punishment for the crimes of those, whose only crime was, that being Men, and the descendants of Britons, they had refused to be Slaves. (p. 44)

Bribed with promises of land, Indian tribes formed alliances equally with the British, Americans and French, their presence adding to the horrors, and the horror-stories, of war. History now relates that the 'massacre' at Wyoming was a fairly regular engagement between British and American forces, both supported by Indians; Brandt (as Campbell later discovered when his son came to England) had been misrepresented, and on this occasion was not even present. War, however, is not Campbell's major concern. Nor is politics. For his purposes it does not matter that Wyoming is on the Susquehannah, where Priestley had settled, and where (as he might, or might not, have known) Coleridge and Southey had intended in 1794 to set up their commune. Drawing on the 1796 *Travels in North America* of Isaac Wild (often 'Weld' in the Notes), Campbell takes trouble with his exotic setting, and his exotic Indian chief, Outalissi; he is preoccupied, however, with relationship, strong simple emotions, bonds of love and loyalty.

Southey's *Thalaba* (1801) was an inspiration to Newman, not as a story of Islam, but as the quest of the individual soul; beneath the surface of *Gertrude of Wyoming* is a story that might have been set in Cumbria. Hazlitt, who had lived in America, and seen as a child the cardinal's brilliant flight, found in the poetry 'a light startling as the red-bird's wing, a perfume like that of the magnolia', but Campbell's landscape is evocative, not localised. It is any paradise anywhere. What matters is that the poignancy of Gertrude's human suffering (like that of

Wordsworth's Vagrant, or Susan, or Margaret) should be heightened –
in a sense, validated – by harmony with the natural world:

> It seem'd as if those scenes sweet influence had
> On Gertrude's soul, and kindness like their own
> Inspir'd those eyes affectionate and glad,
> That seem'd to love whate'er they look'd upon . . .
>
> (p. 29)

With *Gertrude*, Campbell (already famous for the *Pleasures of hope*,
1799) published a group of exquisitely crafted shorter poems and
ballads, *Lochiel* and *Hohinlinden* among them. Hazlitt speaks of
Campbell's perfectionism, his feeling called upon 'to pay the exactest
attention to the expression of each thought, and to modulate each line
into the most faultless harmony'. It is a lyricism, a sad beauty of melody
and cadence, that only Tennyson can match:

> On Linden, when the sun was low,
> All bloodless lay th'untrodden snow;
> And dark as winter was the flow
> Of Iser, rolling rapidly.
>
> But Linden saw another sight,
> When the drum beat, at dead of night,
> Commanding fires of death to light
> The darkness of her scenery.
>
> By torch and trumpet fast array'd,
> Each horseman drew his battle blade,
> And furious every charger neigh'd,
> To join the fearful revelry . . .
>
> (pp. 127–8)

On 3 December 1800 Campbell had watched from a nearby convent as
the French under Moreau defeated the Austrians at Hohenlinden; later
he crossed part of the battlefield by coach. En route the driver stopped to
cut off tails of the dead horses.

## 20

# MARY TIGHE

# Psyche
*with other poems*
1811 (1805)

*Psyche*, with its six cantos of elegant and cogent spenserian narrative, is one of the most accomplished long poems of the Romantic period. Yet Mary Tighe is known only as a disputed influence on Keats. The relationship has been no help to her reputation. After wishing for her blessing in his early poem, *To some ladies*, Keats (the critics note) makes a single disparaging reference to Tighe, in the letter of Christmas 1818 to his brother and sister-in-law. With Beattie – also a writer of spenserians – she is placed among poets whom he has grown out of. Scholars have taken Keats at his word; Tighe has gone unread. No one has asked about the state of mind in which this letter is written.

Keats is preoccupied with human experience and development – perhaps one should say, with male experience and development. Though addressing himself partly to Georgiana, 'little George', he agrees in this mood with Pope, that 'Most women have no characters at all'. There is a world-weariness in his tone that derives from Hamlet, 'Man delights not me – nor women neither, though by your smiling you seem to say so':

The more we know the more inadequacy we discover in the world to satisfy us . . . Mrs Tighe and Beattie once delighted me – now I see through them and can find nothing in them – or weakness – and yet how many they still delight! Perhaps a superior being may look upon Shakespeare in the same light – is it possible – No. This same inadequacy is discerned (forgive me little George you know I don't mean to put you in the mess) in Women with few exceptions – the Dress Maker, the blue Stocking and the most charming sentimentalist differ but in a Slight degree, and are equally smokeable [to be seen through] . . . I never intend hereafter to spend any time with Ladies unless they are handsome.

Tighe, an excellent Latinist, and known to the Ladies of Llangollen, is perhaps a 'blue Stocking'. Or perhaps to Keats at this moment she seems merely a 'charming sentimentalist'. Either way she is a woman. Weakness detected in her poetry is, in this mood, associated with an inadequacy perceived in her sex.

Tighe might surely in other moods have appeared less 'smokeable'. In what sense has Keats grown out of her? If she has truly ceased to delight, has she ceased also to be of interest? Is it mere chance that the *Eve of St Agnes* adopts the same metre as *Psyche* (and Beattie's *Minstrel*)? Could Keats, four months after dismissing Tighe in his Christmas letter, compose his own *To Psyche* – first of the great Odes – without her coming to mind? This poem too is sent in a journal-letter to George and Georgiana (February–May 1819). Keats, we learn, has taken unusual trouble over it, and thinks it may be the richer for his pains. As before he is concerned with spiritual development. This time, though, it is in terms precisely of 'Soul-making': the process by which the intelligence (a 'spark' of God, but lacking identity) is schooled, through the 'provings and alterations and perfectionings' of the heart, to become the 'individual being' that is the Keatsian soul. In Tighe's poem, Psyche, the unformed soul, endures a prolonged series of trials before discovering her true self, and achieving immortality, in a permanent union with Love.

Keats sets great store by his account of soul-making. It is 'a faint sketch of a system of Salvation which does not affront our reason and humanity'. He is 'convinced that many difficulties which christians labour under would vanish before it'. No doubt *Tintern abbey* is in his mind, and the Wordsworthian 'living soul' that is achieved as 'the affections gently lead us on', but Tighe has presented in an allegorical form exactly the process that he describes. Keats' ode begins where Tighe leaves off: like the 'winged boy' whom she is embracing, Psyche is an immortal. From Lemprière's *Classical dictionary*, however, Keats has discovered that Psyche 'was not embodied as a goddess before the time of Apuleius the Platonist'. 'Too late for antique vows', she has not had the worship she deserves. In becoming her (belated) priest, Keats builds for her a temple within his own mind, enacting once again the allegorical finding of the soul:

> Yes, I will be thy priest and build a fane
> In some untrodden region of my mind,
> Where branched thoughts, new grown with pleasant pain
> Instead of pines shall murmur in the wind . . .
> A rosy sanctuary will I dress
> With the wreath'd trellis of a working brain . . .

# Mary Tighe

Keats, of course, shares with Tighe much that is common stock. Apparent borrowings come from Spenser, or some other source known to both poets. Even with the story of Psyche, both have read Apuleius (Keats, in Adlington's translation). The central fact of the central stanza of *Ode to a Grecian urn*, however, comes straight out of *Psyche*. It is Tighe who inspires the bold lover, frozen in his moment of expected bliss, the unwearied piper, 'For ever piping songs, forever new':

> Oh, how unlike the pure transparent stream,
> Which near it bubbles o'er its golden sands!
> The impeding stones with pleasant music seem
> Its progress to detain from other lands;
> And all its banks inwreathed with flowery bands,
> Ambrosial fragrance shed in grateful dew;
> There young Desire enchanted ever stands,
> Breathing delight and fragrance ever new,
> And bathed in constant joys of fond affection true.
>
> (p. 19)

Given 'young Desire' standing there, and the echo, 'ever . . . ever new', we are at liberty to hear allusions and connections in other lines as well. An obvious case points forward to Keats's fourth stanza, reminding us how creatively influence works where it is no longer imitative:

> And all its banks inwreathed with flowery bands    (Tighe)

> And all her silken flanks with garlands dresst    (Keats)

Transmuted, the flower-wreathed stream from *Psyche* becomes the garlanded sacrificial heifer of the *Urn*. Repetition alerts us in the first two words ('And all' / 'And all'); 'flanks' in Keats's line is a rhyming recollection of 'banks' (moved up a space to avoid identity of sound); remaining words in the two lines *sound* different, but *mean* the same. Such detail will be interesting chiefly to those who enjoy listening to the intricacies of echo and allusion. But Tighe's ambrosial stream has implications for Keats's thinking as well as his language. It is the stream of unalloyed pleasure, happiness that is denied to common humanity:

> not to mortals is it e'er allowed
> To drink unmingled of that current bright . . .
>
> (p. 20)

*Psyche*

Mortals can drink only when the clear waters are mingled with those of 'dull sorrow's' adjacent stream. Their tasting of joy will always be marred. Psyche, though she will finally achieve the immortality craved by Keats, cannot at this stage partake of the ideal. Though her lover is divine, hers is the 'aching forehead and [the] parching tongue' of human experience.

A number of poets – Thomson in the *Castle of indolence*, Chatterton in the *Excellent balade of charitie*, Wordsworth in *Resolution and independence* – have successfully adapted spenserian stanzas to a quirky personal use; Tighe has the rare distinction of producing a memorable poem while writing in Spenser's own idiom. We move enjoyably through a landscape, peopled, as Spenser's is, by allegorical personages whose unreality is part of their attractiveness. Tighe's language pleasurably reminds us of the *Faerie queene*, without ever seeming to be pastiche:

> Mid the thick forest was a lonely dell,
> Where foot of man was seldom known to tread,
> The sloping hills all round in graceful swell
> The little green with woods environed;
> Hither the dove their passive course had led;
> Here the thin smoke blue rising mid the trees
> Where broad and brown the deepest umbrage spread,
> Spoke the abode of safe retired ease,
> And Psyche gladly there her dove descending sees.
>
> (p. 92)

The style is simpler, less encrusted than Spenser's, carrying the poetry forward with strong, fluent rhythms. Narrative moves well, never (by virtue of the veiled presence of allegory) deeply involving us, yet always capable of holding our attention:

> Scarce on the altar had she placed the urn,
> When lo! in whispers to her ravished ear
> Speaks the soft voice of Love! 'Turn, Psyche, turn!
> And see at last, released from every fear,
> Thy spouse, thy faithful knight, thy lover here! . . .'
>
> Two tapers thus, with pure converging rays,
> In momentary flash their beams unite,
> Shedding but one inseparable blaze
> Of blended radiance and effulgence bright,
> Self-lost in mutual intermingling light;
> Thus in her lover's circling arms embraced,

107

# Mary Tighe

The fainting Psyche's soul, by sudden flight,
   With his its subtlest essence interlaced;
Oh! bliss too vast for thought! by words how poorly traced!

(p. 205)

Scudamour and Amoret come together at the end of the 1590 three-canto *Faerie queene* in a tenderly erotic reunion:

But she faire Lady, overcommen quight
Of huge affection did in pleasure melt,
And in sweete ravishment pourd out her spright . . .

Delicately present in Spenser's imagery is the Elizabethan pun on dying into an afterlife of sexual fulfillment, used by Shakespeare and by Donne ('We're tapers too, and at our own cost die', *Canonization*, 21). Tighe's extension of the image requires an equal delicacy, and a more exalted merging of the physical within the abstract. Psyche does not merely pour forth a human spirit in her lover's arms, allegorically she *is* the soul. Tighe achieves in her language the blending of sensual and spiritual that the narrative implies. Sexual innuendo, such as Donne's, she would naturally avoid; yet the losing and finding of the soul as it is 'interlaced' with the 'subtlest essence' of love cannot be wholly chaste. Psyche *the human-being* receives immortality as she merges with the divine, in the arms of Cupid; Psyche *the soul* is released from the merely human as she takes on, within an act of love, the fullest implications of mortality. What Keats thought we don't know. The coming together of Porphyro (near rapist) and Madeline (near saint) in the spenserian *Eve of St Agnes* has its own peculiar blending of the spiritual and erotic:

Into her dream he melted, as the rose
Blendeth its odour with the violet,
Solution sweet . . .

(ll. 320–2)

There is an element of wish-fulfillment in *Psyche*, with its faithful love and final happiness. Mary Tighe herself married her first cousin in 1793 and led a short, sad life, dying of T.B. at Woodstock, County Wicklow, aged 37, in 1810. Parts of her diary are transcribed by another cousin in her journal, *Anecdotes of our family written for my children*, preserved at the National Library of Ireland (Patrick Henchy, Bibliographical Society of Ireland vi, 6, 1957). Tighe knew from the first that she did not love her husband, and in her unpublished novel, *Selena*, ascribes the heroine's

108

similar marriage to the meddling of parents. *Psyche* was written in 1802–3, and printed in a tiny Irish edition (occasionally seen with a London titlepage) in 1805. Minor poems published after Tighe's death with the four London editions of *Psyche*, 1811–16 (Philadelphia, 1812), are more openly personal, and no less accomplished. She is writing for herself, not, as are so many women writers of the period, to support a family. Henry Tighe, her husband, was an Irish member of Parliament with a comfortable private income, who took her to Dublin and London and fashionable watering-places. She was admired, and met interesting people (Tom Moore among them), and wrote a poetry of secret grief:

> Oh, my loved Harp! companion dear!
>   Sweet soother of my secret grief,
> No more thy sounds my soul must cheer,
>   No more afford a soft relief . . .
>
> Forced to forego with thee this spot
>   Endeared by many a tender tie,
> When rosy pleasure blessed my lot,
>   And sparkled in my cheated eye.
>
> Yet still thy strings, in Fancy's ear,
>   With soothing melody shall play;
> Thy silver sounds I oft shall hear
>   To pensive gloom a silent prey.
>       (*Address to my harp*, pp. 238–40)

It is no surprise to hear the tones of Gray in Tighe's concluding line. Often she is writing within the elegiac tradition, yet she never sells out to pensive gloom. Looking back in *Written at Scarborough, August 1799*, she thinks bleakly of 'days of sorrow, and some hours of joy' (p. 220). *Verses written in sickness, December 1804* speaks of 'nights of horror, days of pain' that deride 'The baffled opiate's force' (p. 259). As she grows more ill, Tighe's thoughts turn again to soul-making, and to allegory, in the beautiful though conventional image of the lily-bulb:

> The careless eye can find no grace,
>   No beauty in the scaly folds,
> Nor see within the dark embrace
>   What latent loveliness it holds.
>       (*The lily*, p. 303)

Always the religious poems have a personal application, but they are surprisingly strong, surprisingly flexible. Few would be able to place the grand sound-effects and emotional control of her 'imitation' of *Jeremiah*:

# Mary Tighe

Hark, the voice of loud lament
  Sounds through Ramah's saddened plain!
There cherished grief, there pining discontent,
  And desolation reign.
  There, mid her weeping train
See Rachel for her children mourn
  Disconsolate, forlorn!
  The comforter she will not hear,
And from his soothing strains she hopeless turns her ear.
  Daughter of affliction peace,
  Let, at last, thy sorrows cease . . .

(p. 297)

Tighe is a poet of many voices. We are aware at times in her writing of Spenser, Milton, Pope, Gray, Cowper (in some excellent blank verse), Charlotte Smith, perhaps Scott (in the skilful late ballads). Yet none of these ever takes her over. She is herself. Never more so than in the concluding lines of *Psyche*, where she bids farewell to her dreams, and her second self, in tones so wistful that they could be Lamb:

Dreams of Delight farewel! your charms no more
Shall gild the hours of solitary gloom!
The page remains – but can the page restore
The vanished bowers which Fancy taught to bloom?
Ah, no! her smiles no longer can illume
The path my Psyche treads no more for me;
Consigned to dark oblivion's silent tomb
The visionary scenes no more I see,
Fast from the fading lines the vivid colours flee!

Tighe was last published in 1846. There has never been a Collected Works. Such poetry should not be consigned to dark oblivion. Some is still in manuscript, with her novel and her cousin's invaluable journal, at the National Library of Ireland.

# 21

# WILLIAM WORDSWORTH

## The excursion
*being a portion of The recluse, a poem*
1814

For almost a hundred years *The excursion*, published in 1814, was
Wordsworth's major poem. Until 1850, and the posthumous appearance
of his autobiography, *The prelude*, there was no competition. Thereafter,
*The excursion* was gradually displaced. The twentieth century has had no
doubt that *The prelude* (finished in 1805, but set on one side by the poet) is
the more impressive work. And so it is. Apart from the marvellous first
book, telling the story of Margaret, and written in 1797–8, *The excursion*
belongs to the years 1810–12; by contrast, *The prelude* as a whole belongs
to Wordsworth's early creative period, 1798–1805. From a twentieth-
century point of view, subject-matter too favours the autobiography.
Though out-of-date by the standards of its Victorian first readers (for
whom the new poem was *In memoriam*), *The prelude* has appealed to more
recent audiences as a study of consciousness. *The excursion*, with its third-
person narrative, its weightier preoccupations and open didacticism,
does not so easily break free of its period.

It is *The excursion*, however, that was read by Byron, Shelley, Keats,
Hazlitt, Lamb, and, in later generations, by Tennyson, Arnold, Ruskin,
George Eliot. Shelley was disappointed (mainly for political reasons),
Byron was mischievous:

> And Wordsworth, in a rather long 'Excursion'
> (I think the quarto holds five hundred pages)
> Has given a sample from the vasty version
> Of his new system to perplex the sages;
> 'Tis poetry – at least by his assertion . . .
> *(Don Juan*, Dedication)

Yet Keats thought *The excursion* one of the three great wonders of the age, and Lamb described his first reading as 'A day in heaven.' Hazlitt had his reservations, but the poem brought out in him some of his greatest and most sensitive criticism:

It is less a poem on the country, than on the love of the country. It is not so much a description of natural objects, as of the feelings associated with them . . . [Wordsworth] does not present the reader with a lively succession of images or incidents, but paints the outgoings of his own heart, the shapings of his own fancy. He may be said to create his own materials; his thoughts are his real subject . . . He hardly ever avails himself of striking objects or remarkable combinations of events, but in general rejects them as interfering with the workings of his own mind, as disturbing the smooth, deep, majestic current of his own feelings. (*Examiner*, 21 August 1814)

Despite the impression given by Jeffrey's opening words in the *Edinburgh* – 'This will never do' (November 1814) – three-quarters of the original reviews of *The excursion* were favourable. Those that weren't, tended to show a grumpy awareness of the poem's stature. For Byron's friend Merivale, it contains 'innate qualities of genius' which not even Wordsworth has the 'powers wholly to conceal' (*Monthly review*, February 1815). Jeffrey was not going to give up his crusade against the Lakers. His review of Southey's *Thalaba* in 1802 had been followed by a scornful attack on Wordsworth's *Poems* 1807. He felt himself to be upholding standards. By the time of *The excursion*, however, he was himself becoming isolated. Instead of carrying other critics with him, he was neatly put in his place by an anonymous writer in the *British review* (August 1815):

To this poem it is necessary that the reader should bring a portion of the same meditative disposition, innocent tastes, calm affections, philosophical habits, which characterize the poet himself; for readers of another kind we greatly fear (and we deeply sympathize in the author's shame and mortification) that this poem 'will never do'.

There were, of course, many readers in 1814 without a share of Wordsworth's philosophical temperament. *The excursion* could never be fashionable: sales of Byron and Scott were not likely to be threatened. Yet the poem is surprisingly varied in its appeal. Jeffrey might speak dismissively of 'a tissue of moral and devotional ravings', but Margaret's story in Book I is among the great English tragic narratives. The dramatization in Books II-IV of the effects of the French Revolution is interesting both for the poet's own experience, and for the intellectual history of the age.

Though *The excursion* does not give comparable space to the Industrial Revolution, it is difficult not to be moved by Wordsworth's passionate concern in Book VIII. The stories of Book VI, 'The churchyard among the mountains', have dignity at the least. 'Ravings' seems a harsh word to describe the Solitary's cloudscape vision in Book II, or the corresponding Grasmere scene of IX. Nor could it justly be applied to 'Despondency corrected' (Book IV), which lies at the centre of *The excursion*.

In Lamb's view, indeed, this openly didactic section is 'the most valuable portion of the poem':

For moral grandeur; for wide scope of thought and a long train of lofty imagery; for tender personal appeals; and a *versification* which we feel we ought to notice, but feel it also so involved in the poetry, that we can hardly mention it as a distinct excellence; it stands without competition among our didactic and descriptive verse. (*Quarterly*, January 1815)

Though the message is clear, the prose falters, reflecting either Gifford's editorial revisions (of which Lamb bitterly complains), or the fact that this is Lamb's earliest published review. Thanking Wordsworth when first he received *The excursion* in August 1814, he had been his ebullient self:

I cannot tell you how pleased I am with the great Armful of Poetry which you have sent me . . . It is the noblest conversational poem I ever read. A day in heaven . . . My having known the story of Margaret . . . even as long back as I first saw you at Stowey, did not make her reappearance less fresh.

Lamb's memory of meeting Wordsworth at Nether Stowey, and hearing the first version of *The ruined cottage* (later *Excursion* Book I), goes back to summer 1797. Six months after his visit, Coleridge and Wordsworth had drawn up their scheme for *The recluse* (the 'system to perplex the sages', that would encompass *The excursion* and *The prelude*, but never be completed). *The ruined cottage*, newly revised, was now to form the nucleus of a great millenarian poem, 'On Man, on Nature, and on Human Life'.

'I know not anything', Wordsworth commented on 6 March 1798, 'that will not come within the scope of my plan'. Margaret's tragic story evidently came within the scope, but more important in the long run – as *The ruined cottage* develops into *The excursion* – is the Pedlar who tells the story and acts as spokesman for the poet himself. Renamed the Wanderer, the Pedlar in 1814 dominates the early parts of *The excursion*, causing Jeffrey to ask amusingly:

# William Wordsworth

Did Mr Wordsworth really imagine, that his favourite doctrines were likely to gain any thing in point of effect or authority by being put into the mouth of a person accustomed to higgle about tape, or brass sleeve buttons?

The answer is, yes and no. The Pedlar as itinerant observer, moving alone amid the countryside on rounds that brought him back periodically to the same villages, seemed to Wordsworth not just a suitable spokesman, but a 'second self'. It is Jeffrey's imagination, not the poet's, that creates the higgling and tape.

As the plan of *The excursion* developed, two further 'selves' were added: the Solitary, as representative of Wordsworth's early political idealism, and the Pastor, as the voice of Anglican reassurance. The Solitary, or his story at least, seems to have been envisaged as early as 1804. 'Time may come', Wordsworth commented to Coleridge in *Prelude* Book X,

> When some dramatic story may afford
> Shapes livelier to convey to thee, my friend,
> What then I learned – or think I learned – of truth,
> And the errors into which I was betrayed . . .

As the 'dramatic story', *The excursion* was to stand back from the French Revolution, placing it in a larger, more general, perspective than the personal memories and involvements of *The prelude*. Wordsworth's concern was not with history, but with the emotional experience of a generation. Readers above the age of forty had been marked by the Revolution – sharing, or repudiating, its exultation; suffering, or crowing, over its betrayal of principles. Younger ones had grown up with a confused sense of its aspirations and failure. The Solitary experiences the exultation of the younger Wordsworth, but cannot pull out of the corresponding despair. He is sensitive, creative, deserving, but doomed:

> 'The powers of song
> I left not uninvoked; and, in still groves . . .
> I sang Saturnian Rule
> Returned, a progeny of golden years
> Permitted to descend, and bless mankind.'
>
> (p. 129)

The power of the poetry, and of the Solitary's characterisation, is the power of Wordsworth's awe for one whose fate could have been his own. In *Prelude* Book X he had glimpsed the possibility of joining forces with the Girondins, perishing in France 'A poor mistaken and bewildered offering'; now he entered instead into drawn-out suffering and disillusion. To the Solitary he gave even his most recent and terrible sorrow, the deaths of the two children (Catharine and Thomas) who died as the poem was being written. And yet *The excursion* is never autobiography. The poet keeps his distance. He has the resilience that this other self is lacking. He can even offer him advice. The pattern of *The prelude* – Imagination Impaired and Restored – is reenacted in the more evidently moral terms of Despondency Corrected. The man, we are told, who

> commenes with the Forms
> Of Nature, who with understanding heart,
> Doth know and love, such Objects as excite
> No morbid passions, no disquietude,
> No vengeance, and no hatred, needs must feel
> The joy of that pure principle of love
> So deeply, that, unsatisfied with aught
> Less pure and exquisite, he cannot choose
> But seek for objects of a kindred love
> In Fellow-natures, and a kindred joy . . .
> [He] seeks for good; and finds the joy he seeks;
> Until abhorrence and contempt are things
> He only knows by name; and, if he hear
> From other mouths, the language which they speak,
> He is compassionate; and has no thought,
> No feeling, which can overcome his love.
>                    (p. 195; sixth line omitted by printer, 1814)

Appropriately it is the Wanderer who speaks. The lines, with their message of love and sharing, had been written for him (in his former guise, as the Pedlar) back in 1798, in the very month when *The recluse* was planned. They had from the first embodied the poem's central belief, and they continued to do so. We may think that the Wordsworth of 1814 was changed. He didn't think so himself.

Time had moved on, however. *The excursion* has scope to take account both of abiding qualities, values, landscapes, and of social change that the poet saw around him. Communities such as those the Pastor celebrates in Books VI and IX were being destroyed by an irreversible revolution in technology. Wordsworth is aware, even proud, of economic achievements:

> Hence is the wide Sea peopled, – and the Shores
> Of Britain are resorted to by Ships
> Freighted from every climate of the world
> With the world's choicest produce.
>                    (p. 365)

But he sees the appalling cost, as cotton-mills work day and night in valleys 'Where not a habitation stood before', destroying the rhythms of family life, depriving adults of the occupations that brought stability and hope, depriving children of the birthright of a country childhood:

> The Boy, where'er he turns,
> Is still a prisoner; when the wind is up
> Among the clouds and in the ancient woods,
> Or when the sun is rising in the heavens,
> Quiet and calm . . .
> His raiment, whitened o'er with cotton flakes,
> Or locks of wool, announces whence he comes.
> Creeping his gait and cowering – his lip pale –
> His respiration quick and audible . . .
>
> (p. 373)

The child of Shakespeare's 'Seven Ages' was to be seen 'Creeping like snail / Unwillingly to school', but did so with a 'shining morning face'; the child of the Industrial Revolution creeps home, pale and cowering, from the factory, his lungs already choked with the cotton-fibres that will cause his early death.

For his final Book Wordsworth has reserved the great images of oneness that make *The excursion* a poem of spiritual hope. Prompted by Wilson's comment on 'the utter absence of revealed religion', he would, late in life, introduce new pieties (Margaret of Book I becomes, in 1849, 'the meek sufferer', her eyes fixed upon the Cross). The text of 1814, however, rests largely upon the pantheism celebrated in *Tintern abbey*, the life-force that (in Coleridge's words), rolls through the material universe 'in organizing surge'. Book IX opens with the sequence, 'There is an active principle alive in all things', spoken by the Wanderer (Pedlar), and written for *The recluse* in March 1798:

> From link to link
> It circulates, the Soul of all the Worlds.
> This is the freedom of the Universe . . .
>
> (p. 388)

As we move towards the conclusion we come upon the snow-white ram on the river-bank, his two-fold image 'Blended in perfect stillness to our sight':

## The excursion

> Most beautiful,
> On the green turf, with his imperial front
> Shaggy and bold, and wreathed horns superb,
> The breathing Creature stood; as beautiful,
> Beneath him, shewed his shadowy Counterpart.
> Each had his glowing mountains, each his sky,
> And each seemed centre of his own fair world . . .
>
> (p. 407)

There follows the sunset over Grasmere, as the Pastor and his companions look back across the Lake from Loughrigg Terrace. The moment is symbolic, but not crudely so. The Solitary's cloudscape vision in Book II had offered apocalyptic Christian imagery of New Jerusalem ('Fabric it seemed of diamond and of gold') in place of the mountain grandeur of the Climbing of Snowdon (*Prelude*, Book XIII). In its concluding vision, *The excursion* is more modest. Instead of rivalling Snowdon, it offers important thematic connections. For the second time Wordsworth is to be seen ending 'a portion of *The recluse*' with a landscape of abnormal beauty that images for the reader an interplay of the divine and human imaginations. In the yet-unpublished *Prelude* there had been room for hesitation as to where the true power lay. Feeding 'upon infinity', the human mind had experienced

> The sense of God, or whatso'er is dim
> Or vast in its own being . . .
>
> (1805 *Prelude*, xiii, 72–3)

In 1814 such an alternative would be impossible. The poetry no longer asserts the godlike in man. But nor is it yet dogmatic, inflexible, as it will sometimes be in Wordsworth's later years.

'Sinking with less than ordinary state' (the disappointment is purely Wordsworthian), the sun sets behind the mountains. Suddenly the clouds above are transfused with rays from an 'unapparent Fount of glory'. 'Multitudes of little floating clouds' become, in this moment, 'Vivid as fire'. In their interaction they offer, for the last time in the poem, an image of social harmony, interfused by the presence of God:

> clouds separately poized,
> Innumerable multitude of Forms
> Scattered through half the circle of the sky,
> And giving back, and shedding each on each,

William Wordsworth

With prodigal communion, the bright hues
Which from the unapparent Fount of glory
They had imbibed, and ceased not to receive.

(p. 414)

'That which the heavens displayed', the poet adds, 'the liquid deep /
Repeated; but with unity sublime!' The human mind, imaged in 'the
bosom of the steady lake' (*There was a boy*), renders back the glory it
receives, creating as it does so 'unity sublime' that could not otherwise
exist. *The excursion* may no longer seem to us the 'day in heaven' it
seemed to Lamb; it is nonetheless a great Wordsworthian 'Poem of the
Imagination'.

# 22

# SAMUEL TAYLOR COLERIDGE

## Christabel

*Christabel: Kubla Khan, a vision:*
*The pains of sleep*
1816

'Coleridge', Lamb wrote to Wordsworth in a delightful letter of 26 April 1816:

is printing *Xtabel* by Ld Byron's recommendation to Murray, with what he calls a vision, *Kubla Khan* – which said vision he repeats so enchantingly that it irradiates and brings heaven and Elysian bowers into my parlour while he sings or says it.

The thought of Coleridge chanting *Kubla Khan* in the parlour has a marvellous and magical incongruity:

> Weave a circle round him thrice,
> And close your eyes with holy dread:
> For he on honey-dew hath fed,
> And drank the milk of Paradise.

Lamb was his ideal audience, but knew enough of the ways of reviewers to fear for the poem when it was brought to light:

there is an observation, Never tell thy dreams, and I am almost afraid that *Kubla Khan* is an owl that won't bear day light; I fear lest it should be discovered by the lantern of typography . . . no better than nonsense or no sense.

Lamb was not wrong, but *Christabel*, when it came to the point, was received with quite as much incomprehension. Not all the reviews were hostile. The *Critical*, for instance, retells the story in May 1816 with sympathy, concluding that *Christabel* is a 'very graceful and fanciful poem . . . enriched with more beautiful passages than have ever been before included in so small a compass.' More typical, however, are the tones of the *British review* ('We really must make a stand somewhere for the rights of common sense') and the pompous *Anti-jacobin*: 'gravely to discuss so wretched a performance is beneath the dignity of criticism'. An essay in the *Edinburgh* regards the whole volume 'as one of the most notable pieces of impertinence of which the press has lately been guilty'. It is 'utterly destitute of value'. The reviewer (commonly thought to be Moore) is prepared to 'defy any man to point out a passage of poetical merit in any of the three pieces which [the book] contains'.

Moore's friend, Byron, would certainly have accepted the challenge. On 18 October 1815 he had written to Coleridge:

[Scott] repeated to me a considerable portion of an unpublished poem of yours – the wildest and finest I ever heard in that kind of composition – the title he did not mention – but I think the heroine's name was Geraldine . . . [it] took a hold of my imagination that I never shall wish to shake off.

The tones recall Lamb's comment to Wordsworth on the *Ancient mariner* in January 1801: 'I was never so affected with any human Tale. After first reading it, I was totally possessed with it for many days'. Byron's purpose, however, was to ask whether the two completed sections of *Christabel* (Part I, 1798, Part II, 1800) were to be included in *Sibylline leaves* (printed 1815, published two years later). Learning that they weren't, he at first urged Coleridge to complete the poem, then arranged with Murray to publish it as it stood. Six months later, in April 1816, *Christabel* was in print, sharing a slim octavo with *Kubla Khan* and the beautiful, yet terrible, *Pains of sleep*.

No answer has been preserved to Byron's letter of October 1815. Coleridge was probably too deferent to remark the lapse of memory that made Geraldine hero of *Christabel* (and her creator 'a member of the devil's party'), but he seems to have had strong words to say about Scott's plagiarism in the *Lay of the last minstrel*. Answering Coleridge's complaints on 27 October, Byron is tactful and judicious: 'though I cannot contradict your statement . . . all I have ever seen of [Scott] has been frank – fair and warm in regards to you'. Scott had memorized parts of *Christabel* as early as 1802, when it was repeated to him in Edinburgh by Coleridge's friend (and Hazlitt's future brother-in-law), John Stoddart. The effect on the *Minstrel* (1805) is there for all to see. Critics might grumble that *Christabel* was unfinished and unintelligible, but Coleridge's fellow poets had no doubts as to its power. Wordsworth drew on it in the *Waggoner* and *White doe of Rylstone*, Scott in the *Minstrel*, Keats in *Eve of St Agnes* and *Lamia*; Byron, meanwhile, found himself telling Coleridge that similarities between *The siege of Corinth* and *Christabel* were merely

chance. Perhaps they were. But Coleridge's poem, with its strange
metre and strange supernatural goings-on, was quietly pervasive.

Lamb's views of *Kubla Khan* are echoed, in a rather less generous tone
of voice, by Hazlitt in the *Examiner* of 2 June 1816:

*Kubla Khan*, we think, only shews that Mr Coleridge can write better *nonsense*
verses than any man in England. It is not a poem, but a musical composition.

> A damsel with a dulcimer
> In a vision once I saw:
> It was an Abyssianian maid,
> And on her dulcimer she play'd,
> Singing of Mount Abora.

'We could repeat these lines to ourselves', Hazlitt adds ungraciously,
'not the less often for not knowing the meaning of them.' Meaning is a
preoccupation with the reviewers. By presenting *Kubla Khan* as a vision
and 'a psychological curiosity', Coleridge has disclaimed responsibility
for its content. Josiah Conder in the *Eclectic review* (June 1816) is
especially indignant: 'We could have informed Mr Coleridge of a
reverend friend of ours, who actually wrote down two sermons on a
passage in the Apocalypse, from the recollection of the spontaneous
exercise of his faculties in sleep.'

*Christabel* (though it did at least tell a story) was again deliberately
enigmatic. Hazlitt, who saw it gruesomely as containing 'something
disgusting at the bottom . . . like moon-beams playing on a
charnel-house, or flowers strewed on a dead body', was exercised that
Coleridge should have left out of the printed text a line in the manuscript
describing Geraldine's side and bosom as 'lean and old and foul of hue'.
The line, he asserts,

is necessary to make common sense . . . 'It is the key-stone that makes up the
arch'. For that reason Mr Coleridge left it out.

On both counts Hazlitt is right, but he must have been surprised to find
himself siding with the *British review* as the champion of common sense.
Disapproval of Coleridge's politics has been allowed too obviously to
affect his critical judgment. Mystery is essential to poetry, doubly so to
poetry of the supernatural. Geraldine's nakedness must remain 'A sight to
dream of, not to tell', just as the war prophesied by 'ancestral voices' in
*Kubla Khan* must forever remain enigmatic. As it happens, the enigma of
*Christabel* is at its most pronounced in the text of 1816. Not only has

# Samuel Taylor Coleridge

Coleridge cut the one gratuitously informative line, he has yet to insert the passage that offers his clearest hints as to Geraldine's nature – possessed, surely, rather than evil:

> Yet Geraldine nor speaks nor stirs;
> Ah! what a stricken look was hers!
> Deep from within she seems half-way
> To lift some weight with sick assay,
> And eyes the maid and seeks delay;
> Then suddenly, as one defied,
> Collects herself in scorn and pride,
> And lay down by the Maiden's side . . .

Printed on its own alongside two of Coleridge's three masterpieces, *The pains of sleep* (1803) might seem a little exposed. Where *Christabel* and *Kubla Khan* have individual prefaces (the second so compelling in its myth of inspiration and interruption as to be inseparable from the poem ever after), *Pains of sleep* has a single sentence:

As a contrast to this vision [*Kubla Khan*], I have annexed a fragment of a very different character, describing with equal fidelity the dream of pain and disease.

As with *Kubla Khan*, the word 'fragment' is used as a kind of self-deprecation, an attempt to ward off criticism. *Pains of sleep* (1803) is beautifully rounded, a perfect whole. Once again, however, it is a kind of poetry for which the critics had no precedent. Coleridge, in what is almost the last of his great poems, has found a way to express in personal terms the horrors, yearnings, guilt and confusion, that we sense in the *Ancient mariner*. The poem is not a fragment, and not a dream, and is by no means solely concerned with 'pain and disease', but it does have a marvellous fidelity. This is what it was like to experience the nightmare alternations of Coleridge's opium years:

> Ere on my bed my limbs I lay,
> It hath not been my use to pray
> With moving lips or bended knees;
> But silently, by slow degrees,
> My spirit I to Love compose . . .
> But yester-night I pray'd aloud
> In anguish and in agony,
> Upstarting from the fiendish crowd
> Of shapes and thoughts that tortured me . . .

*Christabel*

'My sleep,' De Quincey would tell his readers in the final words of *Confessions*, 'is tumultuous, and like the gates of Paradise to our first parents . . . is still (in the tremendous line of Milton): "With dreadful faces throng'd and fiery arms." ' If opium had provided an entry to the paradise of *Kubla Khan*, it was associated far more surely with sin and eviction. In Coleridge's conclusion we hear first the desperate pleading of the adult poet, then the voice of the unloved child within:

> Such punishments, I said, were due
> To natures deepliest stain'd with sin:
> For aye entempesting anew
> Th'unfathomable hell within
> The horror of their deeds to view,
> To know and loathe, yet wish and do!
> Such griefs with such men well agree,
> But wherefore, wherefore fall on me?
> To be beloved is all I need,
> And whom I love, I love indeed.

# 23

## CHARLES ROBERT MATURIN

———————————

# Bertram
### *or, The castle of St Aldobrand*
1816

When Monk Lewis's *Castle spectre* appeared in December 1797, Coleridge's *Remorse* (then titled *Osorio*) had just been turned down by Covent Garden; when Maturin's *Bertram* appeared in May 1816, *Remorse* had had a successful run at Drury Lane. Coleridge had failed to cash in with a sequel, however (*Zapolya* being turned down by the selection committee), and *Bertram* was no ordinary success. Like the *Spectre*, it was an affront. Where *Remorse* ran for twenty nights, and went through three editions in the year, *Bertram* ran for sixty, and went through seven. With the *Spectre*, Coleridge confined his chagrin to a point-by-point dismissal of his rival's talents in a letter to Wordsworth (23 January 1798); with *Bertram*, he allowed it to flow out into a series of no less than five letters to the *Courier* (29 August–11 September 1816), which he then edited to form chapter 23 of *Biographia literaria*. The resulting essay is witty in its dismissiveness, solemn in its evoking of moral standards. Though occasioned by sour grapes, it raises important questions about the nature of Romantic drama, and tells us much about the staging of Romantic plays. St Aldobrand makes his exit in Act III, scene ii. 'Well!' Coleridge writes, with evident pleasure,

the husband gone in on the one side, out pops the lover from the other, and for the fiendish purpose of harrowing up the soul of his wretched accomplice in guilt, by announcing to her, with most brutal and blasphemous execrations, his fixed and deliberate resolve to assassinate her husband; all this too is for no discoverable purpose on the part of the author, but that of introducing a series of super-tragic starts, pauses, ˙screams, struggling, dagger-throwing, falling on the ground, starting up again wildly, swearing, outcries for help, falling again on the ground, rising again, faintly tottering towards the door, and, to end the scene, a most convenient fainting fit of our lady's, just in time to give Bertram an opportunity of seeking the object of his hatred, before she alarms the house, which indeed she has had full time to have done before, but that the author rather chose she should amuse herself and the audience by the above-described ravings and startings.

It was Scott who had first noticed Maturin, reviewing his early novel, *Fatal revenge* (published over the pseudonym Dennis Jasper Murphy), for the *Quarterly* in May 1810, and later mentioning *Bertram* 'with great commendation' to Byron, who was on the committee at Drury Lane. Byron's letter to Maturin, of 21 December 1815, is generous both in its enclosure of £50 (Maturin was an impoverished Irish parson), and in its terms of praise. He and a second member of the committee have read the play, and think it 'of great & singular merit as a composition & capable . . . with some alterations & omissions, of being adapted even to the *present* state of the stage – which is not the most encouraging to men of talent'. 'What it seems to want for this purpose', Byron adds 'is *lowering* . . . this for the sake of the physical powers of the actor – as well as to relieve the attention of an audience – no performer could support the tone & effort of continual & sustained passion through five acts'.

What to Byron appeared to be 'sustained passion' appeared to Coleridge as 'super-tragic' ravings. In Venice , where rather surprisingly he seems to have had a copy of *Biographia*, Byron found the attack on *Bertram* and the Drury Lane committee, 'Not very grateful nor graceful on the part of the worthy auto-biographer' (12 October 1817). The two poets' difference of opinion was largely predictable. Moody, passionate and diabolical, Bertram is a Byronic character, even if not a very subtle one. Coleridge was asking instead for Shakespearian sensibility, which isn't there, and isn't intended to be. Coleridge's disapproval went deeper, though. Maturin is guilty in his view of moral, as opposed to political, jacobinism:

I want words to describe the mingled horror and disgust with which I witnessed the opening of the fourth act, considering it as a melancholy proof of the depravation of the public mind. The shocking spirit of jacobinism seemed no longer confined to politics. The familiarity with atrocious events and characters appeared to have poisoned the taste, even where it had not directly disorganized the moral principles, and left the feelings callous to all the mild appeals, and craving alone for the grossest and most outrageous stimulants. The very fact . . . that a British audience could remain passive under such an insult to common decency, nay, receive with a thunder of applause, a human being supposed to have come reeking from the consummation of this complex foulness and baseness . . . pressed as with the weight of lead upon my heart . . .

Turning to the play, it is difficult to say at what point Bertram might have received his 'thunderous applause'. So far from triumphing in his seduction of Imogine, he is to be seen at the opening of Act IV alone beneath the castle walls, addressing to the moon a soliloquy conspicuous for its reticence and self-reproach. It is true that he comes from a consummation, but the reeking that so offends Coleridge is his own creation:

> *Bertram*:  Thou hidest away thy face, and wilt not view me –
> All the bright lights of heaven are dark above me –
> Beneath the black cope of this starless night
> There lurks no darker soul . . .
> I should have bearded him in halls of pride –
> I should have mated him in fields of death –
> Not stol'n upon his secret bower of peace,
> And breathed a serpent's venom on his flower.
>
> (p. 49)

There is an eroticism, certainly, in the overwritten final line; but it is traditional and contains no hint of 'complex foulness and baseness'.

The complexity is Coleridge's. His attack on *Bertram* is printed in *Biographia* alongside *Satyrane's letters* (written originally in 1798–9) as evidence of his unchanging opposition to the drama of excess inspired by Schiller:

Eighteen years ago I observed, that the whole secret of the modern jacobinical drama . . . and of all its popularity, consists in the confusion and subversion of the natural order of things . . . by rewarding with all the sympathies which are the due of virtue, those criminals whom law, reason, and religion have excommunicated from our esteem.

With Charles de Moor of *The robbers* as the great prototype, a drama of the gothic sublime had grown up, in which not merely horror, but admiration, is aroused by a hero who places himself above the moral standards of the day. Singled out by his battle with the elements, Bertram saves himself from the shipwreck of the opening scene, 'With careless, desperate force':

> full many times
> His life was won and lost, as though he recked not –
> No hand did aid him, and he aided none –
> Alone he breasted the broad wave, alone
> That man was saved.
>
> (pp. 6–7)

It goes almost without saying that this man will be powerful, wicked, tormented, doomed, and the leader of a robber band.

Coleridge, who as a married man had spent a lot of time not quite going too far in his passion for Sara Hutchinson, is appalled that Bertram and Imogine, after years of separation, should make the most of the hour they have together. Yet the tendency of the drama is far from recommending adultery. Both lovers suffer for their act. It is the extravagance that causes offence – the fact that because they are larger than life they are permitted to play out their lives according to different rules. Imogine keeps her appointment with Bertram despite the return of St Aldobrand and his goodness to her, despite the loving intervention of her child. By Shakespearian standards there is no characterization to speak of, but there is a force that carries the play along. We accept that she cannot not keep her appointment. And, to Coleridge's indignation, we sympathize with her in the suffering (also larger than life) that follows:

> *Imogine*: There is no human heart can bide this conflict –
> All dark and horrible – Bertram must die –
> But oh, within these walls, before mine eyes,
> Who would have died for him, while life had value –
> He shall not die – Clotilda, ho, come forth –
> He yet may be redeemed, though I am lost . . .
>
> (p. 61)

Even the final scene, full of the grossest improbabilities, in which Bertram (in Coleridge's phrase, 'out-heroding Charles de Moor') cows his executioners and dies in the manner of Othello, is, in its kind, moving.

Coleridge was fighting again the battle that he and Wordsworth had fought in the Preface to *Lyrical ballads*, 1800. Effectively it was against the gothic. The 'invaluable works of our elder writers', characterized by naturalness, morality and the language of the heart, were being driven into neglect by 'frantic novels, sickly and stupid German Tragedies, and deluges of idle and extravagant stories in verse'. The Drury Lane audience did not merely applaud adultery, it was guilty of a 'degrading thirst after outrageous stimulation'.

There had been a time, though, when Coleridge himself might have applauded. 'Who is this Schiller?' he wrote to Southey minutes after his first reading of *The robbers*, 'This Convulser of the Heart? . . . I tremble like an Aspen Leaf . . . Why have we ever called Milton sublime?' (1.0 a.m., 4 November 1794). Byron and Maturin knew, with the 22-year-old Coleridge, that passion takes different forms. *Bertram* is to be read fast, at a single sitting, all disbelief suspended. In the phrase used by Wordsworth of Gottfried Bürger, it offers in these circumstances 'a hurry of pleasure'. Like *Faust* or *Manfred*, it exists because the Romantic period discovered an affinity in opposites. The unreal, the extreme, the gothic sublime, did not, as Coleridge the critic imagined, preclude the elemental. They too were a valuing of states of heightened emotion that showed the human capacity for suffering and love. *Bertram* is as much a product of the spirit of the age as *Lyrical ballads*.

## 24

## ROBERT OWEN

---

# A new view of society

### *or, essays on the formation of the human character*

### 1817 (1813)

'A *New* View of Society' – No Mr Owen, that we deny. It may be true, but it is
not new. It is not coeval, whatever the author and proprietor may think, with the
New Lanark mills . . . It is as old as the *Political Justice* of Mr Godwin, as the
*Oceana* of Harrington, as the *Utopia* of Sir Thomas More, as the *Republic* of Plato;
it is as old as society itself, and as the attempts to reform it by shewing what it
ought to be, or by teaching that the good of the whole is the good of the
individual – an opinion by which fools and honest men have been sometimes
deceived, but which has never yet taken in the knaves and the knowing ones. The
doctrine of Universal Benevolence, the belief in the Omnipotence of Truth, and
in the Perfectibility of Human Nature, are not new, but 'Old, old', Master
Robert Owen; why then do you say that they are new?

Hazlitt is at his brilliant best. His review, published in the *Examiner* on 4
August 1816 and reprinted in *Political essays* (1819), is witty and scathing
from first to last. Owen, for all his achievements and good intentions,
gets not a single word of praise. His ideas are superannuated, dead and
buried; they have been dug up, 'drawn, quartered and gibbeted', and
dispersed in rotten fragments to the winds of heaven. 'In what does the
New Lanark differ from the old Utopia', Hazlitt demands, dropping his
gruesome metaphor,

Does not Mr Owen know that the same scheme, the same principles, the same
philosophy of motives and actions, of causes and consequences, of knowledge
and virtue, of virtue and happiness, were rife in the year 1793, were noised
abroad then, were spoken on the house-tops, were whispered in secret, were
published in quarto and duodecimo, in political treatises, in plays, in poems,
songs, and romances . . . (*Political essays*, pp. 98–99)

The mention of 1793 takes Hazlitt's readers back twenty years to the
period of the French Revolution. More specifically it reminds them of the

publication (in February '93 and two volumes, quarto) of Godwin's *Political justice*. There can be no doubt that Owen is in many ways a Godwinian. He knew Godwin personally, and took his advice. The doctrines on which he founds his system – and which Hazlitt derisively capitalizes (Universal Benevolence, the Omnipotence of Truth, Perfectibility of Human Nature) – all derive from *Political justice*. Yet he is his own man. Where Godwin is Calvinist minister turned atheist and radical philosopher, Owen is factory-manager (latterly owner) turned political thinker. His notions are grandiose – he can solve the problems of the nation, the Empire, the world – but to a large extent he bases them on practical experience. In the 1830s Owen will become associated with trades-unionism and the beginnings of modern socialism; his new view of society in 1816 is the view of a capitalist who sees that a contented, well-fed, well-housed, partly educated work-force will do the job better. He is good-hearted, but not too worried by inequality, and not uneasy at doing well by doing good. As Hazlitt implies, Owen converts the world into a cotton-factory – or converts his cotton-factory into the world.

The mills at New Lanark had been built by a Mr Dale of Glasgow in 1784, at a point where falls on the Clyde provided water-power. There was no existing source of labour. A village was built to attract workers with families from other parts of the kingdom, and a large house erected, 'which ultimately contained about 500 children . . . procured chiefly from workhouses and charities in Edinburgh'. A surgeon was appointed 'to prevent or cure disease', and 'the best instructors . . . to teach such branches of education as were deemed likely to be useful to children in their situation'. 'To defray the expense of these well-devised arrangements', Owen adds,

it was absolutely necessary that the children should be employed within the mills from six o'clock in the morning till seven in the evening, summer and winter; and after these hours their education commenced.

A thirteen-hour day, six days a week, followed by lessons. Any thought that the 'children' might be twelve-year-olds is soon dispelled:

The directors of the public charities, from mistaken economy, would not consent to send the children under their care to cotton mills, unless the children were received by the proprietors at the ages of six, seven and eight. (p. 45)

Owen himself acquired the New Lanark mills (with the aid of partners from Manchester) in 1799. He was 28, and at once set about making improvements. For a start, he encouraged 'permanent settlers with large families' in place of the workhouse apprentices. Parents were advised to allow their children 'to acquire health and education until they were ten years old', before sending them into the mill. That this was a considerable step is suggested by Owen's parenthesis as he tells of his decision: 'It may be remarked that even this age is too early to keep them at constant employment in manufactories, from six in the morning to seven in the evening.' Compassion plays little part in the *New view*. We are told that under Dale, many children 'became dwarfs in body and mind, and some of them were deformed', but not encouraged to ask what proportion lived to complete their apprenticeship, or how the solitary doctor cured or prevented lung-diseases that were commonly fatal. Owen would have had little understanding of Dyer (*Complaints of the poor people of England*, 1793), and less of the satirical Blake:

> But most through midnight streets I hear
>
> How the chimney-sweeper's cry
> Every blackening church appals,
> And the hapless soldier's sigh
> Runs in blood down palace walls
>         (*London*, 8–12)

There are no individuals in Owen's thinking. It is unproductive and therefore irrational to task children beyond their strength. A good work-force is a happy work-force. To get the system right is everything.

Not that Owen has any doubts. The new view that he presents will solve existing problems at a blow. A single fallacy has held back the progress of mankind:

From the earliest ages it has been the practice of the world to act on the supposition that each individual man forms his own character, and that therefore he is accountable for all his sentiments and habits, and consequently merits reward for some and punishment for others . . . This is not a slight mistake which involves only trivial consequences; it is a fundamental error of the highest possible magnitude . . . This error cannot much longer exist; for every day will make it more and more evident *that the character of man is, without a single exception, always formed for him* . . . (pp. 90–91)

Infants brought up in a given social group, adopt its ways even if they were not born into it. Criminals are created by social conditioning – and hanged by judges who would have been criminals themseves had circumstances been reversed. Owen allows for small differences, but asserts confidently that human nature 'is one and the same for all':

It follows that every state, to be well governed, ought to direct its chief attention to the formation of character; and thus the best governed state will be that which shall possess the best national system of education. (p. 149)

Every known form of education, and every current religion, can in Owen's view be superseded by the teaching of a single principle. The principle is not so different from Christ's love of the neighbour, but Owen is a deist, and places no reliance on scripture:

that Power which governs and pervades the universe has evidently so formed man, that he must progressively pass from a state of ignorance to intelligence . . . and in that progress . . . discover, that his individual happiness can be increased and extended only in proportion as he actively endeavours to increase and extend the happiness of all around him. (pp. 22–23)

Education must begin early: 'much of [a child's] temper or disposition is correctly or incorrectly formed before he attains his second year'. The problem of course is how to educate the educators. Like the Coleridge of 1794, who worried that Pantisocracy would be undermined by parents handing down vices brought from the Old World, Owen is concerned that children 'be removed, so far as is at present practicable, from the erroneous treatment of [their] yet untrained and untaught parents'. As soon as he can 'freely walk alone', the child should be introduced into a playground, and told the simple precept that will stay with him for life: 'that he is never to injure his playfellows; but that, on the contrary, he is to contribute all in his power to make them happy'.

Hazlitt's witty invoking of Plato, More and Harrington (though entirely to the point) tends to obscure Owen's relation to the spirit of his age. Determinist thinking could hardly be caused by the Revolution, but was certainly stimulated. From their different standpoints, Priestley, Godwin, Coleridge, Wordsworth (rather briefly), Shelley, and many others, looked forward to a millennium of future happiness when man through education should achieve his true potential. In 1797 Coleridge's benefactor, Tom Wedgwood, announced a 'master-stroke which should anticipate a century or two upon the large-paced progress of human improvement'. Again the emphasis was on the formation of character. But where Owen was concerned mainly with the working-classes, Wedgwood was intent upon creating the new world leader: 'it is my opinion, that in the education of the greatest of these characters, not more than one hour in ten has been made to contribute to the formation of those qualities upon which [their] influence has depended'. Potential leaders would be trained from infancy by a special regime of the correct sense-impressions, and never permitted to encounter that which was unuseful or confusing – the outdoor world, for instance.

How Wedgwood's new leaders would have been eased into their role is not very clear, but Owen required positive cooperation from those whom he was asking to give way. Being by nature a prophet rather than a lobbyist, he offered churchmen a firm new foundation 'on which to erect vital religion, pure and undefiled', and affronted the rich and powerful with the question,

can that system be right, which compels the industrious, temperate, and comparatively virtuous, to support the ignorant, the idle, and comparatively vicious? (p. 142)

In his 1817 Preface, Owen boasts that the *New view* has been 'circulated among the principal political, literary and religious characters in the country and on the continent, as well as among the governments of Europe, America and British India'. One is reminded of the Blake who mounts his exhibition of 1809 as 'the greatest of duties to [his] country'. But Owen is much less easy to place, blending practicality with its opposite in an absurd degree, while remaining evidently sane. His is not a wild scheme, but a local project that has grown out of all proportion. As owner-manager of an isolated factory, staffed by children and members of a subordinate class grateful for even the slightest consideration, Owen sees a vision as to how the universe might be. Like Godwin's, on which it often depends, it is a Romantic vision masquerading as a practical one – an act of faith that didn't for a moment take in 'the knaves and the the knowing ones', but which achieves significance because of the passionate conviction of its author.

Southey, who was shown round the mills at New Lanark by Owen in September 1819 compares him (in friendly tones) to a benevolent slave-owner:

Owen in reality deceives himself. He is part-owner and sole Director of a large establishment, differing more in accidents than in essence from a plantation: the persons under him happen to be white, and are at liberty by law to quit his service, but while they remain in it they are as much under his absolute management as so

# Robert Owen

many negro–slaves. His humour, his vanity, his kindliness of nature (all these have their share) lead him to make these *human machines* as he calls them (and too literally believes them to be) as happy as he can, and to make a display of their happiness. And he jumps at once to the monstrous conclusion that because he can do this with 2210 persons, who are totally dependent upon him – all mankind might be governed with the same facility. *Et in Utopia ego.*

# 25

## HAZLITT AND HUNT

---

# The round table

*a collection of essays on literature,
men, and manners*
1817

No one was ever so often, and so elegantly, right as Hazlitt. Curiously it is not a virtue that is highly regarded. Dr Johnson maintains his reputation as critic and sage despite being frequently, memorably, wrong. Wrongness becomes a source of strength. *Lycidas*, we are told, is 'easy, low, vulgar, and therefore disgusting': Johnson has the pleasure of his obduracy, we have the pleasure of seeing him true to himself. By implication, a smaller man would have been right – and gone unnoticed. Coleridge's vagaries are of a different kind, but similarly have no effect on his standing. He can be marvellously right, but his judgments are bound up with his wishes and his needs and his personal relationships. When he tells us that Wordsworth is the greatest poet since Milton, it is worth reflecting that he had said the same about Southey.

Hazlitt's rightness is unusual. He has his prejudices (in favour of Bonaparte; against the noble poet, Byron), and his occasional blind-nesses (failure to see the greatness of *Christabel*), but in general he sees and reads with imaginative sympathy. Deeply committed as he is to politics and to poetry, he can hardly be said to be dispassionate; yet his judgments achieve something close to disinterestedness by virtue of their concern for the object, poem, topic, before his eyes. He has a sharp tongue, and can be cruelly witty, but he is seldom unjust. His essays offer a profusion of insights, most of them generous, in a style that never ceases to astonish.

*The round table* presents a great writer alongside a good one; the difference is always noticeable. Hunt, as editor of the *Examiner*, seems to have evolved the scheme for a series of articles 'in the manner of the early periodical Essayists, the Spectator and Tatler'. Work was to be undertaken by 'a small party of friends' meeting once a week round a table 'to discuss the merits of a leg of mutton' and the subjects of the next issue. In the event, Hazlitt more or less took the scheme over, though the fiction of numerous diners at the table was preserved by the use of false initials. As published in two volumes, 1817, *The round table* contains forty essays by Hazlitt (over six sets of initials) and twelve by Hunt (over L.H. and H.T.). Just over half of Hazlitt's contributions are from the original series, but *The round table* is his first collection in book-form, and he feels free to include other work from the *Examiner* together with five pieces from the *Morning chronicle*. Hunt's contributions are easy-going, garrulous, a little self-regarding. Though the table is round, he sees himself as the host. He is at his best in the three-part *Day by the fire* ('I am one of those that delight in a fireside, and can enjoy it without even the help of a cat or a tea-kettle') or when he is thinking

of that laborious and inelegant class of the community, *Washerwomen*, and of all the hot, disagreeable, dabbing, smoking, splashing, kitcheny, cold-dining, anti-company-receiving associations, to which they give rise. (ii, 182–3)

It is Montaigne whom Hazlitt regards as the father of 'personal authorship' – the first to write the kind of accomplished and agreeable essay 'in which the reader is admitted behind the curtain, and sits down with the writer in his gown and slippers'. The picture is disarming. Hunt is at ease in his slippers; Hazlitt, if he admits the reader behind the curtain at all, rarely asks him to sit down. If we do get close to him, it will be in the writing, not through personal revelation or the building up of a literary character. A sentence stands out from his praise of Isaac Walton. *The compleat angler*, he tells us, is the best pastoral in the language: 'In the description of a fishing tackle you perceive the piety and humanity of the author's mind.'

That brilliance of style should be allied to such insights is truly remarkable. Hazlitt throws off habitually what would be for others laborious epigrams ('The first Methodist on record was David.' 'Whenever we look at the hands of Correggio's women, or Raphael's, we always wish to touch them.'), and in doing so charms where others would irritate. Why, we ask at once, is David a Methodist? The answer is there. Hazlitt has no pleasure in the merely enigmatic:

[David] was the first eminent person we read of, who made a regular compromise between religion and morality, between faith and good works. After any trifling peccadillo in point of conduct, as a murder, adultery, perjury, or the like, he ascended with his harp into some high tower of his palace; and having chaunted, in a solemn strain of poetical inspiration, the praises of piety and virtue, made his peace with heaven and his own conscience. (i., 163)

The tone is beautifully controlled. David, king of Israel, author of the Psalms, spotted Bathsheba (wife of Uriah the Hittite) from the roof of his palace, washing herself. What follows is entirely disgraceful (*vide* II Samuel, chapter two). Hazlitt's concern, however, is with *The causes of Methodism*. His point has been wittily made. The sect could hardly object to descent from the royal ancestor of Jesus himself (*vide* Matthew, chapter one).

The hands of Correggio's women show – both in Hazlitt's observation and in Correggio's skill – the presence of gusto. The NED fails to note *The round table* and Hazlitt's special usage of the term:

There is gusto in the colouring of Titian. Not only do his heads seem to think – his bodies seem to feel . . . Michael Angelo's forms are full of gusto. They everywhere obtrude the sense of power upon the eye. His limbs convey an idea of muscular strength, or moral grandeur, and even of intellectual [spiritual] dignity . . . Rembrandt has it in everything; everything in his pictures has a tangible character. If he puts a diamond in the ear of a burgomaster's wife, it is of the first water; and his furs and stuffs are proof against a Russian winter. (ii, 21–24)

In Sidney's beautiful phrase, the quality that Hazlitt evokes is 'inward touch', imaginative truth. It seems to be the result of a special kind of caring, but passes beyond the barriers of physical depiction into a moral and spiritual implication:

Claude's landscapes, perfect as they are, want gusto . . . his eye wanted imagination: it did not strongly sympathize with his other faculties. He saw the atmosphere, but he did not feel it. (ii, 25–26)

That Hazlitt should for a moment sound like Wordsworth is presumably something to do with the spirit of the age. The two writers certainly didn't think themselves alike. Yet affinities do exist. Teased in his *Excursion* review by Wordsworth's celebration of 'humble and rustic life', Hazlitt produces the diatribe, 'All country people hate each other', but there is room too in *The round table* for *On the love of the country*, with its purely Wordsworthian associationism:

It is because natural objects have been associated with the sports of our child-hood, with air and exercise, with our feelings in solitude, when the mind takes the strongest hold of things, and clings with the fondest interest to whatever strikes its attention . . . [it is] because they have been one chief source and nourishment of our feelings, and a part of our being, that we love them as we do ourselves. (i, 65–66)

Hazlitt disliked Wordsworth's egotism, and disapproved of his politics, but *On Mr. Wordsworth's Excursion* shows an understanding of the poetry such as no other critic has ever achieved:

He scans the human race as the naturalist measures the earth's zone, without attending to the picturesque points of view, the abrupt inequalities of surface. He contemplates the passions and habits of men, not in their extremes, but in their first elements . . . He only sympathizes with those simple forms of feeling, which mingle at once with his own identity, or with the stream of general humanity. To him the great and the small are the same; the near and the remote; what appears, and what only is. The general and the permanent, like the Platonic ideas, are his only realities. All accidental varieties and individual contrasts are lost in an endless continuity of feeling, like drops of water in the ocean-stream! (ii, 98–99)

Hazlitt's commitment to truth and sense of justice are not confined to seeking out things to praise; they contribute too to a magnificent anger. Burke

who was a half poet and a half philosopher, has done more mischief than perhaps any other person in the world. His understanding was not competent to the discovery of any truth, but it was sufficient to palliate a falsehood . . . Without genius to adorn the beautiful, he had the art to throw a dazzling veil over the deformed and disgusting. (ii, 82–83)

Gifford, editor of the *Quarterly*, deals in more personal mischief. His review of *The round table* is blatant and malicious in its misrepresentation. Strangely Gifford's most cutting remarks about Hazlitt are based on essays (*On washerwomen*, for instance) which he knows to be by Hunt. The cold and measured contempt of Hazlitt's *Letter to William Gifford Esq.* (1819) is a model to all who have scores to repay:

Sir, you have an ugly trick of saying what is not true of any one you do not like, and it will be the object of this letter to cure you of it . . .
    You are a little person, but a considerable cat's-paw, and so far worthy of notice. Your clandestine connection with persons high in office constantly influences your opinions, and alone gives importance to them. You are the *Government Critic*, a character nicely differing from that of the government spy . . . Raised from the lowest rank to your despicable eminence in the world of letters, you are indignant that anyone should attempt to rise into notice, except by the same regular

trammels and servile gradations, or should go about to separate the stamp of merit from the badge of sycophancy. The silent listener in select circles, and menial tool of noble families, you have become the oracle of Church and State. (Howe, ix, 13)

Hazlitt, as usual, was right.

# 26

## THOMAS LOVE PEACOCK

---

# Nightmare abbey

### 1818

It was Shelley who provided Peacock with the epigraph for *Nightmare abbey*, pointing appropriately to a passage in Jonson's *Every man in his humour* (1598):

*Matthew*. Oh! it's your only fine humour, sir. Your true melancholy breeds your perfect fine wit, sir . . . I pray you, sir, make use of my study: it's at your service.
*Stephen*. I thank you, sir, I shall be bold, I warrant you. Have you a stool there, to be melancholy upon?

*Nightmare abbey* is a beautifully shaped and accomplished comedy of humours. The somewhat unwieldy debates of *Headlong hall* (1815) and *Melincourt* (1817) – Foster *versus* Escot, Forester *versus* Fax (broadly, in each case, Godwin/Shelley/optimism *versus* Malthus/Peacock/clear-sightedness) – have been replaced by a single pervasive theme. Though still concerned with contemporary issues, Peacock, like Jonson, is writing a satire of affectation. He is making a stand, he tells Shelley on 30 May 1818, 'against the encroachments of black bile' (cause of melancholy, according to the Elizabethan theory of humours). 'The fourth canto of *Childe Harold*', Peacock continues, 'is really too bad. I cannot consent to be *auditor tantum* of this systematical poisoning of the mind of the reading public.'

Such language could hardly be carried over into comedy. Mr Asterias puts it for us more lightly, and in more general terms: 'A gloomy brow and a tragical voice seem to have been, of late, the characteristics of fashionable manners' (p. 98). In his quest for a 'stool . . . to be melancholy upon', Scythrop takes

his evening seat, on a fallen fragment of mossy stone, with his back resting against the ruined wall, – a thick canopy of ivy, with an owl in it, over his head, – and the *Sorrows of Werter* in his hand. (p. 21)

Mr Flosky, who is later to be discovered writing 'a dismal ballad', speaks of

that new region of the belles-lettres, which I have called the Morbid Anatomy of Black Bile, and which is greatly to be admired and rejoiced at, as affording a fine scope for the exhibition of mental power. (p. 80).

In a speech that comes almost verbatim from *Childe Harold*, Mr Cypress tells Scythrop and Flosky:

I have no hope for myself or for others. Our life is a false nature, it is not in the harmony of things: it is an all-blasting upas, whose root is earth, and whose leaves are the skies which rain their poison-dews upon mankind. (p. 156)

To modern readers Scythrop, Flosky and Cypress exist as caricatures of Shelley, Coleridge and Byron; to an Elizabethan audience they would have been studies of the melancholic, cousins of Jacques and Hamlet. Alongside them Peacock offers a full supporting cast of humour-characters and humour-names: Scythrop's father, Mr Glowry, and Mr Listless (whose names speak for themselves); Marionetta, the puppet, responsive to the strings of circumstance (attracted when Scythrop is distant, distant when he grows warm); Mr Toobad, with his one-liner, 'The devil is come among us'; Mr Hilary (the cheerful one, though not to the point of 'hilarity'); Mr Larynx the clergyman, Raven the butler. More topical in their humours are the scientist, Asterias (whose name relates to starfish, and who has 'penetrated into the watery den of the Sepia Octopus', p. 84), and Celinda, who chooses to be known as Stella, modelling herself on Goethe's voguish play, as Scythrop models himself on Werter.

Though he could have borrowed Raven from *Volpone* (and might indeed have fitted into the play himself, alongside the parrot, Sir Pol), Peacock did not have to go to Jonson for a comedy of humours. It was to be seen in Molière, in Restoration drama, in Fielding the playwright and Fielding the novelist (Allworthy, Thwackum, Square), and in countless other places. In point of fact it had preceded Jonson, not only in Chapman's *Humourous day's mirth* (1597), but in Langland's Lady Meed and the frequent personifications of medieval and renaissance allegory. But Peacock is unusually thorough-going. He does not merely employ humour-characters for convenience, he presents, like Jonson (or, in this respect, like Sterne), an overall vision of human-beings dominated by their humours. Melancholy has taken over. The mind of the reading public has been poisoned by the black bile of the gothic and Byronic. The task of *Nightmare abbey* is to 'bring to a sort of philosophical focus . . . the morbidities of modern literature, and to let in a little daylight on its atrabilious complexion' (to Shelley, 15 September 1818).

It looks very much as if *Nightmare abbey* was provoked by a sequence of seven world-weary stanzas at the end of *Childe Harold* Canto IV – above all, perhaps, by cxxvi:

> Our life is a false nature: 'tis not in
> The harmony of things, this hard decree,
> This ineradicable taint of sin,
> This boundless upas, this all-blasting tree,
> Whose root is earth, whose leaves and branches be
> The skies which rain their plagues on men like dew . . .

Despite this provocation to satire, Cypress plays a relatively small part in *Nightmare abbey* – presumably because Peacock did not know Byron personally, as he did Shelley, or engage with his ideas, as he did with Coleridge's. There was, and still is, a literary pleasure to be had from the interweaving of Byron's best-selling poetry into his speeches. But Cypress will be remembered chiefly for the pronouncement: 'Sir, I have quarrelled with my wife; and a man who has quarrelled with his wife is absolved from all duty to his country' (p. 154).

Flosky is a far more sophisticated portrait. Direct references to *Christabel* (and less direct ones to the *Ancient mariner* and *Kubla Khan*) would have made him easily recognizable, but the ideas parodied in his speeches come from the decidedly non-popular *Statesman's manual* and *Biographia literaria*. The degree of Flosky's affectation is brought out by the marvellous scene in chapter eight where Marionetta asks his advice about Scythrop. He is not unclear in his thinking, but wilfully obscure. From the satirist's point of view he is the most rewarding character. Peacock enjoys him, rather borrowing than creating his voice of learned Coleridgean self-satisfaction:

This distinction between fancy and imagination is one of the most abstruse and important points of metaphysics. I have written seven hundred pages of promise to elucidate it . . . (pp. 112–113)

Except my works, and those of my particular friends, nothing is good that is not as old as Jeremy Taylor: and, *entre nous*, the best parts of my friends' books were either written or suggested by myself. (p. 61)

The beauty of this process [synthetic reasoning] is, that at every step it strikes out into two branches, in a compound ratio of ramification; so that you are perfectly sure of losing your way, and keeping your mind in perfect health, by the perpetual exercise of an interminable quest; and for these reasons I have christened my eldest son Emanuel Kant Flosky. (p. 75)

Scythrop is different again. Unlike Cypress and Flosky, he is not treated as a poet, and not characterized through parody or literary reference. Nor does his story conform to the public facts of Shelley's life. Instead of being sent down from Oxford, he completes his education 'to the high satisfaction of the master and fellows of his college'; he does not declare his atheism, quarrel with his father, elope (twice), get married (twice), fight for the custody of children, or have a wife who commits suicide. No doubt he preserves Shelleyan attributes that Peacock had obseved (craftiness might be one), but he appears chiefly as a type of the impractical idealist. When we first meet him he has published a treatise which he expects will 'set the whole nation in a ferment'. In the event seven copies are sold. Scythrop's thoughts turn to *Revelation*. There is an almost Blakean quality about his response:

'Seven copies', he thought . . . 'Seven is a mystical number, and the omen is good. Let me find the seven purchasers of my seven copies, and they shall be the seven golden candle-sticks with which I will illuminate the world.' (pp. 25–26)

Scythrop does find one golden candle-stick – or rather, she finds him – but the world remains unilluminated. Far from aiding in its regeneration, Stella complicates a situation already dominated by the veering moods of Marionetta. To some extent the two girls must have been related in Peacock's mind to Harriet and Mary Shelley, but in no way do they represent them. Marionetta is far more sophisticated than Harriet, Stella far more dashing than Mary. Nor, unless one takes the connections to be heavily ironic, does Scythrop's position (wishing to preserve the love of both girls, finally turned down by both) square with such equations. From the point of view of *Nightmare abbey*, it is quite as relevant to know that in 1814-15 Peacock himself was part of a triangle that included Marianne de St Croix (related by name at least to Marionetta). And it is probably far more relevant that such triangles existed in both Shelley's early gothic novels, *Zastrozzi* and *St Irvyne*, and in Goethe's *Stella*.

Peacock's characterization is more flexible than it seems at first sight. Where it is useful to do so, he trades on our knowledge of actualities; where facts are unhelpful, he ignores them. Even within the book consistency is not valued. For the sake of parody we hear in chapter six of the naming of Flosky's son, Emanuel Kant (recalling the christening of David Hartley Coleridge, as recorded in *Biographia*); for the sake of the plot, Flosky in chapter 15 is single and free to marry Celinda. Characters similarly are permitted to step outside their roles. It is, for instance, Toobad who is chosen to give expression to Peacock's own values:

We see a hundred men hanged, where [our ancestors] saw one. We see five hundred transported, where they saw one. We see five thousand in the workhouse, where they saw one. We see scores of Bible Societies, where they saw none. We see paper [money], where they saw gold. . . We see children perishing in manufactories, where they saw them flourishing in the fields. (p. 159)

In truth *Nightmare abbey* is a hybrid. Regarded for convenience as a novel, it has links with the prose satires of Rabelais, Swift and Voltaire. In the longer speeches of Flosky, especially, it incorporates parody in the manner of the *Anti-jacobin*. Its use of dialogue, its detailed stage-directions, and great set-piece scenes in Scythrop's tower, all remind us of Peacock's gift for theatre (he had indeed written two plays early on). Scythrop and his two loves – one 'a dancing, laughing, singing, thoughtless, careless, merry-hearted thing' (p. 41), the other 'who had a lively sense of all the oppressions that are done under the sun' (p. 141) – hold the book together. Meanwhile the conversations, central to all Peacock's work, proceed amid interruptions: from Toobad (covered in mud and with fresh proof of the devil's presence), from Asterias (who has sighted a mermaid from the window, thus giving us our first hint of the presence of Stella), from a ghost, 'shrouded in white drapery, with the semblance of a bloody turban on its head' (p. 180).

*Nightmare abbey* insists, as the true novel hardly can, upon its unreality. Within their comedy of humours, Peacock's characters have no inner thoughts, do not develop, cannot change their views. Interaction is minimal, and relationship, one might think, impossible. Yet one relationship does exist, of considerable importance: the unShelleyan one of father and son. 'You are a fox, Scythrop', Glowry says in Chapter 13, taking us by surprise with his blend of pride and tenderness, 'you are an exceedingly cunning fox, with that demure visage of yours' (p. 186). What follows is one of the great English comic scenes. Challenged by his father to explain the woman's voice heard through the door to his tower, Scythrop first delivers a lecture on acoustics and the structure of the ear, then invents, impromptu, a play that he has been rehearsing, supplying exaggerated stage-directions, and taking male and female parts himself. Unable to convince his father ('It won't do, Scythrop. There is a girl concealed in this tower, and find her I will'), he tries to talk him down.

Scythrop's impromptu play – a tragedy of the Great Mogul, 'on the German model' – is a companion-piece to *The rovers* (*Anti-jacobin*, 166–99). But where Canning and Frere require us to be aware of Schiller's background presence, Peacock's imagination frees itself from parody. We pass from mock-drama to the thing itself:

Scythrop now saw that the affair was growing serious . . . having no other subject, he continued his description of the ear, raising his voice continually as Mr Glowry raised his.
'When your cousin Marionetta', said Mr Glowry, 'whom you profess to love – whom you profess to love, sir –'
'The internal canal of the ear', said Scythrop, 'is partly bony and partly cartilaginous. This internal canal is –'
'Is actually in the house, sir; and, when you are so shortly to be – as I expect –'
'Closed at the further end by the *membrana tympani* –'
'Joined together in holy matrimony –'
'Under which is carried a branch of the fifth pair of nerves –'
'I say, sir, when you are so shortly to be married to your cousin Marionetta –'
'The *cavitas tympani* –'
A loud noise was heard behind the book-case, which, to the astonishment of Mr Glowry, opened in the middle, and the massy compartments, with all their weight of books, receding from each other . . . disclosed an interior apartment in the entrance of which stood the beautiful Stella . . . (pp. 190–2)

It is the bond of father and son that enables Peacock to sustain and develop his dramatic situation. Glowry's pleasure at his fox's discomforture amounts to gloating. Love, affectedly regarded by Cypress as 'not an inhabitant of the earth', and shown as wholly unreal in Scythrop's relationships with Marionetta and Stella, appears now in a kind of affectionate mischief:

'I can explain it all', said Scythrop, 'in a most satisfactory manner, if you will but have the goodness to leave us alone.'
'Pray, sir, to which act of the tragedy of the Great Mogul does this incident belong?'
'I entreat you, my dear sir, leave us alone' . . .
Stella threw herself into a chair, and burst into a tempest of tears . . .

Thomas Love Peacock

'I suppose, after all', said Mr Glowry maliciously, 'it is only a phenomenon in acoustics, and this young lady is a reflection of sound from concave surfaces.' (pp. 193–4)

Fittingly Stella and Marionetta have the last say. Or, not quite the last say. Glowry has a final point to make:

'Calm yourself, my dear Scythrop . . . there are yet maidens in England.'
'Very true, sir', said Scythrop.
'And the next time', said Mr Glowry, 'have but one string to your bow.' (p. 217)

As Shelley said, 'The catastrophe is excellent' (to Peacock, 20 June 1819).

# 27

# JOHN KEATS

---

## Endymion
### *a poetic romance*
### 1818

'A thing of beauty (as Mr Keats says, or sings, we know not which, in the first line of his poem) is a joy for ever'! And, 'as the year grows lush in juicy stalks', 'many and many a verse he hopes to write'.

The mockery to which *Endymion* is subjected in the *British critic* (June 1818) turns to scorn and condescension in Lockhart's much longer article for *Blackwood's* two months later. The poetry is debased, and Keats's training as a medical student used to reduce him to the level of shop-assistant:

It is a better and a wiser thing to be a starved apothecary than a starved poet; so back to the shop Mr John, back to 'plasters, pills, and ointment boxes' . . .

Croker's review in the *Quarterly* (dated April, published September) is famously ruder still: 'This author is a copyist of Mr Hunt, but he is more unintelligible, almost as rugged, twice as diffuse, and ten times more tiresome and absurd'.

It seems that Hunt, who had introduced Keats to the literary world through the *Examiner* in December 1816, was not above parading his influence. Told that the four thousand lines of *Endymion* were nearly complete, he boasted to John Hamilton Reynolds that the poem would have been seven thousand but for him. Diffuseness was certainly Keats's problem, and it may well be that Hunt had warned him to curtail it, but during the composition of *Endymion* in summer 1817 Keats kept himself deliberately apart. He was aware of the need to protect his individuality and to create his own style. It was irksome to be the disciple. Writing to Benjamin Bailey on 8 October he predicted what the reviewers would say:

# John Keats

You see Bailey how independant my writing has been – Hunts dissuasion [from writing a long poem] was of no avail – I refused to visit Shelley, that I might have my own unfettered Scope – and after all I shall have the Reputation of Hunt's elevé.

The reputation was partly justified, partly not. Keats had learned his craft from Hunt. *Poems* 1817 is not only dedicated to him, but takes the epigraph to *I stood tiptoe* (on page one) from the *Story of Rimini*, 'Places of nestling green for Poets made'. The lines that follow do not have the jauntiness of Hunt, but show three of the main features associated with the Cockney School, a relaxed use of the heroic couplet (designed to rescue the metre from Pope), a tendency to slightly twee, slightly embarassing, sentimental detail, and a willingness to use or coin self-consciously poetic expressions:

> I stood tip-toe upon a little hill,
> The air was cooling, and so very still,
> That the sweet buds which with a modest pride
> Pull droopingly, in slanting curve aside . . .
> Had not yet lost those starry diadems
> Caught from the early sobbing of the morn.

Hunt, however, is a poet divided against himself. At the same time as gaining a reputation for poetic misuse of language –

> What need I tell of lovely lips and eyes,
> A clipsome waist, and bosom's balmy rise
> (*Rimini* p. 10)

– he announces, in his Preface of 1816, Wordsworthian principles about purity of diction: 'All the merit I claim is that of having made an attempt to describe natural things in a language becoming to them, and to do something towards the revival of what appears to me a proper English versification' (*Rimini* p. xviii). The Keats of *Endymion* inherits from Hunt a desire to get away from Pope and the closed couplet, but is to be seen deliberately flouting his assumptions about diction. 'The proper language of poetry', Hunt writes,

is in fact nothing different from that of real life, and depends for its dignity upon the strength and sentiment of what it speaks. It is only adding musical modulation to what a fine understanding might actually utter in the midst of its griefs or enjoyments. The poet therefore should do as Chaucer and Shakespeare did . . . use as much as possible an actual, existing language. (*Rimini* pp. xv–xvi)

Keats never did restrict himself to the 'existing language' of his time.

His greatest lines – 'Now more than ever seems it *rich* to die' (*Ode to a nightingale*, 1819) – contain expressions that may be classed as Cockney if we choose. They have become a strength, however. The writing of *Endymion* taught him control. The poem out-Hunts Hunt, gets away from him (and earns his criticism) by taking to an extreme the relatively small freedoms with language that he had permitted himself. *Rimini* might scandalize those whose ear was still attuned to Pope, but it is never lax. In providing a new setting for Dante's story of Paulo and Francesca, the narrative (until Hunt's disastrous later revisions) is taut and elegantly handled. 'Clipsome waists' are few. The style, somewhere between Byron (to whom *Rimini* is awkwardly dedicated) and Browning's *Dramatic romances*, is such as Keats might well have chosen to imitate, but didn't:

> Some likeness was there 'twixt the two – an air
> At times, a cheek, a colour of the hair,
> A tone, when speaking of indifferent things;
> Nor, by the scale of common measurings,
> Would you say more perhaps, than that the one
> Was more robust, the other finelier spun;
> That of the two, Giovanni was the graver,
> Paulo the livelier, and more in favour.
>
> (*Rimini* pp. 44–5)

Keats's purpose in writing *Endymion* is described in a letter sent to his brother George in spring 1817 and copied for Bailey in October. Material for the poem consists of one 'bare circumstance': the Latmian shepherd, Endymion's love for the Moon, Cynthia. This he proposes to elaborate over four thousand lines, as a test of his fitness to enter the Temple of Fame:

it will be a test, a trial of my Powers of Imagination and chiefly of my invention which is a rare thing indeed – by which I must make 4000 lines of one bare circumstance and fill them with Poetry . . . Did our great Poets ever write short Pieces? I mean in the shape of Tales . . . This same invention seems indeed of late Years to have been forgotten as a Poetical excellence . . .

Invention led to certain elaborations in the narrative (the meeting with Adonis, Endymion's journey beneath the sea, the story of Glaucus and Scylla, and that of the Indian Maid who turns out to be Cynthia herself), but mostly it consisted in filling lines with poetry, giving to each its sweetness, like Summer 'o'erbrimming' with honey the 'clammy cells' of Autumn's bees:

# John Keats

> Such the sun, the moon,
> Trees old and young, sprouting a shady boon
> For simple sheep; and such are daffodils
> With the green world they live in; and clear rills
> That for themselves a cooling covert make
> 'Gainst the hot season; the mid forest brake,
> Rich with sprinkling of fair musk-rose blooms:
> And such too is the grandeur of the dooms
> We have imagined for the mighty dead . . .
>
> (p. 4)

Whether or not it is charitable, Croker's comment on the passage is excellent criticism:

He seems to us to write a line at random, and then he follows not the thought excited by this line, but that suggested by the *rhyme* with which it concludes . . . He wanders from one subject to another, from the association, not of ideas but of sounds . . . Here it is clear that the word, and not the idea, *moon* produced the simple sheep and their shady *boon*, and that 'the *dooms* of the mighty dead' would never have intruded themselves but for the '*fair musk-rose blooms*'.

Keats's answer would have been an appeal to the sensibility of reader: 'Do not the Lovers of Poetry like to have a little Region to wander in where they may pick and choose, and in which the images are so numerous that many are forgotten and found new in a second Reading?' (8 October 1817). The sensitive reader would enjoy the imagery for its richness and diversity, and not ask whether on occasion it was prompted by rhyme. Similarly, he would have no objection to coinage and extravagant diction – 'the new words with which, in imitation of Mr Leigh Hunt, [Keats] adorns our language' (*Quarterly*).

'We are told', Croker complains, that turtle-doves '*passion* their voices' (p. 15); that 'an arbour was *nested*' (p. 23); and a lady's locks '*gordian'd up*' (p. 32):

to supply the place of the nouns thus verbalized Mr Keats, with great fecundity, spawns new ones; such as 'men-slugs and human *serpentry*' (p. 41); the '*honey-feel* of bliss' (p. 45) . . .

Then he has formed new verbs by the process of cutting off their natural tails, the adverbs, and affixing them to their foreheads; thus, 'the wine out-sparkled' (p. 10); the 'multitude up-followed' (p. 11) . . .

But if he sinks some adverbs in the verbs he compensates the language with adverbs and adjectives which he separates from the parent stock. Thus, a lady 'whispers *pantingly* and close' . . .

*Endymion* has to be read sympathetically or not at all. Keats was twenty-one when he wrote it. He set himself fifty lines a day, and was through in seven months. His feelings are laid open for us in the draft Preface that his friends persuaded him to rewrite:

this Poem must rather be considered as an endeavour than a thing accomplish'd: a poor prologue to what, if I live, I humbly hope to do. In duty to the Public I should have kept it back for a year or two, knowing it to be so faulty: but I really cannot do so; by repetition my favourite passages sound vapid in my ears, and I would rather redeem myself with a new Poem – should this one be found of any interest.

'I have', he adds, 'to apologize to the lovers of simplicity for touching the spell of loveliness that hung about Endymion: if any of my lines plead for me with such people I shall be proud.' Among 'the lovers of simplicity', Wordsworth had already dismissed the *Hymn to Pan* as 'a Very pretty piece of Paganism' (which was stuffy of him). Hunt, though he would write feelingly of *Endymion* after Keats's death, found it 'unnatural' when shown the first book in January 1818, '& made ten objections to it in the mere skimming it over'. Croker, despite 'the fullest stretch of [his] perseverence', was unable to get beyond Book One.

'Touching the spell of loveliness' is a beautiful, and a touching, phrase. Keats knew that his poem had been extravagant, that much of it hadn't worked. It had been necessary to him, however, as a first prolonged attempt to create, 'invent' for himself and for others, the world of his imagination. It was not, in the sense of the word that distinguishes Coleridge's ballads from Wordsworth's, a supernatural world. Nor was it a world of coherent myth or cogent story-telling. *Endymion* is an attempt to create a major work by writing at length, and inappropriately, a poetry charged with lyric intensity. To see the shepherd's love for Cynthia as an allegory of Keats's pursuit of the ideal is heavy-handed, yet at some level the implication has to be there. 'Touching the spell of loveliness', Keats was in every line striving towards the 'fellowship with essence' that he defines in a central passage of Book One, rewritten in January 1818:

> Wherein lies happiness? In that which becks
> Our ready minds to fellowship divine;
> A fellowship with essence, till we shine,
> Full alchymiz'd, and free of space.
>
> (p. 39)

The lines to which this passage is an introduction are described by Keats to his publisher, Taylor, as 'a regular stepping of the Imagination towards a Truth' (30 January 1818). Defined for us is 'a sort of oneness', the Wordsworthian phrase marking not hesistancy, but Keats's unwillingness to be doctrinaire. 'Behold the clear religion of heaven', he begins, and instantly we are returned to earth:

> Fold
> A rose leaf round thy finger's taperness,
> And soothe thy lips: hist, when the airy stress
> Of music's kiss impregnates the free winds,
> And with a sympathetic touch unbinds
> Eolian magic from their lucid wombs:
> Then old songs waken from enclouded tombs;
> Old ditties sigh above their father's grave;
> Ghosts of melodious prophecyings rave
> Round every spot where trod Apollo's foot;
> Bronze clarions awake, and faintly bruit,
> Where long ago a giant battle was;
> And, from the turf, a lullaby doth pass
> In every place where infant Orpheus slept.

'Feel we these things?' Keats asks rhetorically –

> that moment have we stept
> Into a sort of oneness, and our state
> Is like a floating spirit's.

'Fellowship divine' and 'clear religion' tempt us towards an inappropriate transcendental reading. Keats's world of heightened imagination is analogous to religious experience, but not spiritualized, as Wordsworth's is in *Tintern abbey*, or Shelley's (potentially at least) in *Mont Blanc*. 'But there are', Keats goes on, taking us by surprise,

> Richer entanglements, enthralments far
> More self-destroying, leading, by degrees,
> To the chief intensity: the crown of these
> Is made of love and friendship, and sits high
> Upon the forehead of humanity.
>
> (p. 40)

For a moment, as the destruction of self leads not to oneness with the Coleridgean godhead, but to 'the chief intensity', we are in the world of Wallace Stevens. But the emphasis on love and friendship reminds us that it was the writing of *Endymion* that brought Keats to the grandest of all his statements of faith:

*Endymion*

I am certain of nothing but of the holiness of the Heart's affections and the truth of Imagination – What the imagination seizes as Beauty must be truth – whether it existed before or not – for I have the same Idea of all our Passions as of Love they are all, in their sublime, creative of essential Beauty. (22 November 1817)

# 28

# JOHN HOOKHAM FRERE

## Whistlecraft

*Prospectus and specimen of an intended national work, by
William and Robert Whistlecraft, of Stow-market, in
Suffolk, harness and collar makers. Intended to comprise
the most interesting particulars relating to King Arthur and
his round table*

1818

Known to scholars only as the source of Byron's metre in *Beppo* and *Don
Juan*, Frere's *Whistlecraft* is a poem of great wit and charm, showing a
writer completely relaxed and in control, talking to himself and his
audience and his muse about nothing very much. It is the manner that
matters. Thalia, muse of comedy and pastoral, can seldom have led so
amiable and domesticated an existence. 'I've a proposal here from Mr
Murray', Frere tells her at the outset of Canto III, 'He offers handsomely
– the money down.' Why not a stay in the country to calm her nerves as
the two of them get down to writing again:

> 'Tell me, my dear Thalia, what you think;
>     Your nerves have undergone a sudden shock;
> Your poor dear spirits have begun to sink;
>     On Banstead Downs you'd muster a new stock,
> And I'd be sure to keep away from drink,
>     And always go to bed by twelve o'clock.
> We'll travel down there in the morning stages;
> Our verses shall go down to distant ages.
>
> And here in town we'll breakfast on hot rolls,
>     And you shall have a better shawl to wear . . .
> Come, now, fling up the cinders, fetch the coals,
>     And take away the things you hung to air,
> Set out the tea-things, and bid Phoebe bring
> The kettle up.' – *Arms and the Monks I sing.*

> Some ten miles off, an ancient abbey stood,
> Amidst the mountains, near a noble stream . . .
> (III, ii–iv)

There is a deliciousness in the juxtaposition as Frere and Thalia go down to the country by the morning stage-coach, and the poetry goes down with them – to posterity.

No wonder Byron was delighted and inspired. The spenserian stanzas of *Childe Harold*, with their more elaborate rhyme-scheme and lagging final alexandrine, had served their purpose, but were weighty and inflexible by comparison. Here was a form that really lent itself to the speaking voice. And one, too, that had an Italian pedigree. Southey comments on the new development in a letter to Landor of February 1820:

A fashion of poetry has been imported which has had a great run, and is in a fair way of being worn out. It is of Italian growth – an adaptation of the manner of Pulci, Berni, and Ariosto in his sportive mode. Frere began it. What he produced was too good in itself, and too inoffensive to become popular; for it attacked nothing and nobody; and it had the fault of his Italian models, that the transition from what is serious to what is burlesque, was capricious. Lord Byron immediately followed . . .

Byron's interest in Frere's stanza led him in 1820 to translate the first canto of Pulci's *Morgante maggiore*, claiming on 21 February that it was 'the parent not only of *Whistlecraft*, but of all jocose Italian poetry'. So concerned was he to make his point that with infinite pains he translated Pulci line for line, insisting that the original be printed alongside. The giant, Morgante, speaks to his future master:

> 'And let your name in verity be shown;
> Then will I everything at your command do'
> On which the other said, he was Orlando.
> (st. xlvii)

> 'Dimmio del nome tuo la veritade,
> Poi di me dispor puoi al tuo comando';
> Ond' e' gli disse, com' egli era Orlando.
> (st xlvii)

Confronted by a pointless, wandering story about knights and giants and monks, written allegedly by two brother harness-makers from Suffolk, Frere's first readers looked for allegory and political satire. Those who knew him to be the author were aware that he had been responsible, with Canning, for the brilliant parodies and Government propaganda of the *Anti-jacobin*. The giants must surely be the French, recently defeated at Waterloo? The wayward genius of Sir Tristram should make him easy enough to identify. And what of Sir Gawain, with his touches of Dryden's Achitophel:

> Adviser-general to the whole community,
> He serv'd his friend, but watch'd his opportunity.
>
> (I, xxv)

Could Gawain's inability to carry through his plans really have no ulterior meaning:

> Take his own plans, and place him in command,
>     Your prospect of success became precarious:
> His plans were good, but Launcelot succeeded
> And realized them better far than He did.
>
> (I, xxvi)

Wellington must surely be somewhere in all this? Could he perhaps be the 'anti-tintinnabularian' Friar John, saviour of the monastery? But if so, what could the fable of the bells be all about? Why should the monks want 'bells of larger size, and louder tone'? Why should bells arouse in giants 'irrational gigantic anger'? It was, and is, all very perplexing. And delightful.

In a learned and rambling article on *Whistlecraft*, headed 'Narrative and Romantic Poems of the Italians', the *Quarterly* for April 1819 refers its readers to Pulci, Boiardo, Berni, Ariosto and Forteguerri. The writer's quest for origins and resemblances is no great success. More surprisingly, he is prepared to say so: 'Indeed it is not very easy to understand the nature of the part which the poet is acting; nor do we always know how to take him. Sometimes he is *really* Mr Whistlecraft the harness and collar maker'. Not often. Twenty years after his time on the *Anti-jacobin* working (with Pitt as well as Canning) as a bright, brittle, up-to-the-moment tory political satirist, Frere was amusing himself. His choice of the harness-making alias pokes fun at the fashion for labourer poets (Ann Yearsley the Bristol Milk Woman, Burns, Bloomfield and others), but also shows an intention to burlesque Arthurian romance, and national epic pretensions, from an unlettered viewpoint. The intention seems not to have lasted very long. Far from establishing the voice of a rural innocent, Frere found a way, as Lamb would do in *Elia*, of being comfortably himself under another name. As for King Arthur and his Round Table, they scarcely got beyond the title-page.

Southey was probably right that *Whistlecraft*, 'attacking nothing and nobody', was too inoffensive to be popular, but he shows little understanding of the poetry in his objection to caprice. Whether or not it was a fault in Frere's Italian models, it is (as Byron immediately perceived) a strength in the English. There could be no 'transition from what is serious to what is burlesque' without its being made clear which is which. *Whistlecraft* has its values: concern for language, for instance,

> don't confound the language of the nation
> With long-tail'd words in *osity* and *ation*
> (Proem, vi)

(compare Clough's *Uranus* on 'modern *ologistic* fancyings'), and distrust of political process:

> it often happens in the hour of need,
> From popular ideas of utility,
> People are pitch'd upon for mere ability.
> (IV, xviii)

It has its beauties and exquisite observations: of the black and glossy water-skaters, for instance, as the poet and Thalia, their legs 'idly dangling down',

> rest upon the bank, and dip [their] toes
> In the poetic current as it flows . . .
> Or mark the jetty, glossy Tribes that glance
> Upon the water's firm unruffled breast,
> Tracing their ancient labyrinthic dance
> In mute mysterious cadence unexpress'd . . .
> (III, l–lii)

But seriousness, free from caprice, *Whistlecraft* does not, and could not, have.

It is even a little difficult to be sure where there is burlesque. '*Arms and the Monks I sing*' we can all place as a take-off of Virgil ('Arma virumque cano'), but the poem as a whole hardly seems to be mock-epic. There is satire in Frere's portrayal of leadership among the knights, and faction among the monks, but it could never be said to be the point of the poetry. Swift, with the giants of Brobdingnag, makes his position clear on every page. They are crude, at times cruel, at times disgusting, but they nonetheless convict human beings of littleness. Frere's giants exist in no such morally definable universe. They carry off ladies, roast mules and horses, eat a couple of duennas, without anyone seeming to mind. The trick, of course, is evenness of tone. Whatever takes place, the voice that tells the story insists upon a comic detachment. It may be funny, beautiful, shocking, but always (as later with Byron ) it is droll:

> But first I must commemorate in Rhime
>   Sir Tristram's dext'rous swordmanship and might
> (This incident appears to me sublime),
>   He struck a Giant's head off in the fight:

Tough on the giant – but what are giants for? These things are bound to happen in pursuit of the sublime. Frere has not finished with us, though:

> The head fell down of course, but for some time
>   The stupid, headless trunk remain'd upright;
> For more than twenty seconds there it stood,
>   But ultimately fell from loss of blood.
>
> (II, xlviii)

Nowhere does Byron offer cruelty with greater elegance. Why are we not sick? Because vivid and appalling as the scene is to the mental eye, we are still listening to the voice claiming it as comedy. The final line of the stanza (as we have come to expect) turns the scene to comic effect. Grasping with relief at a heartless (headless) joke – only the living fall from loss of blood – we read on, permitted by our sense of the grotesque to remain within the borders of unreality. It is an extreme case of Frere's control, but one among many that remind us of the only preceding English poem that shows a comparable elusiveness, intelligence, elegance, beauty of language and manipulation of poetic style, sense of proportion and power in disproportion – Marvell's *Appleton house* (c. 1650). Marvell too is writing just after a bloody war, and introduces disconcerting violence within the protected world of his poem. He too tempts us with the thought of allegory, defying us to make a definition of his mode of not quite narrative. He too controls the poetry through a voice, urbane, witty, trusted in its values, yet always at a distance.

Surprisingly the one writer with whom Frere could be said to engage is Wordsworth. The ponderousness of his title-page (*Prospectus and Specimen of an intended National Work . . . Intended to Comprise the Most Interesting Particulars Relating to King Arthur and his Round Table*) is surely a guying of the *Excursion*, with its Prospectus to *The recluse* and pretensions to be part of a forthcoming philosophical epic. The Wordsworth whom Frere confronts in the text, though, is at his least pompous. It is the tender, fanciful poem, *To Joanna*, that has taken his fancy, with its laughter echoing among the mountains:

> The rock, like something starting from a sleep,
> Took up the Lady's voice, and laugh'd again:
> That ancient Woman seated on Helm-crag
> Was ready with her cavern; Hammar-Scar,
> And the tall Steep of Silver-How sent forth
> A noise of laughter; southern Loughrigg heard,
> And Fairfield answer'd with a mountain-tone:
> Helvellyn far into the clear blue sky
> Carried the Lady's voice . . .
>
> (ll. 54–62)

Joanna clearly charmed her future brother-in-law. Wordsworth's lines have a gaiety unlike anything that we expect of him. Frere makes from them the high point of his poem, as first the mountain-giants, then the giant-mountains, express their disapproval at the tintinnabulation of the monks:

> Giants abominate the sound of bells,
>      And soon the fierce antipathy was shown,
> The tinkling and the jingling, and the clangor,
> Rous'd their irrational gigantic anger.
>
> (III, xv)

It is extraordinary that such poetry should not be better known: the first line powerfully imaginative, the second mock-heroic in its hint of Pope ('The *strong antipathy* of good to bad'), the third vividly onomatopoeic, the fourth elegant not least in its picking up of the etymology of 'giant' (Anglo Saxon 'gigant'). Friar John, as his fellow monks scurry round setting up their belfry, has felt 'beforehand, for a fortnight near, / A kind of deafness in his fancy's ear' (III, xlv); the mountains, in 'their granite ears', are more deeply troubled:

> Meanwhile the solemn mountains that surrounded
>      The silent valley where the convent lay,
> With tintinnabular uproar were astounded,
>      When the first peal burst forth at break of day:

Feeling their granite ears severely wounded,
> They scarce knew what to think, or what to say;
And (though large mountains commonly conceal
Their sentiments, dissembling what they feel,

Yet) Cader-Gibbrish from his cloudy throne
> To high Loblommon gave an intimation
Of this strange rumour, with an awful tone,
> Thund'ring his deep surprise and indignation;
The lesser hills, in language of their own,
> Discuss'd the topic by reverberation;
Discoursing with their echoes all day long,
Their only conversation was 'ding-dong'.

'Those giant-mountains', Frere continues, at his most playful and enchanting,

> inwardly were mov'd,
But never made an outward change of place:
Not so the mountain-giants (as behov'd
> A more alert and locomotive race),
Hearing a clatter which they disapprov'd,
> They ran straight forward to besiege the place . . .
(III, xvii–xix)

Riddle: how do you tell mountain-giants from giant-mountains? Answer: they are 'A more alert and locomotive race'. Not a lot different, but they move. Frere's is an entirely delightful humour. Cader-Gibbrish (Cader-Idris) and high Loblommon (Ben Lomond) are farcical, with a touch of disrespect for Wordsworth; 'Discussed the topic by reverberation' is a line brilliant by Frere's highest standards (how many of our human colleagues do the same?); and, to crown it all, Frere in this marvellous stanza has rhymed three times – 'intimation', 'indignation', 'reverberation' – on the sound that he (or perhaps, so early in the poem, the harness-maker) expressly forbad.

When all is said and done, Italian models seem to have contributed little to *Whistlecraft* beyond its metre. More to the point is Rabelais. Frere's humour is not, in the accepted sense, Rabelaisian, but as we watch Gargantua eating pilgrims with oil, vinegar and salt 'to refresh himself a little before Supper' there is a comparable incongruity at work:

[He] had already swallowed up five of the Pilgrims, the sixth being in the Platter, totally hid under a Lettice, except for his *Staff* that appeared, and nothing else.

Which Grangousier seeing, said to Gargantua, I think that is the Horn of a Shell-snail, do not eat it. Why not (said Gargantua) they are good all this Month, which he no sooner said, but drawing up the Staff, and therewith taking up the Pilgrim, he eat him very well, then drank a terrible draught of excellent White-wine, and expected Supper to be brought up. (*Works*, trans. Urquhart 1694, I, 153)

In addition to gargantuan fantasy, Rabelais can supply a Friar John (Luther, in the allegory) who single-handed defends an abbey (i, 108ff) – not, it is true, against giants, but against 'the Cake-bakers of Lerne' (popish priests). There is even an episode with bells, as Gargantua decides to carry off those of Our Lady's church at Paris 'for tingling Tantans to hang about his Mare's Neck' (i. 65). It all seems more likely than Pulci to have prompted the imagination. The pilgrims, be it said, escape, as Gargantua is wielding his toothpick, a young walnut-tree.

Byron, first good humouredly in *Beppo*, then with power and a much sharper cutting edge in *Don Juan*, would possess and extend the idiom of *Whistlecraft*. But there are lasting qualities in Frere that go with his more equable temperament and benign observation of human foible. His sense of beauty and sense of disproportion are all his own. Alone among Romantic poets (Lamb the essayist is a parallel), he takes an imaginative pleasure in fancy. Who else, in the space of two stanzas, could play the fisherman, set a picnic in front of us, turn it into a still life for the collector, and, standing back, adopt the tones of the connoisseur showing off his 'cabinet jewel':

> The Monk with handy jerk, and petty baits,
>> Stands twitching out apace the perch and roach . . .
> And soon his motley meal of homely Cates
>> Is spread, the leather bottle is a-broach;
> Eggs, Bacon, Ale, a Napkin, Cheese and Knife,
> Forming a charming Picture of Still-life.
>
> *The Friar fishing* – a design for Cuyp,
>> A cabinet jewel – 'Pray remark the boot;
> And, leading from the light, that shady stripe,
>> With the dark bulrush-heads how well they suit;
> And then, that mellow tint so warm and ripe,
>> That falls upon the cassock . . .
>
> (IV, iii–iv)

# 29

# PERCY BYSSHE SHELLEY

---

# The Cenci
### *a tragedy, in five acts*
### 1819

Tragedies are rare. Many plays, poems, novels, have unhappy endings, but tragic intensity is achieved by few writers, and only in a small proportion of their works. Implied is an intuition into the very nature of suffering. The reader (audience) must identify with pain, yet finally stand outside it. There must be the overwhelming sense of waste identified long ago by A. C. Bradley (*Oxford Lectures on Shakespeare*, 1904), together with admiration and an enhancing sense of human dignity. We must be made to feel both the littleness of man, defeated and transient, and outrage that anything so great should be caused to suffer, permitted to die. We must endure with Lear as he bends in the final scene over the body of Cordelia:

> No, no, no life!
> Why should a dog, a horse, a rat, have life,
> And thou no breath at all? Thou'lt come no more,
> Never, never, never, never, never.
> Pray you undo this button. Thank you, sir.
> Do you see this? Look on her! Look her lips,
> Look there, look there!
>
> *[He dies]*

That Shelley should have such power comes as a surprise. His poetry is full of passion, but does not commonly deal in the sharpness of pain. That he should have written *The Cenci* between Acts Three and Four of *Prometheus unbound* seems more surprising still. The grandeur of *Prometheus*, outside time, unlimited in space, contracts to the history of a single fated household in late renaissance Rome. It is Cenci himself who forms the link. Even the knowledge that he did exist, that there was once such a human being, does not make credible the horror of his actions. He has about him the axiomatic malignity of Jove. We could, if we chose, regard him as a sadist, a psychopath, but we don't – tragedy does not deal in diagnoses – we see him as a force, a prodigious manifestation of hatred. Monstrous as they are, his actions seem less evil than those of the Pope, who condones his murders in return for gold, or of Orsino, who connives and prompts in order to entrap Beatrice for himself. Evil in *The Cenci* consists in hypocrisy and self-serving. The Count stoops to neither.

The question as to what goodness consists of is more difficult. Apart from Cardinal Camillo, who is well-intentioned despite excessive wealth, and Bernardo Cenci (the pardoned younger brother), those with whom we sympathize are murderers. Beatrice, hero of the tragedy, is unhesitating in the decision to kill her father, and never for a moment repents. Whether she is more sinned against than sinning, depends on how one weighs brutality, rape and incest, on the one hand, against parricide on the other. Either way, the innocence in which she entirely believes is of an unusual kind. Of Shelley's numerous reviewers, all but two were profoundly shocked. It is the Reverend George Croly who sets the tone in the *Literary gazette* of 1 April 1820:

Of all the abominations which intellectual perverseness, and poetical atheism, have produced in our times, this tragedy appears to us the most abominable.

According to the *Edinburgh monthly review*, a month later, Shelley has been tempted to 'withdraw the veil from things that ought for ever to remain concealed'.

Even John Scott, in *Baldwin's London magazine* (also May 1820), turns from his praise of sublimity and tenderness in the poetry to consider Shelley's depravity and 'weakness of character'. 'This extraordinary work', he writes,

preserves throughout a vigorous, clear, manly turn of expression, of which [Shelley] makes excellent use to give force, and even sublimity, to the flashes of passion and of phrenzy – and wildness and horror to the darkness of cruelty and guilt. His language, as he travels through the most exaggerated incidents, retains its correctness and simplicity . . .

There are 'the most beautiful images, the most delicate and finished ornaments of sentiment and description'. There is 'the most touching tenderness, graceful sorrow, and solemn appalling misery' that constitutes 'the very genius of poesy', but, strange and lamentable to say, closely connected with [these are] the signs of a depraved, nay mawkish, or rather emasculated, moral taste, craving after trash, filth and poison . . .

Nothing in the play supports this judgment. Lurid details are excluded. There are no erotic or violent scenes. Cenci's abuse of Beatrice takes place off stage, and is never described. Shelley does not so much as mention the word, incest.

Like Byron's *Cain*, in the following year, *The Cenci* is morally offensive to the age in which it is written. Its subject is taboo. Shelley's own view of his material is set out in the Preface, a document of considerable importance in its own right. Far from showing a depraved pleasure in the horrors, he is anxious that they should be treated in a way that plays down their sensationalism. His interest has been aroused by Guido's portrait of Beatrice at the Colonna Palace. He has obtained the copy of a manuscript describing her story, and wishes to tell it, 'endeavouring as nearly as possible to represent the characters as they probably were':

This story of the Cenci is indeed eminently fearful and monstrous: any thing like a dry exhibition of it on the stage would be insupportable. The person who would treat such a subject must increase the ideal, and diminish the actual horror of the events, so that the pleasure which arises from the poetry that exists in these tempestuous sufferings and crimes may mitigate the pain of the contemplation of the moral deformity from which they spring. (p. ix)

The concept of poetry as innate within the 'tempestuous sufferings and crimes' of the past seemed meaningless to at least one of the reviewers, but follows from Shelley's wish to be true – imaginatively true – to the emotion he portrays. 'The Reader cannot be too often reminded', Wordsworth had written in his Note to *The thorn* (1800), 'that Poetry is passion: it is the history or science of feelings'.

Like Wordsworth, Shelley refuses to inculcate a moral. Purpose is innate in his writing, just as poetry is innate in the feelings that he hopes to recreate:

There must . . . be nothing attempted to make the exhibition subservient to what is vulgarly termed a moral purpose. The highest moral purpose aimed at in the highest species of the drama, is the teaching the human heart, through its sympathies and antipathies, the knowledge of itself; in proportion to the possession of which knowledge, every human being is wise, just, sincere, tolerant and kind.

In what might seem a mood of unusual tolerance, Shelley adds, 'If dogmas can do more, it is well: but a drama is no fit place for the enforcement of them.' His characters are 'represented as Catholics', and as such, 'deeply tinged with religion.' Their religion, however, has no bearing on moral conduct, and none on how the play is to be perceived. Catholicism in Italy

pervades intensely the whole frame of society, and is according to the temper of the mind which it inhabits, a passion, a persuasion, an excuse, a refuge; never a check. (p. xi)

Cenci, Shelley records, 'built a chapel in the court of his Palace', dedicated to St Thomas the Apostle, 'and established masses for the peace of his soul'.

Beatrice, her brother and step-mother, were not right to kill Cenci; but nor, in the terms of the tragedy, were they wrong. He was violent, cruel, a murderer many times over. They took the law into their own hands. Giacomo and Lucretia confess at once under torture: Beatrice does not. In her own eyes she is innocent. It is in this larger moral vision that the greatness of the tragedy lies. Beatrice kills her father, as Tess kills Alec D'Urberville, to put right an intolerable wrong. Neither could have behaved otherwise. Hardy goes so far as to subtitle his book, *A pure woman*; Shelley is not (on this occasion) out to shock his critics. He merely gives to Beatrice the tragic stature, and tragic climax, that his contemporaries felt to have been forfeited. 'One thing more, my child', she says to the young Bernardo, in the final scene

> For thine own sake be constant to the love
> Thou bearest us; and to the faith that I,
> Tho' wrapt in a strange cloud of crime and shame,
> Lived ever holy and unstained . . .

Bernard]  I cannot say, farewell!
Camillo]  O, Lady Beatrice!
Beatrice]  Give yourself no unnecessary pain,
> My dear Lord Cardinal. Here, Mother, tie
> My girdle for me, and bind up this hair
> In any simple knot; aye, that does well.
> And yours I see is coming down. How often
> Have we done this for one another; now
> We shall not do it any more. My Lord,
> We are quite ready. Well, 'tis very well.

In the background we hear Lear's 'Pray you undo this button', but it is not an imitation, or a borrowing, it is a beautiful acknowledgement from one great tragic writer to another. Hunt, in the *Indicator* for 26 July 1820, comments that Shelley

reminds us of some of the most strenuous and daring of our old dramatists, not by any means as an imitator, though he has studied them, but as a bold, elemental imagination, and a framer of 'mighty lines'.

To which he adds, conscious no doubt of the affront that it will give,

He possesses also . . . what those to whom we more particularly allude did not possess, great sweetness of nature, and enthusiasm for good; and his style is, as it ought to be, the offspring of this high mixture.

Hunt is thinking of Marlowe ('framer of *mighty lines*'), and Tourneur, and Middleton's *Changeling* (with its very different Beatrice, also wrapped in a 'cloud of crime and shame'); but Shelley's 'great sweetness of nature, and enthusiasm for good' could well be said to distinguish him from Shakespeare too. *The Cenci*'s 'high mixture' of style is carefully devised. Shelley has, he tells us, avoided 'the introduction of what is commonly called mere poetry': 'In a dramatic composition the imagery and the passion should interpenetrate one another, the former being reserved simply for the full developement and illustration of the latter.' Inevitably there are the too Shakespearean moments, but Shelley, like the Byron of *Cain* and *Sardanapalus*, has created a vivid unmetaphorical blank verse that is all his own.

To the strangely open-minded reviewer of the *Theatrical inquisitor* (April 1820) it seemed that there was a 'dark splendor' to Shelley's genius:

As a first dramatic effort, *The Cenci* is unparalleled for the beauty of every attribute with which the drama can be endowed. It has few errors but such as time will amend, and many beauties that time can neither strengthen nor abate.

Hunt thought the play 'undoubtedly the greatest dramatic production of the day' (*Examiner*, 19 March 1820), but was of course writing the year before Byron's *Three Plays* appeared. Mary Shelley commented interestingly, and perhaps rightly, that Act V of *The Cenci* is the greatest thing that Shelley ever wrote. The final speech of Beatrice establishes him among the few great English tragic writers.

# 30

# WILLIAM WORDSWORTH

─────────────

## Peter Bell

*a tale in verse*
1819

*Peter Bell* had the rare distinction of being parodied, under its own name, two weeks before its first appearance in print in April 1819. John Hamilton Reynolds was the anonymous parodist. Keats was amused, and in the know; Byron was amused, but guessed the writer to be Moore; Shelley was amused, and weighed in with *Peter Bell the Third* (sadly not printed till 1839); Coleridge was amused, describing Reynolds's verse as '*morally* fair' and laughing 'heartily' at all the prose; Wordsworth was not amused. But he did go through three editions (as did Reynolds) in a matter of weeks.

It was a Longman announcement in the London press, 'In a few days will be published *Peter Bell, A Tale in Verse*, by William Wordsworth Esq.', that gave Reynolds his cue. Keats, whose moving *Epistle to John Hamilton Reynolds* had been written the previous year, tells the secret of what is afoot to his brother George and Georgiana on 15 April, the day the parody comes out:

Wordsworth is going to publish a Poem called *Peter Bell* – what a perverse fellow it is! Why will he talk of *Peter Bells* – I was told not to tell – but to you it will not be tellings – Reynolds hearing that said *Peter Bell* was coming out, took it into his head to write a skit upon it call'd *Peter Bell*. He did it as soon as thought on; it is to be published this morning, and comes out before the real *Peter Bell*, with this admirable motto from the *Bold stroke for a Wife*, 'I am the real Simon Pure'.

The motto was a brilliant choice. Susannah Centlivre's play (1718, but much revived) was famous for the moment when Colonel Fainwell, impersonating the Quaker, Simon Pure, is unmasked by the real Simon's arrival. At a blow, Wordsworth became the impostor. Added to which, 'Simon' had the advantage of suggesting Peter (*via* the Bible), and simplicity (*via* the nursery-rhyme). And 'Pure' evoked the holier-than-almost-everyone-else stance that Wordsworth had taken to adopting in his public statements.

Not that Reynolds was anti-Wordsworth. His poem shows a knowledge both of the verse and the prose that was not acquired overnight. His publishers were telling the truth when they described him (or rather, described the anonymous author of *Peter Bell, a lyrical ballad*) in a letter to Coleridge as 'a sincere admirer of Mr Wordsworth's poetry'. By the 'Announcement of a new Poem with so untimely a Title as that of *Peter Bell*', Wordsworth has let himself down. The parody will encourage him to renounce 'those Peculiarities which grieve his Friends [and] gladden his Adversaries' (Griggs iv, 934–5n). Reynolds's poem is, as Keats says, a skit. It has no narrative, but offers Peter as a rustic double of the poet, 'rurally related' (Betty Foy is his aunt, Simon Lee his nephew, Alice Fell his niece), and musing on the graves of a country churchyard in a travesty of *Excursion* Book VI:

> Harry Gill is gone to rest,
> Goody Blake is food for maggot;
> They lie sweetly side by side,
> Beautiful as when they died;
> Never more shall she pick faggot.
> (pp. 23–4)

The bathos makes its point, and there is an unexpected twist, as well as bizarre rhyme ('knees' and 'spectac*lees*') in the poem's dénouement. The writing of *Peter Bell, a tale*, we are to assume, has proved fatal to its author:

> And tears are thick with Peter Bell,
> Yet still he sees one blessed tomb;
> Tow'rds it he creeps with spectacles,
> And bending on his leather knees,
> He reads the *Lakeiest* Poet's doom.
>
> The letters printed are by fate,
> The death they say was suicide;
> He reads – 'Here lieth W.W.
> Who never more will trouble you, trouble you':
> The old man smokes who 'tis that died.
> (p. 26)

As Coleridge points out, it is the prose of *Peter Bell, a lyrical ballad* that is inspired. In the 1815 Preface, and Essay Supplementary, the parodist had something substantial to work on. At one point Reynolds achieves his effect merely by quoting Wordsworth, at others he is cruelly funny in his imitation:

My Ballads are the noblest pieces of verse in the whole range of English poetry: and I take this opportunity of telling the world that I am a great man. Mr Milton was also a great man. Ossian was a blind old fool. Copies of my previous works may be had in any numbers, by application at my publisher. (p. v)

Interestingly Taylor and Hessey describe *Peter Bell, a lyrical ballad* as a 'burlesque imitation of the *Idiot boy*'. The author, they claim, 'had never heard a line of *Peter Bell, a tale*'. Some have doubted this, but a glance at the text suggests that it is true. Choosing to base his skit on Wordsworth's most easily, and often, ridiculed poem, Reynolds hit by chance on the metre it shares with the *Tale*. Calling his poem, for the sake of derision, *A lyrical ballad*, he hit by chance on the form of the *Tale*. Above all, he was lucky in the coincidence there proved to be between the opening statement of his Preface (based on the publication date of *Lyrical ballads*), and Wordsworth's Dedication to Southey. 'It is now', he writes,

a period of one-and-twenty years since I wrote some of the most perfect compositions (except certain pieces I have written in my later days) that ever dropped from poetical pen.

The satire would always have been effective, but Wordsworth, it turned out, had also made play with the figure 21:

My Dear Friend,
  The *Tale of Peter Bell*, which I now introduce to your notice, and to that of the Public, has, in its Manuscript state, nearly survived its *minority*; for it first saw the light in the summer of 1798. During this long interval, pains have been taken at different times . . . to fit it for filling *permanently* a station, however humble, in the Literature of my Country.

Change places, and, handy-dandy, which is the parodist, which is the poet? For months the reviewers pretended gravely that they couldn't tell them apart.

Of all things, Wordsworth's poem when it appeared proved to be a comedy – not at all what was to be expected from the poet of the *Excursion* (1814). After the duly pompous prose Dedication (written April 1819), came a verse Prologue (written April 1798) that was openly and happily whimsical:

# William Wordsworth

> There's something in a flying horse,
> And something in a huge balloon;
> But through the clouds I'll never float
> Until I have a little Boat,
> Whose shape is like the crescent-moon.
>
> (p. 1)

To this day, *Peter Bell*, though among the longest and most carefully wrought of Wordsworth's poems, is among the least understoood. Like the *Prelude*, which had its beginnings six months later, it is an exploration of the workings of the mind. The way into it (ironically, considering Reynolds's skit) is through the tender comedy of the *Idiot boy*. And the way into both of them is through Sterne (and Cervantes).

Refusing both the classical Pegasus and the modern hot-air balloon of Montgolfier (celebrated by Erasmus Darwin), Wordsworth takes off on a voyage of the imagination. As readers, we are challenged to follow. 'And now I *have* a little Boat', the Prologue continues,

> In shape a very crescent-moon:
> Fast through the clouds my Boat can sail;
> But if perchance your faith should fail,
> Look up – and you shall see me soon!
>
> The woods, my Friends, are round you roaring,
> Rocking and roaring like a sea . . .
>
> (pp. 1–2)

Some will see the sky-boat at once in the mind's eye, feel the woods rocking around them, and be charmed by the poet's fantasy. Others feel uneasy. Like Sterne, Wordsworth is aware of such differences of response, and plays upon them. His poem has two audiences, both of them bemused, and two openings, both of them abrupt. As the first audience, we are challenged to enter into his world of make-believe:

> Up goes my Boat between the stars
> Through many a breathless field of light . . .
>
> (p. 3)

We then witness the poet failing his own test, returning to earth and ordinariness amid the boat's indignant reproaches:

> Out – out – and, like a brooding hen,
> Beside your sooty hearth-stone cower;
> Go, creep along the dirt, and pick

> Your way with your good walking-stick,
> Just three good miles an hour!
>
> (p. 6)

Finally, we are introduced to the stout earth-bound listeners gathered round the stone table in the poet's garden, who are in some sense our counterparts, and whose confusion we are to share as he plunges into his narrative:

> All by the moonlight river side
> It gave three miserable groans;
> ' 'Tis come then to a pretty pass',
> Said Peter to the groaning Ass,
> But I will *bang* your bones!'
>
> 'Good Sir!' – the Vicar's voice exclaim'd,
> 'You rush at once into the middle';
> And little Bess, with accents sweeter,
> Cried, 'O dear Sir! but who is Peter?'
> Said Stephen, ' 'Tis a downright riddle!'
>
> (p. 15)

As Byron reminds us, 'Most epic-poets plunge *in medias res*'. *Peter Bell*, like the *Idiot boy*, has a mock-heroic aspect which the poet enjoys; but it is all part of a wish to disconcert. How are we to react? Banging of bones is hardly to be taken seriously, but ought the beating of donkeys to be a joke? A reviewer in the *British critic* for June 1819 thought the poet, in striving for dramatic effect, had by mistake used words 'inseparably connected with low and ridiculous associations'. Wordsworth should have 'told us in his own person, and his own language, that Peter beat the ass very unmercifully'. But this is comedy that deliberately refuses to permit a comfortable response. Values are being questioned all the time. Peter is a ruffian. He is hard, cruel and unimaginative:

> A primrose by a river's brim
> A yellow primrose was to him,
> And it was nothing more.
>
> (p. 19)

Yet he is also attractive. Comic exaggeration ('He had a dozen wedded wives', p. 21), and the very quality of the poet's observation –

> His face was keen as is the wind
> That cuts along the hawthorn fence . . .
>
> (p. 23)

– protect him from harsh or dismissive judgments. We watch as Peter finds, steals, and attempts to move, an obstinate donkey, siding with the animal as he maltreats it, but not entirely sure that we are free from Peter's brutal human petulance. Noting, perhaps, the parallel with Balaam's ass (who saves her master from the wrath of God, though misunderstood and three-times beaten, *Numbers* xxiii), we observe the transition as the donkey takes charge of the story, carrying Peter not merely to the home of his drowned master, but through a series of mental terrors and guilty confrontations.

Leigh Hunt, in his *Examiner* review of 2 May 1819, misreads not only the comedy of *Peter Bell*, but its Wordsworthian moral implication. Having written a book on *The folly and danger of Methodism* (1809), he treats the poem as a straightforward Methodist conversion-narrative, denouncing it as a 'didactic little horror', and adding: 'We are really and most unaffectedly sorry to see an excellent poet like Mr Wordsworth returning, in vulgar despair, to such half-witted prejudices'. So far from being 'in vulgar despair' when he wrote *Peter Bell*, Wordsworth had been in high spirits, having just completed the exuberant *Idiot boy* ('I never wrote anything with so much glee!'). Nor was he given to 'vulgar prejudices'. He took the conversion-narrative as the basis for his poem, just as he had taken a medical report as the basis for *Goody Blake and Harry Gill* the previous month (March 1798), because it was evidence, from an unexpected source, of the power of the human imagination. Just as Harry believes himself to be cursed by Goody (or by God, on Goody's behalf), Peter feels himself to be singled out for divine retribution:

> 'Where there is not a bush or tree,
> The very leaves they follow me –
> So huge hath been my wickedness!'
>
> (p. 53)

Peter's conversion, it should be said, is to a life of feeling, not to Methodism as such. Even so it is not Wordsworth's main concern. As with the 'spots of time' and educative processes of the *Prelude*, the means concern him more than the end. He is fascinated by Peter Bell's tormentors, the 'spirits of the mind':

> I know you, potent Spirits! well,
> How with the feeling and the sense

> Playing, ye govern foes or friends,
> Yok'd to your will, for fearful ends –
> And this I speak in reverence!
>
> But might I give advice to you,
> Whom in my fear I love so well,
> From men of pensive virtue go,
> Dread Beings! and your empire show
> On hearts like that of Peter Bell.
>
> (p. 58)

The 'fearful ends', the poet's unexpected 'reverence', the line 'Whom in my fear I love so well', all point to the fact that *Peter Bell* differs from the other ballads in its relation to personal experience:

> Your presence I have often felt
> In darkness and the stormy night;
> And well I know, if need there be,
> Ye can put forth your agency
> When earth is calm, and heaven is bright.
>
> Then, coming from that wayward world,
> That powerful world in which ye dwell,
> Come! Spirits of the Mind! and try
> Tonight, beneath the moonlight sky,
> What may be done with Peter Bell!
>
> (p. 59)

Like the spirit-world that governs the poet's own development in Part One of the 1799 *Prelude*, these forces work on the mind both through the sublime (the stormy night) and the beautiful (when earth is calm and heaven bright). They belong, though, to a 'wayward world', a 'powerful world', that has more than a touch of the fairy world of Mab and Puck. Beside them, the *Prelude* spirits seem stiff and literary, little more than a metaphor for the poet's sense of having been chosen and guided:

> I believe
> That there are spirits which, when they would form
> A favored being, from his very dawn
> Of infancy do open out the clouds . . .
>
> (1799 Prelude, i, 68 ff)

Peter is to be 'tried' by less impersonal forces. In one sense, of course, they are his own thoughts, his own guilty associations. But they have taken on the imaginative quality that Coleridge defines in *Biographia literaria* as 'analogous to the supernatural' (chapter 14), and that Wordsworth points his readers to in the Dedication to Southey:

the Imagination not only does not require for its exercise the intervention of supernatural agency, but . . . may be called forth as imperiously . . . by incidents within the compass of poetic probability. (p. iv)

   Though not perhaps in the usual sense, *Peter Bell* is very much a 'Poem of the Imagination', a poem of power and strangeness that concerns itself on different levels, and in different aspects, with mental process. Wordsworth wishes us to believe that he is writing a poetry of ordinariness heightened into the imaginative:

> The dragon's wing, the magic ring,
> I shall not covet for my dower,
> If I along that lowly way
> With sympathetic heart may stray
> And with a soul of power.
>
> (p. 10)

Within 'the compass of poetic probability' we have, for instance, the tenderly observed overgrown chapel:

> Dying insensibly away
> From human thoughts and purposes,
> The building seems, wall, roof, and tower,
> To bow to some transforming power,
> And blend with the surrounding trees.
>
> (p. 64)

But then there is the vivid opposite extreme, not merely in the Prologue –

> Haste! and above Siberian snows,
> We'll sport amid the boreal morning . . .
>
> (p. 7)

– but in the unconstrained imagination of the stanza borrowed by Shelley from Hunt's review as starting-point and epigraph to *Peter Bell the third*:

> Is it a party in a parlour?
> Cramm'd just as they on earth were cramm'd –
> Some sipping punch, some sipping tea,
> But, as you by their faces see,
> All silent and all damn'd!
>
> (p. 39)

Between these extremes, at the verge of probability, the borderline of natural and supernatural, come the high imaginative moments induced in Peter by spirits of the mind. It is the 'sweet and playful Highland girl', deceived into becoming his sixth wife (and mother of the unborn Child of Sorrow, Benoni), whose memory chiefly preys upon him. At one moment he sees not merely her wraith, but his own, being literally 'beside himself':

> And now the Spirits of the Mind
> Are busy with poor Peter Bell . . .
>
> Close by a brake of flowering furze
> (Above it shivering aspins play)
> He sees an unsubstantial creature,
> His very self in form and feature,
> Not four yards from the broad highway;
>
> And stretch'd beneath the furze he sees
> The Highland girl – it is no other;
> And hears her crying, as she cried
> The very moment that she died,
> 'My mother! oh my mother!'
>
> (pp. 68–9)

'The more he may love the sad embroidery of the *Excursion*', Keats wrote of Reynolds in his brief review (copied for George and Georgiana), 'the more he will hate the coarse samplers of Betty Foy and Alice Fell.' Though he had no more read it than Reynolds himself (or Shelley), by implication Keats would have added *Peter Bell* to his list. Probably he never did discover that, amongst its many moods, Wordsworth's ballad was capable of the saddest embroidery. Its name had low associations, and that was enough: 'What a perverse fellow it is! Why will he talk of *Peter Bells*?'

## LORD BYRON

---

# Don Juan
*cantos I and II*
1819

*Don Juan* Cantos I and II must be as handsome a book as ever crept into print without the name of either writer or publisher on the title-page. If Byron's friends had had their way the poem wouldn't have been published at all. 'I have my doubts about *Don Juan*', Hobhouse records in his Diary for 27 December 1818, 'the blasphemy and bawdry and the domestic facts overpower even the great genius it displays.' By 8 January Hobhouse had sounded other members of what Byron, in distant Venice, called his 'cursed puritanical committee': Frere (author of *Whistlecraft*), Kinnaird (business adviser) and Scrope Davies (boon companion). All agreed with him and Murray ('that most nervous of God's booksellers') that Byron must be advised not to publish. By 1 February, Moore too had been brought into line.

At this stage Byron's 'committee' had seen only Canto I. Though the Dedication, with its attacks on Southey and Castlereagh, alarmed them, as did the sexual freedom of Juan and Julia, and the parody of the Ten Commandments ('Thou shalt believe in Milton, Dryden, Pope . . .'), it was 'the domestic facts' that were their chief concern. Julia's mamma, Donna Inez, was older than Lady Byron, and more worldly wise, but shared her unusual turn for mathematics. She was also curiously determined to place her 'loving lord' in a madhouse:

> For Inez call'd some druggists, and physicians,
>     And tried to prove her loving lord was *mad*,
> But as he had some lucid intermissions,
>     She next decided he was only *bad*;
> Yet when they ask'd her for her depositions,

# Don Juan

> No sort of explanation could be had,
> Save that her duty both to man and God
> Required this conduct – which seem'd very odd.
>
> (I, xxvii)

As *Blackwood's* pointed out, in tones of high moral indignation, such details were immediately recognizable:

> Those who are acquainted (as who is not?) with the main incidents in the private life of Lord Byron . . . will scarcely believe, that the odious malignity of this man's bosom should have carried him so far, as to make him commence a filthy and impious poem, with an elaborate satire on the character and manners of his wife. (August 1819)

The 'filthy and impious poem' had been started on 3 July 1818, two and a quarter years after the poet's separation from Annabella Milbanke. On 19 September Byron tells Moore that Canto I is complete. The new poem is 'in the style and manner of Beppo . . . and meant to be a little quietly facetious upon every thing'. 'I doubt', Byron adds,

> whether it is not – at least, as far as it has yet gone – too free for these very modest days. However, I shall try the experiment, anonymously, and if it don't take, it will be discontinued. It is dedicated to S[outhey] in good, simple, savage verse . . .

On 11 November Hobhouse is warned to expect Canto I, together with *Mazeppa* and the *Ode to Venice*. Ten weeks later a letter to Hobhouse and Kinnaird defending *Juan*'s morality, and prohibiting cuts, tells us that II also has been finished in draft:

> *Don Juan* shall be an entire horse or none. If the objection be to the indecency, the Age which applauds the *Bath Guide* & Little's poems – & reads Fielding & Smollett still – may bear with that; if to the poetry – I will take my chance. I will not give way to all the Cant of Christendom . . . There is another Canto written – but not copied – in two hundred & odd Stanzas, if this succeeds . . . (19 January 1819)

Canto I was to be the test. Byron at first accepted his committee's advice that it could not be published ('Give my love to Frere and tell him – he is right – but I never will forgive him nor any of you'; to Kinnaird, 27 January), then decided to hold out for a private edition of fifty copies, and finally demanded full publication: 'After mature consideration I have determined to have *Don Juan* published (*anonymously*) and I Venture to request that you will bargain with Mr Murray for that . . . Don't answer me with any more damned preachments from Hobhouse – about public opinion – I never flattered that & and I never will' (to Kinnaird, 6 March). Hobhouse continued to preach. Murray was so anxious that he dared not write: 'I have had no answer from him . . . for these three months', Byron told Kinnaird on 9 March, 'if the tradesman don't understand civility – change him'. Canto II, meanwhile, was copied and sent off, Byron instructing Murray on 3 April that there should be '*no mutilations* in either', and adding on the 6th, 'I will permit no curtailments except those mentioned about Castlereagh & the two '*Bobs*' in the introduction. You shan't make *Canticles* of my Cantos.'

Quite what was the relation in Byron's mind between 'canto', 'canticle', 'cant', and 'testicle', is not clear, but, under pressure from London, he had himself performed a little gelding of the 'entire horse', *Don Juan*. Already cut were two offensive parts of the Dedication: the obscene pun on Southey as a 'dry Bob', and the attack on Castlereagh, as 'intellectual eunuch' (more castration) and betrayer of the Irish reform movement,

> Cold-blooded, smooth-faced, placid miscreant!
> Dabbling its sleek young hands in Erin's gore . . .
> (Dedication, st. 12)

On 6 May the whole Dedication was sacrificed (on the grounds that to attack Southey anonymously would be 'reviewer's work', and to attack Castlereagh from a distance would prevent his doing the gentlemanly thing and issuing a challenge). At the same time, however, Byron added three new stanzas to the Donna Inez portrait, the first (I, xv, omitted) including a callous allusion to 'Sir Samuel Romilly . . . Whose suicide was almost an anomaly' (and who, though paid a retainer by the poet, had sold his legal services to Lady Byron). With the arrival of proofs, Byron was under new pressure. 'Mr Hobhouse', he told Murray on 15 May,

is at it again about indelicacy – there is *no indelicacy* – if he wants *that*, let him read Swift – his great Idol – but his Imagination must be a dunghill . . . to engender such a supposition about this poem. For my part I think you are all crazed.

Byron had won his fight, conceding little beyond the Dedication, and actually enhancing the section on Donna Inez. 'About the bitch my wife', he had written to Kinnaird on 25 January, 'I differ from you entirely'. To Hobhouse on 17 May he made still plainer his feelings on this 'cursed subject':

What are you so anxious about Donna Inez for? . . . is a ludicrous character of a tiresome woman in a burlesque poem to be suppressed or altered because a contemptible and hypocritical wretch may be supposed to be pointed at? Do you suppose that I ever will forgive – or forget – or lose sight of her or hers – till I am nothing? You will talk to me of prudence – and give me good reasons 'for one's own sake' &c &c – you will have the satisfaction of giving good advice – and I that of not taking it. Excuse my warmth – it is the cursed subject which puts me out of temper.

With the cutting of the Dedication, the Inez stanzas took a large stride towards the front of the poem. There was no literary or political feuding now to distract and delay the reviewer's attention. Byron was no doubt sorry to lose his 'good, simple, savage verse' on Southey; he was not sorry that Inez, with her distinctive traits, should take the eye:

> Her favourite science was the mathematical,
>   Her noblest virtue was her magnanimity . . .
>                                    (I, xii)

Anger and pain were compelling motives in the early stages of *Don Juan*. That such verse would lead to trouble with the reviewers, Byron was well aware: 'I know that I shall have your *Quarterly* and your *Edinburgh* too about my ears – and all your *reading world* – and all your writing *other world*; be it so . . .' (to Kinnaird, 20 May).

Cantos I and II of *Don Juan* appeared on 15 July 1819. Murray was so worried about their likely reception that he withheld his name from the title-page of the most important book he was ever to publish. There was little point. *Juan* had been long awaited (Keats, for instance, reporting to his brother on 14 February 'another satire is expected from Byron, called *Don Giovanni*'), and its publisher's anxieties were the talk of the town. Croker went so far as to write to Murray on 15 September:

I told you from the first moment that I read *Don Juan*, that your fears had exaggerated its danger. I say nothing about what may have been suppressed; but if you had published *Don Juan* without hesitation or asterisks, nobody would have ever thought worse of it than as a larger *Beppo*, gay and lively and a little loose.

Byron noticed the asterisks too, plus the excision of the Romilly stanza and one on the pox, but was inclined to be forgiving. Murray he accuses on 9 August of being a 'chicken-hearted–silver-paper Stationer', but his thoughts are on Teresa Guiccioli, and his spirits are high. Kinnaird on 26 October is challenged with delighted exuberance:

As to *Don Juan* – confess – confess – you dog – and be candid – that it is the sublime of *that there* sort of writing – it may be bawdy – but is it not good English? – it may be profligate – but is it not *life*, is it not *the thing*? Could any man have written it – who has not lived in the world – and tooled in a post-chaise? in a hackney coach? in a Gondola? against a wall? in a court carriage? in a vis a vis? on a table? – and under it?

'I have written about a hundred stanzas of a third Canto', Byron continues, in tones that seem half serious, 'but it is damned modest – the outcry has frightened me.'

The outcry had been restrained at first, newspaper reports taking the view that *Juan* was neither as licentious, nor as personal in its attacks, as rumour had predicted. ''Tis simply a tale', the *Morning post* commented on 16 July, 'and *righte merrie conceit*, flighty, wild, extravagant – immoral too, it must be confessed; but no arrows are levelled at innocent bosoms, no sacred family peace invaded'. The *Morning herald* told its readers that for all the sins of Byron's muse, 'comic force, humour, metaphysics . . . boundless fancy and ethereal beauty, and curious knowledge, curiously applied, have never been blended with the same felicity in any other poem'. To the *Literary gazette*, *Juan* is a case in which appearances might be expected to be deceptive, and aren't:

There is neither author's nor publisher's name to this book; and the large quarto title-page looks quite pure, with only seventeen words scattered over its surface: perhaps we cannot say that there is equal purity throughout; but there is not much of an opposite kind, to offend even fastidious criticism or sour morality . . . Never was English festooned into more luxurious stanzas than in *Don Juan*. Like the dolphin sporting in its native waves, at every turn, however grotesque, displaying a new hue and a new beauty, the noble author has shown an absolute control . . . (17 July)

It was the example of *Blackwood's* that pointed the reviews towards 'fastidious criticism' and 'sour morality'. Unable to get an article ready for the July issue, the editors printed a note referring obliquely to Murray's absence from the title-page and adding, for the benefit of future sales: 'a Work so atrocious must not be suffered to pass into oblivion without the infliction of that punishment on its guilty author due to such a wanton outrage on all most dear to human nature.' Returning to the attack a month later, the writer (assumed by Byron to be Wilson) offers *Juan* as containing 'a more thorough and intense infusion of genius and vice – power and profligacy – than in any poem which [has] ever before been written in English':

The moral strain of the whole poem is pitched in the lowest key – and if the genius of the author lifts him now and then out of his pollution, it seems as if he regretted the elevation, and made all haste to descend again . . . It appears, in short, as if this miserable man, having exhausted every species of sensual gratification – having drained the cup of sin even to its bitterest dregs, were resolved to shew us that he is no longer a human being, even in his frailties, but a cool unconcerned fiend, laughing with a detestable glee over the whole of the the better and worse elements of which human life is composed – treating, well nigh with equal derision the most pure of virtues, and the most odious of vices – dead alike to the beauty of the one, and the deformity of the other . . .

Byron's comment to Murray on 10 October, 'I like & admire Wilson . . . *he* should not have indulged himself in such outrageous license – it is overdone and defeats itself', seems very just. As does the question, 'what would he say to the grossness without passion – and the misanthropy without feeling – of *Gulliver's travels?*' *Blackwood's* was an extreme case, obscured by rhetoric and self-righteousness, of the problem that most readers felt (many still feel) of placing *Don Juan*, reconciling its moments of beauty and pathos with the ironic banter and pleasure in sardonic undercutting. Shelley's response, as one might expect, is almost the opposite of Wilson's, yet he turns out to have much the same difficulty. Julia's letter, he tells Byron on 26 May 1820, 'is altogether a masterpiece of portraiture; of human nature laid with the eternal colours of the feeling of humanity.' 'I cannot say', he continues,

I equally approve of the service to which this letter was appropriated; or that I altogether think the bitter mocking of our common nature, of which this is one of the expressions, quite worthy of your genius.

For Shelley the mocking is belied, and thus redeemed, by 'the power and the beauty and the wit'; for Hazlitt, it is, and remains, a desecration:

*Don Juan* indeed has great power; but its power is owing to the force of the serious writing, and to the oddity of the contrast between that and the flashy passages with which it is interlarded . . . [Byron] hallows in order to desecrate; takes pleasure in defacing the images of beauty his hands have wrought; and raises our hopes and our beliefs in goodness to Heaven only to dash them to the earth again, and break them to pieces the more effectually . . . (*Spirit of the age*, 173–4)

It may well be that among Byron's contemporaries Hunt understood him best. He too notes the alternations: 'you are sometimes surprised and moved by a touching piece of human nature, and again startled and pained by the sudden transition from loveliness or grandeur to ridicule or the mock-heroic' (*Examiner*, October 1819). And he too feels that Byron, on occasion, trifles with our feelings, recklessly 'turning to ridicule or hopelessness . . . the fine ideas he has excited'. Yet he notices also the opposite process taking place, as sudden beauty emerges mid the satire and bedroom farce at the end of Canto I:

> Julia did not speak,
> But press'd her bloodless lip to Juan's cheek.
>
> He turn'd his lip to hers, and with his hand
> Call'd back the tangles of her wandering hair;
> Even then their love they could not all command,
> And half forgot their danger and despair.
>
> (I, clxix–clxx)

In Byron's ironic stance Hunt perceives an underlying bitterness, the residue of painful experience. A destructive force, he suggests, rises within the mind causing the poet to disperse emotions that cannot be contained. Byron's temperament 'is not naturally satirical'; hence 'the frequent veins of passion and true feeling'. These are explored till the writer

is no longer able to bear the images conjured up by his fine genius . . . it is to get rid of such painful and 'thick-coming' recollections, that he dashes away and relieves himself by getting into another train of ideas, however incongruous or violently contrasted with the former.

The two cantos of 1819 seem to Hunt a progression, 'an evident struggle . . . in the feelings of the writer', leading to 'a much less interrupted strain of rich and deep beauty'.

It is a romantic, and a Romantic, reading. There is much truth in it, but Byron does not merely 'dash away' from the painful. The manuscripts show that this is poetry he reworked again and again. Its formal patterning is extremely important. As Hazlitt noticed, its power resides not merely in the serious writing, but in 'the oddity of the contrast' between that and what he termed 'the flashy passages with which it is interlarded'. Hazlitt disliked the voice that drew back from the story, asserting its own presence, refusing the comfortableness of narrative. But he was aware of a power in incongruity – a power which in these first two cantos may be at times compulsive and a little raw, but which is nevertheless exploited with delight. The greatness of the 1819 volume, like the greatness of Wordsworth's two-part *Prelude* of 1799 (or, for that matter, the greatness of Langland's two-passus *Piers Plowman* of the 1360s), is that it gives form to an original creative impulse, establishing an idiom that is later to be developed at length, but achieving in the process a poetry that will not be surpassed.

There is a satisfactoriness in the balance of Cantos I and II not obvious until one has read *Don Juan* in this, its original, form. The poem's first readers did not know what would be the fate of Juan and Haidee, they knew only that love mid the sophisticated constraints of Canto I had given place to love in an earthly paradise:

> And now 'twas done – on the lone shore were plighted
>   Their hearts; the stars, their nuptial torches, shed
> Beauty upon the beautiful they lighted:
>   Ocean their witness, and the cave their bed,
> By their own feelings hallow'd and united . . .
>
>                                    (II, cciv)

Both loves are tender, both beautiful, both gently ironized, but where Julia in Canto I is a married woman who should have known better, and did –

> A little still she strove, and much repented,
> And whispering 'I will ne'er consent' – consented.
>
>                                    (I, cxvii)

– Haidee is 'Passion's child . . . Made but to love'. Irony that plays, however indulgently, upon Julia's self-deception, acts rather as a protection for Haidee, reminding us of values by which she and her lover remain untouched:

> Alas! for Juan and Haidee! they were
>   So loving and so lovely – till then never,
> Excepting our first parents, such a pair
> Had run the risk of being damn'd for ever . . .
>
>                                    (II, cxciii)

The temptation, of course, is to say that Canto I offers society, artifice, the world that Byron had known in Regency England, Canto II, nature and innocence. It won't quite do. At least, it will do only if we concede that it is as natural to eat, as to love, one's neighbour:

> The seventh day, and no wind – the burning sun
>   Blister'd and scorch'd, and, stagnant on the sea,
> They lay like carcases; and hope was none,
>   Save in the breeze that came not; savagely
> They glared upon each other – all was done,
>   Water, and wine, and food, – and you might see
> The longings of the cannibal arise
> (Although they spoke not) in their wolfish eyes.

# Lord Byron

> At length one whisper'd his companion, who
>     Whisper'd another, and thus it went round,
> And then into a hoarser murmur grew,
>     An ominous, and wild, and desperate sound,
> And when his comrade's thoughts each sufferer knew,
>     'Twas but his own, suppress'd till now, he found:
> And out they spoke of lots for flesh and blood,
> And who should die to be his fellow's food.
>
>                                        (II, lxxii–lxxiii)

Byron nowhere writes more brilliantly, more appallingly. So much for the noble savage. So much for humanity. Man, made in God's image, turns wolfish on the seventh day (the sabbath of God's labours):

> None in particular had sought or plann'd it,
>     'Twas nature gnaw'd them to this resolution . . .
>
>                                        (II, lxxv)

Byron need not, of course, have had the sailors tear up Julia's touching letter to make the lots – any more than he needed earlier to have Juan succumb to sea-sickness as he was reading it. For Shelley such 'bitter mocking of our common nature' is unworthy of Byron's genius. For Wilson it shows 'a cool unconcerned fiend laughing with a detestable glee'. Both positions now seem a misunderstanding of Byron's idiom. It is not that they are solemn about what is essentially a comic poem, but that the comedy is of an unprecedented kind. Even Hunt, though perceptive about the psychology of alternating mood, is not able to see beauty and destructiveness as elements in a larger vision of incongruity. In common with other Romantics, Byron portrays human emotion as beautiful, sacred, transient, but he sees the comic side of the tragedy of its impermanence:

> But now at thirty years my hair is gray –
>     (I wonder what it will be like at forty?
> I thought of a peruke the other day)
>     My heart is not much greener; and, in short, I
> Have squandered my whole summer while 'twas May . . .
>
>                                        (I, ccxiii)

Like other great poets, Byron had (in Wordsworth's phrase) to create the taste by which he was enjoyed. In his minor work, the Turkish tales, he did so effortlessly. *Childe Harold* too was in keeping with the times. *Juan* was not. Raw feelings and hatred of cant caused Byron deliberately to offend 'Victorian' pieties coming into vogue twenty years before Victoria ascended the throne. More important, beneath the witty display of his poetry, Byron's relation to his own creativity asked from the audience a response of unaccustomed subtlety. *Don Juan*, Hazlitt remarked in a rare footnote, 'has been called a *Tristram Shandy* in rhyme: it is rather a poem written about itself' (*Spirit of the age*, 174).

## 32

## PERCY BYSSHE SHELLEY

---

# Adonais
### *an elegy on the death of John Keats*
### 1821

> For Lycidas is dead, dead ere his prime,
> Young Lycidas, and hath not left his peer.
> Who would not sing for Lycidas? He knew
> Himself to sing, and build the lofty rhyme.
> He must not float upon his watery bier
> Unwept . . .
>
> (ll. 8–13)

It was more or less inevitable that Shelley should see the death of Keats in terms of *Lycidas* and the pastoral elegy. His relationship to the fellow-poet, 'dead ere his prime', broadly resembled Milton's to Edward King (drowned in 1637). And it happened that he had translated two of the Greek pastorals that *Lycidas* drew upon, Moschus's *Lament for Bion* and Bion's *Elegy on the death of Adonis*:

> I mourn Adonis dead – loveliest Adonis –
> Dead, dead Adonis – and the Loves' lament . . .

Shelley took to the pastoral elegy with ease, producing rapidly what he saw at once to be 'a highly wrought *piece of art*, perhaps better in point of composition than anything [he had] written' (5 June 1821). The fifty-five spenserian stanzas of *Adonais*, with their verbal beauty and formal elegance, were composed in under a fortnight. On 5 June Shelley had been at work a matter of days; on the 8th, he announced the new project to Ollier, his London publisher; by the 11th he was finished, and on the 16th arrangements were made for the poem to be printed in Pisa and sent in sheets to London. To Ollier he commented significantly, 'It is a lament on the death of poor Keats, with some interposed stabs on the assassins of his peace and of his fame.'

*Adonais*

*Lycidas* offered precedent even for Shelley's 'stabs', incorporating moods of satire alongside lament, and appearing in 1645 over a headnote that pointed to its double purpose: 'In this monody the author bewails a learned friend . . . and by occasion foretells the ruin of our corrupted clergy'. Playing the part of the 'corrupted clergy' for Shelley in 1821 were contributors to the tory journals, with their Government links and their power to destroy lives and reputations. Shelley believed (and seems even to have persuaded Byron to believe) that Keats's fatal illness had been brought on by the anonymous review of *Endymion* in the *Quarterly* (September 1818). The *Quarterly* thus becomes in his poem the boar that has killed the new Adonis.

More confusingly, Adonais in Shelley's poem has for his 'mighty Mother', or patron, Urania (epic muse of Milton and Wordsworth), in the guise of Venus, who should one feels be his lover. Myth fortunately is to be of little importance. Shelley plays with it at the opening of the poem, then lets it fade. Literary tradition has a more lasting relevance, because the connections it makes are more substantial, more allied to the poet's moods. Like *Lycidas*, *Adonais* is vehemently partisan; in each case the writer's identification with the subject of his lament takes the poetry over, straining the pastoral framework, yet remaining within it. The effect is of artifice charged with personal intensity, beauty that can barely contain its passionate utterance.

Keats had died of tuberculosis in Rome on 23 February 1821. Though Shelley had known him in London through Hunt in 1816–18, they had not become close friends (partly because Keats was trying to distance himself from Hunt and the Cockney influence that reviewers derided in his work). Learning of Keats's illness, Shelley had sent him on 27 July 1820 a letter that mingles sympathy with jocular unease:

My dear Keats,
    I hear with great pain the dangerous accident that you have undergone, and Mr. Gisborne who gives me the account of it, adds that you continue to wear a consumptive appearance. This consumption is a disease particularly fond of people who write such good verses as you have done . . . I do not think that young and amiable poets are at all bound to gratify its taste . . .

It is Shelley's hope that Keats will come and stay in the neighbourhood of Pisa to recover his health. Turning to *Endymion*, he permits himself to adopt the role of elder, more experienced poet: 'I have lately read your *Endymion* again and ever with a new sense of the treasures of poetry it contains, though treasures poured forth with indistinct profusion. This, people in general will not endure . . .'

The comments are moderate and just – as, more surprisingly, are those Shelley makes in November 1820 in his letter of reproach to the editor of the *Quarterly*. What prompts the letter we do not know. Keats is by now on his way to Rome, but seems not to have been in contact with Shelley since replying to his invitation (in rather confusing terms) on 23 August. 'I am willing to confess', Shelley writes, temperately,

that the *Endymion* is a poem considerably defective, and that perhaps it deserved as much censure as the pages of your review record against it. But, not to mention that there is a certain contemptuousness of phraseology from which it is difficult for a critic to abstain, in the Review of *Endymion*, I do not think that the writer has given it its due praise. Surely the poem with all its faults is a very remarkable production for a man of Keats's age and the promise of ultimate excellence is such as has rarely been afforded . . .

Shelley is neither defensive about the faults of *Endymion*, nor openly indignant about the *Quarterly*'s reviewer (whom he assumes to be Southey, though in fact it was Croker). The tones of his letter are controlled. Though not intended to do so, the article has embittered Keats's life, causing (or at least contributing to) his fatal illness: 'The agony of his sufferings at length produced the rupture of a blood vessel in the lungs, and the usual process of consumption appears to have begun.'

The mood of *Adonais* is very different. Keats of course is dead; more important, though, is the fact that Shelley (encouraged by Milton's example) now identifies with the writer whose work and fate he had viewed with such discerning distance the year before:

> I weep for Adonais – he is dead!
> Oh, weep for Adonais! though our tears
> Thaw not the frost which binds so dear a head . . .
>> (stanza 1)

> Where wert thou mighty Mother, when he lay,
> When thy Son lay, pierced by the shaft which flies
> In darkness?
>> (stanza 2)

> To that high Capital, where kingly Death
> Keeps his pale court in beauty and decay,
> He came; and bought, with price of purest breath,
> A grave among the eternal. Come away!

> Haste, while the vault of blue Italian day
> Is yet his fitting charnel-roof! while still
> He lies, as if in dewy sleep he lay;
> Awake him not! surely he takes his fill
> Of deep and liquid rest, forgetful of all ill.
>
> (stanza 7)

Shakespearean echoes from *Richard II* –

> within the hollow crown
> That rounds the mortal temples of a king
> Keeps Death his court . . .
>
> (III, ii. 160–2)

combine with those from Shelley's own *Ode to the west wind* –

> this closing night
> Will be the dome of a vast sepulchre,
> Vaulted . . .
>
> (ll. 24–6)

to create for Keats a resting-place that is fitting, beautiful, and envied: 'A grave among the eternal'.

Rome, the Eternal City, with its catacombs, its tradition, its heroic dead, confers upon Keats the immortality that consists in timelessness: he is buried (in Shelley's words) 'under the pyramid which is the tomb of Cestius, and the massy walls and towers, now mouldering and desolate, which formed the circuit of ancient Rome'. 'The cemetery is an open space among the ruins', Shelley continues, 'covered in winter with violets and daisies. It might make one in love with death, to think that one should be buried in so sweet a place' (Preface to *Adonais*, p. 3). The echo of Keats's 'many a time / I have been half in love with easeful Death' is tender and appropriate, yet reminds us of differences between the two poets that go deep:

> Call'd him soft names in many a mused rhyme,
> To take into the air my quiet breath;
> Now more than ever seems it rich to die,
> To cease upon the midnight with no pain . . .
> (*Ode to a nightingale*, stanza 6)

For Keats, as he listens to the song of the nightingale, death has the richness of the ultimate sensuous experience. It is, however, to be 'easeful', a painless 'ceasing', not the anguish through which he has nursed his brother, Tom, six months before (and which he will suffer himself two years later). Death is a sort of wish fulfillment, in effect an avoidance of dying. Shelley's death wish is something altogether more powerful and strange. *Adonais* builds gradually to the full realization of its power, as Shelley plays first with his myths and Miltonic parallels, then expends his indignation: 'Thou noteless blot on a remembered name' (addressed to Croker, whose review has come to be 'noted' wherever the story of Keats is told). Taking his cue from *Lycidas* Shelley turns and counterturns, stressing loss and injustice, death and continuance:

> Nor let us weep that our delight is fled
> Far from these carrion kites that scream below;
> He wakes or sleeps with the enduring dead . . .
> (stanza 38)

> Peace, peace! he is not dead, he doth not sleep –
> He hath awakened from the dream of life . . .
> (stanza 39)

> He has outsoared the shadow of our night;
> Envy and calumny and hate and pain,
> And that unrest which men miscall delight,
> Can touch him not and torture not again . . .
> (stanza 40)

As the poem mounts towards its conclusion the poetry becomes more and more powerful, Shelley more and more personally identified: 'What Adonais is, why fear we to become?' The subdued platonism of *Mont Blanc* and *Hymn to intellectual beauty* appears for the first, and last, time as a dominant force in Shelley's verse. Milton's Christian vision, with its charming extravagance –

> There entertain him all the Saints above,
> In solemn troops and sweet Societies
> That sing, and singing in their glory move,
> And wipe the tears forever from his eyes.
> (*Lycidas*, 178–81)

– is replaced by a pantheism that is no less touching:

> He is made one with Nature: there is heard
> His voice in all her music, from the moan
> Of thunder, to the song of night's sweet bird;
> He is a presence to be felt and known
> In darkness and in light, from herb and stone,

> Spreading itself where'er that Power may move
> Which has withdrawn his being to its own . . .
>
> He is a portion of that loveliness
> Which once he made more lovely . . .
>
> (stanzas 42–3)

It is pantheism of an unusual immediacy. Wordsworth in *Tintern abbey* has '*felt / A presence* that disturbs [him] with the joy / Of elevated thoughts'; Adonais is himself '*a presence to be felt* and known'. Despite his reunion with the all-pervading Power, Keats achieves something very like a personal immortality. The fact of his voice being heard in 'the song of night's sweet bird' is a reminder that on one important level the immortality is that of the writer. As poet, Keats (to adapt Shelley's lines) continues to make more lovely the loveliness of which he is a portion.

The magniloquence of Shelley's conclusion is famous – who else could have written,

> Life, like a dome of many-coloured glass,
> Stains the white radiance of Eternity . . .
>
> (stanza 52)

Yet, in terms of the poem as a whole, still more impressive is the urgency that hastens him on to immolation – 'Die, / If thou wouldst be with that which thou dost seek':

> Why linger, why turn back, why shrink, my Heart?
> Thy hopes are gone before: from all things here
> They have departed; thou shouldst now depart! . . .
>
> (stanzas 52–3)

Even at this moment, when earnestness seems to be giving way to desperation, there can be a sudden gentleness –

> The soft sky smiles, the low wind whispers near:
> 'Tis Adonais calls!

– but it can only be a lull. In the final stanza Shelley gives his sails wholly to the tempest. The voice we hear in the background is that of Webster's Vittoria Corombona:

> My soul, like to a ship in a black storm,
> Is driven, I know not whither.
>
> (*White divel* V, vi, 248–9)

But this storm we feel is generated within:

# Percy Bysshe Shelley

The breath whose might I have invoked in song
Descends on me; my spirit's bark is driven,
Far from the shore, far from the trembling throng
Whose sails were never to the tempest given . . .
I am borne darkly, fearfully, afar . . .

'Highly wrought' *Adonais* may be, as a '*piece of art*', but no poem takes us closer to the inner life that we recognize in Shelley's letters and the surviving details of his biography. Keats in the final line 'Beacons from the abode where the Eternal are'. A year later, Shelley responds to his signal, drowning in the Gulf of Spezia in a needless shipwreck that unites the circumstances of *Lycidas* to the imagery and the yearning of *Adonais*.

# 33

## WILLIAM WORDSWORTH

## A description of the lakes

*A description of the scenery of the lakes
in the north of England*
1822

Wordsworth was pleased with his prose *Description of the scenery of the lakes*. First published on its own in 1822, it had been written in 1810 as an introduction to *Select views in Cumberland, Westmoreland and Lancashire* by the Reverend Joseph Wilkinson. 'I'm very happy', the poet told Lady Beaumont on 10 May 1810,

that you have read the Introduction with so much pleasure . . . I thought the part about the Cottages well done; and also like a sentence where I transport the Reader to the top of one of the Mountains, or rather to the Cloud chosen for his station, and give a sketch of the impressions which the Country might be supposed to make on a feeling mind, contemplating its appearance before it was inhabited.

Wordsworth, whose early impressions had been shaped by West and Gilpin in the 1780s, had been thinking of writing his own guide to the Lakes at least since 1807. Wilkinson's commission was welcome. The watercolours he wished to publish were limited in technique and not very imaginative, but he didn't require that Wordsworth's text should be a commentary. The poet now had five children to support and couldn't afford to be choosy. Household economies had got to the point where Dorothy wondered if they should give up drinking tea.

'For once the Muse's help will we implore', Wordsworth had written in 1804 as he manoeuvred into position to describe London's Bartholomew Fair,

> And she shall lodge us – wafted on her wings
> Above the press and danger of the crowd –
> Upon some showman's platform. What a hell

# William Wordsworth

For eyes and ears, what anarchy and din
Barbarian and infernal . . .

(1805 *Prelude*, vii, 656–60)

The sentence that he liked in *Description of the lakes* offers a rural equivalent. The vantage-point is higher, London has been exchanged for the north, hell for mountain solitude:

To begin, then, with the main outlines of the country; I know not how to give the reader a distinct image of these more readily, than by requesting him to place himself with me, in imagination, upon some given point; let it be the top of either of the mountains, Great Gavel, or Scawfell; or, rather, let us suppose our station to be a cloud hanging midway between those two mountains, at not more than half a mile's distance from the summit of each . . . (p. 3)

Wordsworth is enabled to give his reader a sense of the shape of the district – 'see stretched at our feet a number of vallies, not fewer than eight, diverging . . . like spokes from the nave of wheel' – but he is also symbolically standing above his work, surveying his task and refusing to be drawn into the ground-level activities of the writer of guides.

That Wordsworth should single out for Lady Beaumont his discussion of cottages is entirely consistent. The section is not merely 'well done', it embodies his sense of the countryman at one with his natural surroundings. Unlike the houses of the gentry, cottages have a life of their own, a special appropriateness to the landscape: 'They are scattered over the vallies, and under the hill sides, and on the rocks'. The subject of Wordsworth's sentence might so easily have been sheep, or trees, or violets. We feel in his phrases the animating quality of imagination. Cottages, he tells us, seem to the contemplative mind

rather . . . to have grown than to have been erected; – to have risen, by an instinct of their own, out of the native rock – so little is there in them of formality, such is their wildness and beauty. (p. 56)

Built of 'rough unhewn stone' and roofed with slates in which 'the seeds of lichens, mosses, ferns, and flowers' have lodged, they 'in their very form call to mind the processes of nature'. This is the language, not of the guide-book, but of great Wordsworthian poetry. 'Clothed with this vegetable garb', lakeland cottages 'appear to be received into the bosom of the living principle of things, as it acts and exists among the woods and fields . . .' (p. 57).

As a poet Wordsworth is seldom descriptive. Both in *The prelude*, and in the shorter poems, we hear far more about his response than about the natural scene to which he is responding. Writing a guide offered him the chance to present numerous personal observations, some lofty ('Sublimity is the result of Nature's first great dealings' with the earth, the tendency 'of her subsequent operations is towards the production of beauty', p. 23), others vivid in a way that lets us share the life he is so contentedly living:

The rain here comes down heartily, and is frequently succeeded by clear, bright weather, when every brook is vocal, and every torrent sonorous . . . Vapours exhaling from the lakes and meadows after sun-rise, in a hot season, or, in moist weather, brooding upon the heights, or descending towards the vallies with inaudible motion, give a visionary character to every thing around them . . . (p. 35)

Amid his 'mists and clouds, and storms', the inhabitant of the Lakes has no need to envy 'the cerulean vacancy of Italy' (p. 36). There can be no doubt that Wordsworth's stance is partisan (he himself came to think he had gone too far in praising the three-thousand foot Lake District fells at the expense of the Alps), but his perceptions are not the less sharp, and some of his best prose is charged by indignation. Oblivious of its history, the new owner of St Herbert's Island on Derwentwater has had it planted

with Scotch firs, left to spindle up by each other's side – a melancholy phalanx, defying the power of the winds, and disregarding the regret of the spectator . . . (p. 68)

*A description of the lakes* is by no means the first guide to protest against the gentrification of the Lake District. Hutchinson, West and Gilpin had all complained about the development of Belle Isle on Windermere. Wordsworth's tones are different, however:

Could not the margin of this noble island be given back to nature? Winds and waves work with a careless and graceful hand: and, should they in some places carry away a portion of the soil, the trifling loss would be amply compensated by the additional spirit, dignity, and loveliness, which these agents and the other powers of nature would soon communicate to what was left behind. (p. 70)

In his concern to preserve not merely the beauty of the district, but the vanishing way of life of the 'estatesman' (smallholder), Wordsworth shows himself truly an environmentalist. He condemns ostentatious new building, white houses that stand out against the landscape, the introduction of exotic plants (unless kept within a few yards of the house), and, above all, the desecration of the fells with larch plantations:

Let me then entreat that the native deciduous trees may be left in complete possession of the lower ground; and that plantations of larch, if introduced at all, may be confined to the highest and most barren tracts. Interposition of rocks would there break the dreary uniformity . . . (p. 95)

While not protesting directly against industrialisation (as he does in *The excursion*), Wordsworth notes, as one of the main causes of change in the environment, the invention of mechanized spinning and collapse of the cottage industry. Families can no longer gain a secondary income by spinning their own wool. Farms that have for centuries been handed down from father to son are being merged into larger units. Mansions for the new owners are built 'out of the ruins of the ancient cottages, whose little enclosures, with all the wild graces that grew out of them, disappear' (p. 100). Unexpectedly, and inobtrusively, Wordsworth has returned to the cottages that had earlier carried his message of human life in accord with 'the living principle of things'. In his now elegiac mood it is the phrase, 'wild graces', that stands out, beautifully evoking the loss of innocence and harmony. 'It is probable', he tells us, 'that in a few years the country on the margin of the Lakes will fall almost entirely into the hands of Gentry' (p. 101).

It is in the context of this lament that Wordsworth makes his reference to the Lake District as 'a sort of national property'. In his plea to the 'new proprietors' to maintain where possible the beauty and simplicity of the past, he will be joined

by persons of pure taste throughout the whole Island, who, by their visits (often repeated) to the Lakes in the North of England, testify that they deem the district a sort of national property, in which every man has a right and interest, who has an eye to perceive and a heart to enjoy. (p. 101)

It was a completely new way of thinking. Revised in 1835 to form *A guide through the district of the lakes*, Wordsworth's text was many times reprinted. Conservationism, however, was slow to gain political support. The Commons, Open Spaces and Footpaths Preservation Society was founded in 1865, and in the same year California declared Yosemite a State Park. The first National Park was Yellowstone, Wyoming (1872). Wordsworth's vision of the Lake District was not realized – or ratified – until 1951.

# 34

## CHARLES LAMB

---

## Elia

*Essays which have appeared under that*
*signature in the London magazine*
1823

Then there is Charles Lamb, a long way from his friend Hazlitt in ways and manners; he is very fond of snuff, which seems to sharpen up his wit every time he dips his plentiful fingers into his large bronze-coloured box, and then he . . . throws himself backwards on his chair and stammers at a joke or pun with an inward sort of utterance ere he can give it speech . . .

Back in Helpstone after his 1824 visit to London, John Clare is recalling the literary scene. Hazlitt 'sits a silent picture of severity', now and then intervening 'with a sneer that cuts a bad pun or a young author's maiden table-talk to atoms'. Lamb, by contrast, is 'a good sort of fellow, and if he offends it is innocently done'. 'Who is not acquainted with Elia?', Clare continues, giving to his question almost a Miltonic ring ('Who would not sing for Lycidas?'),

as soon as the cloth is drawn, the wine and he become comfortable. His talk now doubles and threbles into a combination, a repetition, urging the same thing over and over again, till at last he leaves off, with scarcely a 'goodnight' in his mouth, and disappears, leaving his memory like a pleasant ghost hanging above his vacant chair.

Clare's impressions of London were entered in a private journal (here punctuated, and at times respelt). Lamb did not see them, but would have been delighted by their imaginative quality. Especially sensitive is the account of Lamb's relationship to Mary, the elder sister on whom he totally depended, and who (in her sad recurrent madness) totally depended on him:

his sister Bridget [is] a good sort of woman, though her kind cautions and tender admonitions are nearly lost upon Charles, who, like an undermined river bank, leans carelessly over his jollity and receives the gentle waves of the lappings of woman's tongue unheedingly till it ebbs, and then in the same careless posture sits and receives it again.

Clare's observation of the snuff-taking and the 'inward sort of utterance', his images of the 'pleasant ghost' and the precarious river-bank, catch for us as no one else has done the sense of what Lamb was like. They also blur any distinction that might be perceived between Lamb and Elia (or Mary and Bridget).

Twentieth-century criticism has been unwilling to accept Elia as merely a pseudonym. Lamb, we are told, created, on the basis of his own personality, a separate fictional character. The truth is simpler and more elegant. Lamb marketed himself as a fiction. The personality to which Clare responded with such affection in 1824 was offered to the public (first in articles for the *London magazine*, 1820–22, then in the collected *Essays of Elia*), to be enjoyed as a literary creation. Wordsworth, Coleridge, De Quincey, as writers of Romantic auto-biography, claimed reliance on fact, but tended to fictionalize; Lamb did the opposite, presenting as fiction experiences and opinions that in no important way deviate from his own.

This did not of course prevent Lamb's playing games with his public and his double self. In January 1823, as a prelude to collecting the essays, he published Elia's obituary: *A character of the late Elia. By a friend.* Having printed in 1818 his *Recollections of Christ's Hospital*, he amused himself in the third of the Elia essays (*Christ's Hospital five and thirty years ago*) by having one self comment on the other. 'I remember L. at school', Elia writes, 'and can well recollect that he had some peculiar advantages, which I and others of his schoolfellows had not'. To sustain the joke a certain distancing was needed between the two selves. Elia's early history became, for the purposes of this single essay, a composite, the country upbringing of Coleridge being grafted onto Lamb's own London experience. The process, however (like that by which Lamb's siblings, John and Mary, became the cousins, James and Bridget Elia) involved no borrowing, or fictionalizing, of personality. As regards all but a few unimportant details of 'biography', Elia is Lamb. He has Lamb's age (45 in 1820), Lamb's school, Lamb's lifetime experience of the Inner Temple, Lamb's friends, Lamb's lack of wife and family, Lamb's love of books and the past, Lamb's habits, tendencies and

198

opinions, of every kind. Even the uneasy self-deprecations are there. At one point Elia refers to himself as a 'stammering buffoon'.

It might seem logical to associate Elia with a particular phase in Lamb's development, a creative and nostalgic moment reached in the early 1820s, partly as a result of writing the *Essays*. Both letters and publications, however, show Elia to be fully formed at a very early stage. On 30 January 1801, Lamb (aged 25) writes to Wordsworth:

My attachments are all local, purely local . . . The rooms where I was born, the furniture which has been before my eyes all my life, a book case which has followed me about (like a faithful dog, only exceeding him in knowledge) wherever I have moved – old chairs, old tables, streets, squares, where I have sunned myself, my old school – these are my mistresses . . .

Among the *Essays* published in 1823, *A bachelor's complaint of the behaviour of married people* ('the display of married happiness . . . is throughout pure, unrecompensed, unqualified insult') is surely the funniest, the most indignantly and unmistakeably Elia. So far from being an inspired product of the Elia period, however, it was first printed in the *Reflector* in 1811, nine years before Lamb started to use his famous pseudonym:

what I have spoken hitherto is nothing to the airs which these creatures [married people] give themselves when they come, as they generally do, to have children. When I consider how little of a rarity children are, – that every street and blind alley swarms with them, – that the poorest people commonly have them in most abundance, – that there are few marriages that are not blest with at least one of these bargains, – how often they turn out ill, and defeat the fond hopes of their parents, taking to vicious courses, which end in poverty, disgrace, the gallows, &c – I cannot for my life tell what cause for pride there can possibly be in having them. (pp. 292–3)

To some extent Elia, like other pseudonyms, is a form of self-protection:

If these speculations seem fantastical to thee, reader (a busy man, perchance), if I tread out of the way of thy sympathy . . . I retire, impenetrable to ridicule, under the phantom cloud of Elia. (p. 65)

Though the essay is signed by Elia, Lamb, as writer, uses the first person, informing the reader confidentially that his pseudonym is a 'phantom cloud'. At the same time he makes clear that it is a useful cover. Less ingenuously, a recent editor permits himself to ascribe to Elia (rather than Lamb) the racism of *Imperfect sympathies*:

# Charles Lamb

I am . . . a bundle of prejudices – made up of likings and dislikings – the veriest thrall to sympathies, apathies, antipathies. In a certain sense, I hope it may be said of me that I am a lover of my species. I can feel for all indifferently, but I cannot feel towards all equally . . . I cannot *like* all people alike.

I have been trying all my life to like Scotchmen, and am obliged to desist from the experiment in despair. (pp. 134–5)

Lamb, we are to assume, has imagined himself into the position of one who can't stand Caledonian decisiveness: the Scotsman 'has no falterings of self-suspicion. Surmises, guesses, misgivings, half-intuitions, semi-consciousnesses, partial illuminations, dim instincts, embryo conceptions, have no place in his vocabulary.'

The Scots can take care of themselves. Lamb is after all describing a particular temperament, which we recognize, and like or dislike, but do not attach firmly to a particular race. The problems arise as we turn the page:

I have, in the abstract, no disrespect for Jews. They are a piece of stubborn antiquity, compared with which Stonehenge is in its nonage. They date beyond the pyramids. But I should not care to be in habits of familiar intercourse with any of that nation . . . Old prejudices cling about me. I cannot shake off the story of Hugh of Lincoln. Centuries of injury, contempt, and hate, on the one side, – of cloaked revenge, dissimulation, and hate, on the other, between our, and their fathers, must, and ought, to affect the blood of the children. I cannot believe it can run clear and kindly yet . . . (pp. 140–1)

Worse is to come. Lamb is determined to have prejudice – not Elia's prejudice, but his own, and therefore perhaps the reader's – out into the open:

In the Negro countenance you will often meet with strong traits of benignity. I have felt yearnings of tenderness towards some of these faces . . . that have looked out kindly upon one in casual encounters in the streets and highways. I love what Fuller beautifully calls – these 'images of God cut in ebony'. But I should not like to associate with them, to share my meals and my good-nights with them – because they are black. (pp. 142–3)

The last four words are typical of Lamb's emotional honesty. He doesn't think he is in the right, either as a Christian or as a compassionate human-being, but he is not going to stay silent or prevaricate. We are at once shocked and impressed. Even in this extreme case, where his opinions fill us with dismay, Lamb is to be trusted. There is no humbug. To use his own criterion of liking, he stands with Keats, and less certainly with Scott, as truly likeable among the great Romantics. Hazlitt and Byron we admire, but they are discomfortably clever; Blake, Wordsworth, Coleridge, Shelley, De Quincey, belong (though in differing degrees) to worlds that are not ours. Conversation would not be easy – though there would be the odd harangue. With Lamb and Keats (more especially Keats the letter-writer) we could share our meals and our good-nights.

To read the *Essays of Elia* is to be part of a conversation that never ceases to delight. Writing gives to Lamb the fluency that his stammer denied in speech. With each new theme – grave or gay, ruminative or boisterous – we sense the moment noted by Clare, as 'the cloth is drawn' and the wine and Lamb 'become comfortable'. The talk 'doubles and threbles', urging upon us Lamb's preoccupation of the moment. Phrases too good to let pass halt us as we read: 'the quick pulse of gain' (*South Sea house*), 'those indispensable side intelligencers' (*A chapter on ears*), 'We house together, old bachelor and maid, in a sort of double singleness' (*Mackery End*), 'He was a grand fragment; as good as an Elgin marble' (*Decay of beggars in the metropolis*), 'I have a kindly yearning towards these dim specks – poor blots – innocent blacknesses' (*Praise of chimney-sweepers*). In every phrase, in every detail, we respond to the love of life. Heaven for Lamb will be dull unless the ghosts can share his jokes and his books are there to hug:

Sun, and sky, and breeze, and solitary walks, and summer holidays, and the greenness of fields, and the delicious juices of meats and fishes, and society, and the cheerful glass, and candle-light, and fire-side conversations, and innocent vanities, and *irony itself* – do these things go out with life?

Can a ghost laugh, or shake his gaunt sides, when you are pleasant with him?

And you, my midnight darlings, my Folios! must I part with the intense delight of having you (huge armfuls) in my embraces? (p. 67)

Even in Lamb's more satirical moods there is an imaginative sympathy. 'Why are we never quite at ease', he asks, 'in the presence of a schoolmaster?' Answer:

because we are conscious that he is not quite at ease in ours. He is awkward, and out of place in the society of his equals. He comes like Gulliver from among his little people, and he cannot fit the stature of his understanding to yours. (p. 122)

The observations are sharp, yet leave the schoolmaster – ponderous as he is, and prone to talk down to us – with his dignity intact. He has been

## Charles Lamb

understood, not undermined. It is the same witty, compassionate, often affectionate, vision that we see in Lamb's portraits – Thomas Coventry, 'whose person was quadrate, his step massy and elephantine, his face square as the lion's' (*Old benchers*); George Dyer, 'busy as a moth over some rotten archive' (*Oxford in the vacation*); Aunt Hetty, 'a steadfast, friendly being, and a fine *old Christian*':

> The only secular employment I remember to have seen her engaged in, was the splitting of French beans, and dropping them into a China basin of fair water. The odour of those tender vegetables to this day comes back upon my sense, redolent of soothing recollections. (p. 162)

Aunt Hetty, it seems, tended to read her bible while others did the housework. Seated with her beans, and her 'basin of fair water', she is a 'spot of time', a precious moment of the past, revisited by memory, with power to 'live and serve the future hour'. 'Soothing recollections' may seem unWordsworthian (as does the associative power of smell), but, like the poet, Lamb, through his 'spot', re-enters the world of the child's imagination, and in doing so finds a renewal of strength. It is in his lament for the once-magical Old Benchers that we see most impressively his awareness of change and continuity:

> Fantastic forms, whither are ye fled? Or, if the like of you exist, why exist they no more for me? Ye inexplicable, half-understood appearances, why comes in reason to tear away the preternatural mist, bright or gloomy, that enshrouded you? . . . Let the dreams of classic idolatry perish – extinct be the fairies and fairy trumpery of legendary fabling – in the heart of childhood, there will, for ever, spring up a well of innocent or wholesome superstition – the seeds of exaggeration will be busy there, and vital – from every-day forms educing the unknown and the uncommon. (pp. 205–6)

'While childhood', Lamb concludes, 'and while dreams, reducing childhood, shall be left, imagination shall not have spread her holy wings totally to fly the earth.'

# 35

## WILLIAM HAZLITT

—————

# Liber amoris
### *or, the new Pygmalion*
1823

*Liber amoris*, published in early May 1823, played into the hands of Hazlitt's political enemies. Both the *Examiner*, on the 11th, and *The Times*, on the 30th, reviewed it favourably as the anonymous novel it purported to be, but on 9 June it was denounced by *John Bull* (motto, 'For God, and King, and People') as 'the beastly trash of BILLY HAZLITT'. Not content with a single intervention, the tory upholders of public decency kept up the attack for three consecutive weeks. 'The heroine of the LIBER AMORIS', readers are informed on the 16th,

is, from all the reports we are able to collect, 'a very pretty, innocent girl, of 17 or 18 years of age' – this latter was appointed to wait upon MR HAZLITT, her father's lodger – what follows, the book written by this very HAZLITT himself shews *in part*, but WE will shew *entirely*.

As examples of 'folly and idiotism', excerpts from the book's opening Conversations are presented in dramatic form:

SCENE – The Tailor's House.
DRAMATIS PERSONAE
MR BILLY HAZLITT / SALLY (*The Landlord's Daughter*)

S.    Mrs E – has called for the book, Sir.
H.    Oh; it is there. Let her wait a minute or two. I see it is *a busy-day with you*. How *beautiful your* arms look in *those short sleeves* . . .

'Little more can be wanting', the writer comments, 'to display this lecturer upon SHAKESPEARE in his proper colours . . . The fool, when he wrote this trash, was fifty years old and upwards'.

*John Bull*'s promise to show more fully than Hazlitt himself the details of his two years' infatuation with Sarah Walker must have sounded like an empty threat. In addition to getting reports on Sarah's innocence, however, the editors proved to have come by one of Hazlitt's original letters to her, printed in *Liber amoris* in a cut-down form. Making great play with the cuts, they published both versions in their third attack, of 23 June. Having, as they claimed, disposed of the 'foolery' of the book the previous week, they were now directing 'public attention to [its] baseness and wickedness'.

Though far from uncritical, Benjamin Robert Haydon takes a more compassionate view of Hazlitt's relationship. Not surprisingly, his *Diary* shows him to be shocked on 5 August 1822 by his friend's trip to Scotland to commit adultery ('with a strumpet *one eyed from disease*'), and get a divorce. On the 7th he records bluntly, 'Hazlitt called last night in a state of absolute insanity about the girl who has jilted him'. Hazlitt's talk was no doubt infuriating, but in writing to Mary Russell Mitford next day Haydon gives himself time to stand back. Sarah he regards as 'a lodging-house hussy', yet there is considerable sympathy for her lover:

Hazlitt's torture is beyond expression; you may imagine it. The girl really excited in him devoted and intense love. His imagination clothed her with that virtue which her affected modesty induced him to believe in, and he is really downright in love with an ideal perfection, which has no existence but in his own head! He talks of nothing else day and night.

'He has written down', Haydon continues, in terms that suggest that he has already seen a version of *Liber amoris*,

all the conversations without colour, literal [*sic*] as they happened; he has preserved all the love-letters, many of which are equal to anything of the sort, and really affecting; and I believe, in order to ease his soul of this burden, means, with certain arrangements, to publish it as a tale of character. He will sink into idiotcy if he does not get rid of it.

The judgement that Hazlitt's love-letters 'are equal to anything of the sort' ranks them presumably with letters in the epistolary novels of the day. Crabb Robinson, though wholly unsympathetic, takes the comparison a stage further:

Finished early Hazlitt's disgusting *New Pygmalion*. One can tolerate the passion of a St Preux or a Werther as it is set off by the eloquence of Rousseau or Goethe, but such a story as this is nauseous and revolting. It ought to exclude the author from all decent society. He has been exposed in *John Bull*, and I should think will feel the effects of his exposure of himself in being slighted by many who tolerated him before. (*Diary*, 23 June 1823).

Superficially the *New Pygmalion* does indeed resemble *La nouvelle Héloïse*

(*Eloisa*) and the *Sorrows of Werter*. Each of the three portrays a total, hopeless, obsessional love, virtually unaffected by the behaviour of the woman who is its object. But this is to ignore the powerful hybrid form of *Liber amoris*, in which life and art are in an abnormally close relation.

The first part of *Werter*, we know, is based on personal experience; the fact that the second – suicide and all – follows the history of Goethe's friend, Jerusalem, offers, for those who wish it, a sort of authentication. *Liber amoris* is odder. 'Arrangements' made in the Advertisement to present the book as fiction (talk of the author's emigration and death) are perfunctory, but nevertheless point to its being read as 'a tale of character', a novel. With the exception of the opening Conversations, however (which are reconstruction, documentary), *Liber amoris* is made up of letters that really were letters. Its component parts functioned as private correspondence before they functioned as art. But then, they were private correspondence written by a great artist in the first place. We are unusually close to a Romantic ideal of spontaneity.

Parted from the company of Sarah, Hazlitt in Scotland goes through fluctuations of hope and despair, planning one moment for the future, subject the next to appalling (and not unwarranted) jealousy:

Alas! alas! that this, the only hope, joy, or comfort I ever had, should turn to a mockery, and hang like an ugly film over the remainder of my days! – I was at Roslin Castle yesterday. It lies low in a rude, but sheltered valley . . . The straggling fragments of the russet ruins, suspended smiling and graceful in the air as if they would linger out another century to please the curious beholder, the green larch-trees trembling between the blue sky and white clouds, the wild mountain plants starting out here and there, the date of the year on an old low door-way . . . The exquisite beauty of the scene, with the thought of what I should feel, should I ever be restored to her, and have to lead her through such places as my adored, my angel-wife, almost drove me beside myself. For this picture, this ecstatic vision, what have I of late instead as the image of reality? Demoniacal possessions. I see the young witch seated in another's lap, twining her serpent arms round him, her eye glancing and her cheeks on fire . . . (pp. 89–90)

Ruins, 'suspended smiling and graceful in the air' (in the russet brown so often to be seen in Turner's abbeys and castles), give place to a Fuseli nightmare as Hazlitt tortures himself with a vision of Sarah, the young witch, twining 'serpent arms' of beauty and betrayal about another's neck. The writing has all that we could wish, credible in its moods and interweavings, pleasurable in fancy and cadence, arresting in visual detail: the 'old low door-way', for instance, its date conferring upon the scene a human pathos of past, completed lives.

Though writing from amidst his experience, having little time for recollection, none for tranquillity, Hazlitt has the true artist's ability to create space for himself. Not detachment, but the space that is implied in the giving of form to inchoate emotions. His is a literary intelligence, and a literary training. In moments of deepest feeling he steadies himself by allusion and association, and by the natural eloquence that is always his:

The sky is marble to my thoughts; nature is dead around me, as hope is within me; no object can give me one gleam of satisfaction now, nor the prospect of it in time to come. I wander by the sea-side; and the eternal ocean and lasting despair and her face are before me. Slighted by her, on whom my heart by its last fibre hung, where shall I turn? I wake with her by my side, not as my sweet bedfellow, but as the corpse of my love, without a heart in her bosom, cold, insensible, or struggling from me; and the worm gnaws me, and the sting of unrequited love, and the canker of a hopeless, endless sorrow. (pp. 78–79)

Significantly, the first reference that Hazlitt makes to *Liber amoris* comes in his opening letter to Patmore, at the beginning of Part II:

N.B. I have begun a book of our conversations (I mean mine and the statue's) which I call *Liber amoris*. I was detained at Stamford and found myself dull, and could hit upon no other way of employing my time so agreeably. (pp. 52–53)

The book need not have been intended at first for publication, and we cannot know how soon the letters came to be thought of as part of the scheme, but Hazlitt very early on is thinking in literary terms. As Pygmalion he has created the statue with whom he fell in love, and as writer he will create the Book of Love that conserves the experience. Self-consciousness is to be expected in every part of the resulting work. The letters, as they evoke and give lasting value to the writer's emotions, form a kind of Romantic apologia, to be put alongside *The prelude* and *Biographia literaria* and *The confessions of an English opium-eater*. But where Wordsworth, Coleridge and De Quincey shape the past to give substance to their present selves, Hazlitt gives form to the present. His book, like all great Romantic art, is a record of imaginative experience, the creation of an ideal. The ideal was flawed: Sarah did not give her kisses solely to Hazlitt, would not finally marry him, and would not have turned out to be perfection had she done so. The unreality brought with it pain, but it brought also depths of feeling, enhancing glimpses of what might have been: 'To be with her is to be at peace. I have no other desire. The air about her is serene, blissful; and he who breathes it is like one of the Gods!'

It is appalling to think that writing of such passion and beauty could be debased by the likes of *John Bull*. Hazlitt was, as Robinson predicted, 'slighted by many who tolerated him before'. There was, after all, much to be said for Haydon's view that he was 'in a state of absolute insanity' about Sarah. He was not the 'impotent sensualist' that *John Bull* described, but *Liber amoris* is completely without reticence, and, whatever moral position one takes, does not always show him in an attractive light. It took courage to stand by him in public. Lamb, with characteristic integrity, chose to reestablish his own friendship with Hazlitt at the moment when others were falling away. His words delicately take note of the fact that W.H. has not been himself, yet affirm a lifetime's admiration and regard:

I should belie my own conscience, if I said less than that I think W.H. to be, in his natural state, one of the wisest and finest spirits breathing. So far from being ashamed of that intimacy which was betwixt us, it is my boast that I was able for so many years to have preserved it entire; and I think I shall go to my grave without finding, or expecting to find, such another companion. (*Letter to Southey, London magazine*, October 1823)

# 36

## PERCY BYSSHE SHELLEY

---

# Posthumous poems

### 1824

'Never did the remorseless deep engulph so gentle, so angelic, so melodious a Lycidas as Percy Bysshe Shelley' – Horace Smith is writing in the *Paris monthly review* for August 1822. 'Yet never', he continues, 'was there a name associated with more black, poisonous and bitter calumny than his.' To his admirers Shelley was angelic and maligned, to others he was a blasphemer. News of his death had been announced by Leigh Hunt from Pisa in a letter that did nothing to play down the differences:

Shelley, my divine-minded friend – your friend – the friend of the Universe – he has perished at sea! . . . God bless him! I cannot help thinking of him as if he were alive as much as ever, so unearthly he always appeared to me, and so seraphical a thing of the elements. (*Morning chronicle*, 12 August)

Quoting Hunt's letter a week after its publication, *John Bull* was disgusted that the *Chronicle* 'should descend to the insertion of such nauseating nonsense as this eulogium upon Mr Shelley's friendship for the universe'. Hunt had dared to invoke the blessing of God upon a self-confessed atheist, the author of *Queen Mab*.

Shelley's friends have in common with his far more numerous critics a certainty of their own rightness. Accused by *John Bull* of impiety, Hunt turns on the *Courier* with a counter-accusation of gloating:

'SHELLEY, the writer of some infidel poetry, has been drowned', says the *Courier*, '*now* he knows whether there is a God or no' – meaning, that the writer has the satisfaction of thinking the Divine Being will burn Mr Shelley in everlasting flames for holding the same opinions as Spinoza and Bacon. (*Examiner*, 3 November)

With the two sides embattled and intransigent, it was Mary who tried to make peace. *Posthumous poems of Percy Bysshe Shelley* is a setting right, a tribute to the husband from whom she had long been distanced emotionally, but whose reputation would from now on be her chief concern.

It is Mary who copies from the notebooks Shelley's unpublished poetry, much of it in fragments and rough drafts. It is she who chooses, edits and arranges, the contents of the volume. And it is she who, in the absence of Hunt (still in Italy), composes the Preface, quietly rewriting the past. The Shelley to whom she introduces us could never have become the centre of controversy. His life, we are told,

was spent in the contemplation of nature, in arduous study, or in acts of kindness and affection. He was an elegant scholar and a profound metaphysician: without possessing much scientific knowledge, he was unrivalled in the justness and extent of his observations on natural objects; he knew every plant by its name . . . He made his study and his reading-room of the shadowed copse, the stream, the lake and the waterfall.

It is the Shelley who might have been. Nothing that Mary says is without truth. There was indeed a mild, nature-loving side to Shelley's character, and it is interesting to reflect that he must have been a much better botanist than Wordsworth. But were there not days when he performed rather few 'acts of kindness and affection' – not to mention days when his affections went astray? Mary's account is startling in its omissions. She has begun the myth-making that will lead in the four-volume 1839 edition of the *Poems* to pure adulation:

Whatever faults he had, ought to find extenuation among his fellows, since they proved him to be human; without them, the exalted nature of his soul would have raised him into something divine.

We do learn from *Posthumous poems* that Shelley, 'like other illustrious reformers', has been 'pursued by hatred and calumny', but Mary's instinct is not to confront. Hunt, had he been available to write the Preface, would have faced the accusers – and no doubt made matters worse. Mary offers her readers the poet they would like to have met, the husband it would have been more comfortable to have. Reviewers were not convinced. 'There is peace, there is pardon, there is tenderness, in the grave', the *Literary gazette* begins promisingly on 17 July 1824. 'That which in life is denominated crime', the writer continues,

is by death almost softened into error, and Pity goes hand in hand with

Reprobation. It is with these feelings that we take up this last record of Shelley. Like his other productions, in it are blended beauty and blasphemy, trash by the side of some fine poetry . . .

The reviewer is delighted by his forbearance, yet feels that he owes it to himself not quite to soften crime into error. In his comments on beauty and blasphemy there is little sign of peace, pardon or tenderness. Even the journals that are most sensitive to Shelley as a writer, find it necessary to distance themselves on moral grounds. To the *Edinburgh magazine*, *Posthumous poems* is

the last memorial of a mind singularly gifted with poetical talent, however it may have been obscured, and to many, we doubt not, absolutely eclipsed by its unhappy union with much that is revolting in principle and morality.

Shelley's reputation at the time of his death took no account of changes in his writing and thinking. He was the poet who had travelled on the Continent with, not one, but two, unmarried teenage girls, the poet who had subscribed himself 'atheos' in alpine visitors' books and been denied the custody of his children on grounds of irreligion. Above all, he was the author of *Queen Mab*. Those who knew of Shelley at all, were likely to know that *Mab* (written when he was nineteen, and privately printed in 1813) had been pirated in 1821 for dissident working-class readers. Despite prosecution by the Society for the Suppression of Vice, the book was in 1824 being offered by Carlile at a reduced price, and reaching a wide audience. In her creation of the nature-loving, unpolitical Shelley, Mary had more than prejudice to overcome.

It was possible of course to reject Mary's view of Shelley from a broadly sympathetic point of view. After the 1839 Preface, the poet's surviving friends, Hogg, Peacock, Trelawny, would protest in turn against the myth-making; in 1824 it was Hazlitt who publicly refused to accept it. His article on *Posthumous poems* in the *Edinburgh review* (July 1824) should really have gone into the *Spirit of the age*. It is full of important insights, but not especially generous. With their passionate belief in political freedom, and their friendship with Hunt, Shelley and Hazlitt might seem to have much in common. Yet Hazlitt was distrustful. He himself belonged to no party, but Shelley was too much the individualist: 'His nature was kind and his sentiments noble; but in him the rage of free inquiry and private judgment amounted to a species of madness'(Howe, xxi, 267). His style is to poetry what astrology is to natural science – a passionate dream, a straining after impossibilities, a record of fond conjectures, a confused embodying of vague abstractions – a fever of the soul, thirsting and craving after what it cannot have . . . (ibid., 265)

Hazlitt did find much to praise, but saw Shelley as the poet of isolated images and successful minor poems:

He has single thoughts of great depth and force, single images of rare beauty, detached passages of extreme tenderness; and, in his smaller pieces, where he has attempted little, he has done most. (ibid., 266)

The first collected *Shelley* would appear in 1829 in the great single-volume Galignani *Poetical works of Coleridge, Shelley, and Keats*, printed in Paris. Meanwhile, *Posthumous poems* was the nearest thing to a collection that the public had seen. Earlier volumes had tended to present single major poems, accompanied perhaps by a group of lyrics. Now for the first time there was a fair cross-section of the poetry: *Alastor* (reprinted in *Posthumous poems* on grounds of unavailability), *Mont Blanc* (reprinted from the *Six weeks' tour*), together with *Julian and Maddalo*, *The witch of Atlas* and *Triumph of life* (all published for the first time). Among the great lyrics were *Lift not the painted veil*, *Stanzas written in dejection, near Naples* and *The pine forest* (Mary's conflation of *To Jane: an invitation* and *A recollection*):

> Dearest, best and brightest,
> Come away,
> To the woods and to the fields!
> Which like thee to those in sorrow,
> Comes to bid a sweet good-morrow
> To the rough year just awake
> In its cradle in the brake.

Among the Fragments and Translations were *Ginevra* and the *Scenes from Faust*.

Publication of the *Masque of anarchy* would have to wait until 1832, when Hunt, to whom Shelley had sent the poem in 1819, decided the world was ready to receive it. *Peter Bell the third* (Shelley's brilliant parody of Wordsworth), and the *Defence of poetry*, Mary kept back until the 1839 edition. Of the beautiful songs to Jane Williams written in the last weeks of Shelley's life, *To Jane with a guitar* was published by Medwin in 1832; *She left me at the silent time* did not appear until 1862.

Meanwhile, Mary's fight to establish Shelley's reputation had to contend not only with reviewers intent on saving the moral health of the nation, but with her unforgiving father-in-law. Sir Timothy, on whom she relied for money to bring up her remaining child, Percy Florence Shelley, insisted that *Posthumous poems* be withdrawn. Five hundred copies had been printed; 309 were already sold, 191 were destroyed.

# 37

## JOHN CLARE

---

# The shepherd's calendar
## *with village stories, and other poems*
### 1827

'At the risk of exciting misunderstanding and a sneer', Edwin Paxton Hood writes in 1851, 'we may call Clare the Wordsworth of Labour.' It is an interesting statement. Wordsworth had died the previous year, honoured, and time-honoured, and Poet Laureate to Queen Victoria. Clare, after being taken up by the literary world in 1820, had sunk back into the poverty of his early years as a frequently unemployed farm-labourer. In 1851 he was still alive, and still in fact writing, but in the madhouse at Northhampton. While hastening to mention the poets' 'great distance both of attainment and position', Hood makes a serious attempt to compare them:

All that learning, travel, education in the most sublime scenery of Nature, leisure, solitude, association with the most gifted spirits, long life – all that these combined could do was lavished upon [Wordsworth]. The reverse of all these forms the history of Clare; yet in him we notice the same intense affection for the simplest things in Nature – the same disposition to self-communion – the same power to reflect back a lesson, and to treat Nature in all her visible manifestations as an intimation and a prophecy; the same exuberant overflowing of tenderness and love . . . (*Literature of labour*, p. 161)

Though born to such different lives, the two poets, in Hood's view, draw together in the middle-ground of their poetry and their response to Nature. It is not entirely convincing, but nor is it entirely untrue. Like his Scottish counterpart, James Hogg, who moved in Edinburgh literary circles despite his almost complete lack of education as a child, Clare is by no means the illiterate peasant. 'The man of taste', he comments in one of the Natural History Letters (here punctuated for convenience):

looks on the little Celandine in Spring & mutters in his mind some favourite lines from Wordsworths address to that flower; he never sees the daisy without thinking of Burns; & who sees the taller buttercup carpeting the closes in golden fringe without a remembrance of Chatterton's beautiful . . . 'The kingcup brasted with the morning dew'? (Tibble, pp. 175–6)

We may be surprised that Clare should think of himself as 'a man of taste', yet he continues impressively, 'to look on nature with a poetic eye magnifies the pleasure, she herself being the very essence & soul of Poesy'.

The final comment, made in the mid-twenties at the time of the writing of the *Shepherd's calendar*, is a reminder of the acuteness of Clare's literary observations. Of Keats he remarks shrewdly and amusingly:

He keeps up a constant allusion or illusion to the grecian mythology & there I cannot follow . . . behind every rose bush he looks for a Venus & under every laurel a thrumming Apollo. In spite of all this his descriptions of scenery are often very fine, but as it is the case with other inhabitants of great cities he often described nature as she appeared to his fancies & not as he would have described her had he witnessed the things he describes. (ibid., p. 223)

Coleridge, Lamb, Hazlitt, De Quincey, Clare had met at London parties in 1822 when his publisher, Taylor, was showing off his new prodigy. Coleridge he describes in the *Autobiography* as tenderly as he would a birdsnest: 'his words hung in their places at a quiet pace from a drawl in good set marching order so that you would suppose he had learned what he intended to say before he came'. Playfulness and a sense of drama keep us in enchanted expectation as he writes:

A little artless simple-seeming body something of a child overgrown in a blue coat & black neckerchief . . . with his hat in his hand steals gently among the company with a smile turning timidly round the room. It is De Quincey the Opium Eater & that abstruse thinker in logic & metaphysic X.Y.Z. (ibid., p. 91)

No doubt to others Clare was himself a 'simple-seeming body'. When compared to the learning of Coleridge, or the breeding of Byron, so of course was Wordsworth. The difficulty of sustaining Hood's comparison lies not so much in their different backgrounds as in their different casts of mind. Hood's talk of 'the same disposition to self-communion' shows a willingness to fudge, as does his reference to both poets seeing in Nature 'an intimation and a prophecy'. On the other hand, the stereotype that has Wordsworth working in an exalted spiritual realm, and Clare restricted to painting word-pictures of actuality, won't do either. It is a striking fact that Wordsworth, in his preoccupation with the mind and its responses almost never describes the natural world that he so admires. But Clare, even at his most descriptive, is a painter of moods rather than objects. Personal response is incorporated in everything he writes, together with a profound imaginative sympathy.

In the *Shepherd's calender* the task of bringing out the moods of the months as they pass is achieved with an extraordinary blend of observation and delicate fantasy. On the green hills of April, the lambs 'basking lie / Like spots of ling'ring snows' (p. 40). The 'sleeping' landscapes of July and November are beautifully paired and played off against each other:

> Save the waggon rocking round,
> The landscape sleeps without a sound.
> The breeze is stopt, the lazy bough
> Hath not a leaf that dances now;

(*Christabel* it is that produces the echo: 'The one red leaf, the last of its clan / That dances as often as dance it can')

> The tottergrass upon the hill,
> And spiders' threads, are standing still;
> The feathers dropt from moorhen's wing,
> Which to the water's surface cling,
> Are steadfast, and as heavy seem
> As stones beneath them in the stream . . .
>
> (p. 65)

> The landscape sleeps in mist from morn till noon;
>  And, if the sun looks through, 'tis with a face
>  Beamless and pale and round, as if the moon,
>  When done the journey of her nightly race,
>  Had found him sleeping, and supplied his place.
>  For days the shepherds in the fields may be,
>  Nor mark a patch of sky – blindfold they trace
>  The plains, that seem without a bush or tree,
> Whistling aloud by guess, to flocks they cannot see.
>
> (p. 88)

Taylor tidied this poetry up, cutting and rearranging stanzas, correcting grammar and dialect, and adding punctuation. Manuscripts show both that it needed doing, and that in his anxiety about changing patterns of taste he went a lot further than we should think necessary. Annuals, keepsake-books, collections of poetic gems, were the new fashion. Watching the market, Taylor held the *Shepherd's calendar* back for three years, and then published it with none of the enthusiasm and careful puffing that ushered in *Poems descriptive of rural life* (1820) and the *Village minstrel* (1821). With the *Calendar* he offered the public an interesting and diverse group of poems: love-stories with a kind of earnest gracefulness, seasonal poetry with some of the reflective personal quality of Burns –

> But I'm no more akin to thee,
>    A partner of the Spring;
> For Time has had a hand with me,
>    And left an alter'd thing . . .
>       (*To the cowslip*, p. 207)

– and the great apocalyptic *Dream*, which follows upon Byron's *Darkness* and should put paid to any view that Clare is not an imaginative poet:

> Stars drunk with dread roll'd giddy from the heaven,
> And staggering worlds like wrecks in storms were driven;
> The pallid moon hung fluttering on the sight,
> As startled bird whose wings are stretched for flight;
> And o'er the east a fearful light begun
> To show the sun rise – not the morning sun,
> But one in wild confusion, doom'd to rise
> And drop again in horror from the skies.
>
> (p. 215)

# 38

FELICIA HEMANS

Records of woman
*with other poems*
1828

'Now there is Miss F. D. Browne', Shelley writes to Thomas Hogg in July 1811, 'certainly a tyger'. Hogg, whose complicated emotions will lead him to fall in turn for Shelley's two wives, and finally to marry Jane Williams, fancies himself at this early stage in love with Shelley's sister, Elizabeth. Felicia Browne is put forward as an alternative, partly on the grounds of being a better poet. How Shelley came to regard her as a tyger is not clear, but a letter of March 1811 in the Bodleian Library implies that they have written to each other a number of times, and that her mother, alarmed by his atheism, has forbidden the correspondence.

Felicia, now seventeen, had published her first two books of poetry aged fourteen in 1808. Shelley, aged nineteen, has published his gothic novel, *Zastrozzi, Original poetry by Victor and Cazire* (with Elizabeth) and *The necessity of atheism* (for which he was duly sent down from Oxford). The Bodleian letter shows that he has written to Felicia admiringly, flirtatiously, but with an earnest desire to disabuse her of Christianity and correct her attitude to war. That he should speak also of her reforming his errors sounds less convincing:

I read, I repeated your Poems, I admired them, it gave me much regret to find among so many beauties one fault, one glaring fault. I wrote to you, I informed you of it; your letter entirely removed the only cause of complaint, a fear that you approved of fatal sanguinary war – Your last letter, the plaintive verses it contained, induced me, nay compelled me to solicit your correspondence – I take the liberty of persisting in that request, I desire to reform my errors, to instruct my mind by your lessons . . . if you refuse any other request, grant this one, this final wish, let not the amiable Felicia think very ill of her affectionate Philippe Sidney.

To play Stella to Shelley's Sidney might well have been unwise, but

Felicia Hemans

within a year Felicia was married to Captain Alfred Hemans (pronounced Hemmons), who left her in 1818 with four sons, and about to
have a fifth. When she died, aged forty-one, in 1835, she had brought
out twenty-five major publications and collections. Wordsworth
mourned her in his *Extempore effusion* alongside James Hogg (the Ettrick
Shepherd), Scott, Coleridge, Lamb and Crabbe:

> but why,
> O'er ripe fruit, seasonably gathered,
> Should frail survivors heave a sigh?
>
> Mourn rather for that holy Spirit,
> Sweet as the spring, as ocean deep;
> For Her, who ere her summer faded,
> Has sunk into a breathless sleep.
> (ll. 35–40)

It comes as a surprise to the modern reader that as a poet she had outsold
them all – even Scott – many times over. Only Byron had comparable
popularity. Edition after edition of her work appeared, on both sides of
the Atlantic, throughout the nineteenth century. Yet now she is known,
if at all, for the Victorian party-piece, *The boy stood on the burning deck*.

Despite its uncompromising title, *Records of woman* (1828) is in some
ways the most personal of Felicia Hemans's collections. She is using
fiction and quasi-historical narrative to explore the values that matter to
her as a woman writer. Neither marriage nor fame has brought her
happiness. The death of her mother in 1827 has cut her off finally from
childhood and from the life of the family that has provided her support.
The poetry is resolute and resilient, at times even heroic, but it is about
being alone. From its marvellous opening line – ''Twas but a dream! I
saw the stag leap free' – *Arabella Stuart* is a beautifully controlled
dramatic monologue. Tennyson and Browning, who were to explore
the form in the early 1830s, were Victorian intellectuals, concerned with
psychology and inadvertent revelation; Felicia Hemans is a Romantic.
*Arabella Stuart* is a poem of fluctuating moods: tenderness and reproach,
hope, despair and final resolve. In its emotional turns and counter-turns
it reminds us of Wordsworth's *Complaint of the forsaken Indian woman* and
the original version of Coleridge's *Dejection, an ode*.

Descended from Henry VIII's daughter, Margaret, Arabella is
imprisoned by her distant cousin, James I, and separated from her
husband Edward Seymour:

218

My friend, my friend! where art thou? Day by day,
Gliding, like some dark mournful stream, away,
My silent youth flows from me . . .          (p. 13)

Thou hast forsaken me! I feel, I know,
There would be rescue if this were not so.
Thou'rt at the chase, thou'rt at the festive board,
Thou'rt where the red wine free and high is pour'd,
Thou'rt where the dancers meet . . .          (p. 16)

> Peace be on thy noble head,
Years of bright fame, when I am with the dead!
I bid this prayer survive me, and retain
Its might, again to bless thee, and again!
Thou hast been gather'd into my dark fate
Too much . . .          (p. 19)

We may if we choose see in Arabella's separation from Seymour, Felicia's from Hemans; but (as with Wordsworth) it is the empathy, the understanding of the emotion, not the having experienced it, that matters. It is interesting, though, that Arabella should wish upon Seymour 'Years of bright fame'. Her own distinction, royal blood, has been the cause of her suffering; he, however, is to receive fame as his due – *bright* fame. There is no question of his being unable to handle it, or buying it at too dear a price. By contrast, Joan of Arc stands in the cathedral at Rheims, victor in a man's world, saviour of France, yet vulnerable, incapable of valuing the fame that she has won. 'Never before', Felicia writes,

> and never since that hour,
Hath woman, mantled with victorious power,
Stood forth as *thou* beside the shrine did stand,
Holy amidst the knighthood of the land . . . (p. 112)

The admiration is genuine, but the story has been told as a celebration not of woman's highest hour, but of the values of love, home, childhood, that make fame for her in some sense inappropriate:

> The shouts that fill'd
The hollow heaven tempestuously, were still'd
One moment; and in that brief pause, the tone,
As of a breeze that o'er her home had blown
Sank on the bright maid's heart . . .          (p. 113)

Joan's father and brothers are among the congregation. Her instinct is to return with them 'To the still cabin and the beechen-tree' of childhood. The author's final comment is perhaps needlessly explicit:

> bought alone by gifts beyond all price,
> The trusting heart's repose, the paradise
> Of home with all its loves, doth fate allow
> The crown of glory unto woman's brow.  (p. 115)

Felicia Hemans was circumspect when it came to meeting admirers and revealing details of her private life. We cannot know to what extent success as a writer did indeed undermine her marriage – or to what extent she thought it had. It is the dramatic monologue, *Properzia Rossi*, that tells us most of her relation to her art. Properzia is a renaissance sculptor and unrequited lover:

> It comes, – the power
> Within me born, flows back; my fruitless dower
> That could not win me love. Yet once again
> I greet it proudly, with its rushing train
> Of glorious images: they throng – they press –
> A sudden joy lights up my loneliness, –
> I shall not perish all!
>               The bright work grows
> Beneath my hand, unfolding, as a rose,
> Leaf after leaf, to beauty; line by line,
> I fix my thought, heart, soul, to burn, to shine,
> Thro' the pale marble's veins. It grows – and now
> I give my own life's history to thy brow,
> Forsaken Ariadne!                    (p. 49)

It is a great piece of writing, akin to the Byron of *Childe Harold*, Canto III –

> 'Tis to create, and in creating live
> A being more intense, that we endow
> With form our fancy, gaining as we give
> The life we image . . .
>
>                         (ll. 46–9)

– but Coleridgean in its relating of creativity to the sense of human loss:

> Now fair thou art,
> Thou form, whose life is of my burning heart!
> Yet all the vision that within me wrought,
>    I cannot make thee! Oh! I might have given
> Birth to creatures of far nobler thought,

220

> I might have kindled, with the fire of heaven,
> Things not of such as die! But I have been
> Too much alone . . .                    (p. 51)

It is fitting that *Records of woman* should end with two poems that move out of narrative and monologue into the openly personal mode of lyric. The first concerns a Cumbrian memorial of parting, the second an Irish grave. Both, as might be expected, seek to assuage. The Countess's Pillar was erected in 1656 at the spot where, forty years before, Ann, Countess of Pembroke, had parted from her mother to go south and be married. Felicia's poem is the last tribute to her own mother, among many in the volume that bear on her loss:

>                         no other eye
> Could give thee back thine infancy.
>
> No other voice could pierce the maze
>     Where deep within thy breast,
> The sounds and dreams of other days,
>     With memory lay at rest;
> No other smile to thee could bring
> A gladd'ning like the breath of spring.    (p. 58)

Thus far we have the beauty and poignancy of lament. The tones we hear will be heard again twenty years later in Emily Bronte, but have no obvious source. By contrast, the lines that follow are unmistakeably Wordsworth. He would have been proud to write them.

> Yet, while thy place of weeping still
>     Its lone memorial keeps,
> While on thy name, midst wood and hill,
>     The quiet sunshine sleeps,
> And touches, in each graven line,
> Of reverential thought a sign;
>
> Can I, while yet these tokens wear
>     The impress of the dead,
> Think of the love embodied there,
>     As of a vision fled?
> A perish'd thing, the joy and flower
> And glory of one earthly hour?        (p. 159)

That consolation will finally be Christian is never in doubt, but it is defined movingly as the 'loftier faith we need below / Life's farewell words to bear'. If the *Memorial pillar* assuages Felicia's loss of her mother, and through her of the primal scene, *Grave of a poetess* is to have the final say in reconciling the poet to her art. Mary Tighe, author of *Psyche* (third ed., 1811), and the beautiful *Address to my harp*, had been buried at Woodstock, near Kilkenny:

> I stood beside thy lowly grave;
>   Spring-odours breath'd around,
> And music, in the river-wave,
>   Pass'd with a lulling sound. . .
>
> Fresh leaves were on the ivy-bough
>   That fring'd the ruins near;
> Young voices were abroad – but thou
>   Their sweetness couldst not hear.
>
> And mournful grew my heart for thee,
>   Thou in whose woman's mind,
> The ray that brightens earth and sea,
>   The light of song was shrined.
>
>                               (p. 160–1)

Again and again in *Records of woman* art has been disruptive. The gift of song and the gift of fame have undercut the emotional life on which the woman writer's human happiness is based. We can see this as weakness in Felicia Hemans, a lack of self-sufficiency; or we can see it as the conditioning of her age. More simply we can put it down to the honesty with which she confronts her own inevitable pain at being pulled in two directions. Either way, there is a yearning in the last words of her volume, as she stands over the grave of one who has been through it all:

> Now peace the woman's heart hath found,
>   And joy the poet's eye.

# 39

## ALFRED TENNYSON

---

# Poems, chiefly lyrical

### 1830

*Poems chiefly lyrical* was to have been the *Lyrical ballads* of its day, published jointly by Tennyson and Arthur Hallam, as *Lyrical ballads* had been published jointly by Wordsworth and Coleridge. Hallam's father disapproved, however, and Tennyson went ahead on his own. In a way it was a good thing. Hallam was enabled to write the magnificent review in the *Englishman's magazine* (August 1831) which, more than any other piece of writing, bridges for us Romantic and Victorian assumptions about poetry. It is as if Coleridge had been free in 1798 to write an immediate commentary on the newness of *Lyrical ballads*, rather than mingling grumpiness and praise twenty years later in *Biographia literaria*.

Hallam's place in literary history is of course guaranteed by his death in September 1833, aged twenty-two, and Tennyson's lament in *In memoriam* (1850); he lived long enough, however, to show that he was extremely distinguished in his own right. When *Poems, chiefly lyrical* appeared in June 1830, he had been Tennyson's close friend for over a year. No one can have known better than he did what were the aims of this new poetry. And though he is evidently partial, he is also discerning as to the nature and extent of its achievements. 'As the poem proceeds', he writes of *Recollections of the Arabian nights*:

all is in perfect keeping. There is a solemn distinctness in every image, a majesty of slow motion in every cadence, that aids the illusion of thought, and steadies its contemplation of the complete picture. Originality of observation seems to cost nothing to our author's liberal genius; he lavishes images of exquisite accuracy and elaborate splendour, as a common writer throws about metaphorical truisms, and exhausted tropes.

Hallam writes with an extraordinarily sure sense of his criteria, taking what we should now (with a knowledge of letters then unpublished) perceive as a Keatsian position: 'Whenever the mind of the artist suffers itself to be occupied, during its periods of creation, by any other predominant motive than the desire for beauty, the result is false in art.' The relation of Wordsworth to this thinking is an unresolved question. Hallam refers to him frequently, and seems broadly to depend upon his views. He sees both the poetry and the Preface to *Lyrical ballads* as 'awakening the minds of men, and giving a fresh impulse to art'. Yet he is wary of the Wordsworthian emphasis on reflection: 'much has been said by him which is good as philosophy, powerful as rhetoric, but false as poetry'. It is Shelley and Keats, 'both poets of sensation rather than reflection', who are cited as Tennyson's forerunners:

Susceptible of the slightest impulse from external nature, their fine organs trembled into emotion at colours, and sounds, and movements, unperceived or unregarded by duller temperaments . . . Other poets *seek* for images to illustrate their conceptions; these men had no need to seek; they lived in a world of images . . .

Wordsworth may or may not have 'trembled into emotion', but hardly seems to be excluded by this account of responsiveness to the natural world. At least partly aware of this, Hallam redefines what he perceives as the dangerous alternative to sensation. It is not so much reflection that introduces falsity in art, as 'purely intellectual contemplation'. *Daffodils* (a reflective poem if ever there was) is quoted in what is in effect a manifesto for the new criteria:

where beauty is constantly passing before 'that inward eye, which is the bliss of solitude'; where the soul seeks it as a perpetual and necessary refreshment to the sources of activity and intuition; where all the other sacred ideas of our nature, the idea of good, the idea of perfection, the idea of truth, are habitually contemplated through the medium of this predominant mood . . . there is little danger that . . . the energetic principle of love for the beautiful [will] sink, even for a brief period, to the level of a mere notion in the understanding.

Hallam, in discussing Tennyson's embodiment of this 'energetic principle', quotes in full *Recollections of the Arabian nights* and the *Ballad of Oriana*. For third place he considers *Ode to memory*, *Confessions of a second-rate sensitive mind*, *Sea fairies* and *Mariana*, but gives the choice finally to *Adeline*. It is an interesting group. Hallam's reserves would now be thought stronger than his top three. *Mariana* would be at the head of everybody's list; many would concede a place to *Confessions*, and most would bring into play the *Kraken* and *Song: a spirit haunts the year's last hours*, unmentioned by Hallam. Yet Hallam's choice is instructive. *Recollections of the Arabian nights* is a beautiful poem, and the terms of Hallam's praise are beautifully chosen. We should be listening for 'a solemn distinctness in every image, a majesty of slow motion in every cadence, that aids the illusion of thought':

> When the breeze of a joyful dawn blew free
> In the silken sail of infancy,
> The tide of time flowed back with me
>    The forwardflowing tide of time;
> And many a sheeny summermorn,
> Adown the Tigris I was borne,
> By Bagdat's shrines of fretted gold,
> Highwalléd gardens green and old;
> True Mussulman was I and sworn,
>    For it was in the golden prime
>       Of good Haroun Alraschid.
>
> Anight my shallop, rustling through
> The low and blooméd foliage, drove
> The fragrant, glistening deeps, and clove
> The citronshadows in the blue . . .   (pp. 48–49)

The poetry sounds like – and is – an interim stage between Southey's influential *Thalaba* (1801) and *In memoriam*. Lines 3–4 have the theme, the weightiness, the cadence, of Tennyson's greatest elegiac verse; the opening of the second stanza, with its powerful rhyming verbs, points forward unmistakeably to the last-but-one quatrain of *By night we lingered on the lawn*:

> And gathering freshlier overhead,
>    Rock'd the full-foliaged elms, and swung
>    The heavy-folded rose, and flung
> The lilies to and fro . . .
>                               (*In memoriam*, xciv)

Just as *Recollections* distils an essence from the *Arabian nights*, rejecting mere imitation, so *Oriana* is (in Hallam's words) a 'happy seizure of the antique spirit', accompanied by 'no foolish self desertion':

> My heart is wasted with my woe,
>    Oriana.
> There is no rest for me below,
>    Oriana.
> When the long dun wolds are ribbed with snow,

# Alfred Tennyson

> And loud the Norland whirlwinds blow,
>> Oriana,
> Alone I wander to and fro,
>> Oriana.                    (p. 131)

'The author is well aware', Hallam comments,

> that the art of one generation cannot *become* that of another by any will or skill:
> but the artist may transfer the spirit of the past, making it a temporary form for
> his own spirit, and so effect, by idealizing power, a new and legitimate
> combination.

Tennyson's inspiration in *Oriana* is Scott's *Minstrelsy of the Scottish
border* (1802), and especially *Helen of Kirkconnell*. Hallam's thoughts,
however, have a more general application, as Tennyson 'by idealizing
power' creates his new combinations from the art of the previous
generation. In both *Recollections* and *Oriana* we see a high Romanticism
merging into the later idiom: 'the long dun wolds are ribbed with snow'
could easily be 1850, it couldn't be 1810. *Adeline*, by contrast, we feel to
be a Victorian poem – and not a strong one:

> Mystery of mysteries,
>> Faintly smiling Adeline,
>> Scarce of earth nor all divine,
> Nor unhappy, nor at rest,
>> But beyond expression fair
>> With thy floating flaxen hair;
> Thy roselips and full blue eyes
>> Take the heart from out my breast;
>> Wherefore those dim looks of thine,
>> Shadowy, dreaming Adeline?      (p. 69)

Hallam responded also to 'airy-fairy Lilian', 'revered Isabel' and
'Madeline, with her voluptuous alternation of smile and frown'. He was
in love with Tennyson's sister, and found these chaste celebrations of the
mystery of womanhood more erotic than we do. No doubt he was
impressed too that they were a new departure in poetry, owing little to
the previous generation (except perhaps to Leigh Hunt).

In passing, Hallam says enough about *Mariana* to suggest that he
knew it should have had *Adeline*'s place. *Ode to memory*, with its distant
Wordsworthian intimations, he sees as impressive juvenilia. *Confessions*
makes him uneasy. He doesn't like the title, he doesn't think the mind
portrayed is second-rate, he sees in the two opposed sections of the

poem the same 'sensitive sceptic'. Behind the criticism we hear echoes of long-dead conversations: 'we should not despair of convincing Mr Tennyson, that such a position of intellect would not be the most elevated'. And underneath it all, is Hallam's difficulty in convincing himself that the poem conforms to the ideals of the volume: 'It is exquisitely beautiful to see . . . how the feeling of art is kept ascendant in our minds over distressful realities'. For the modern reader (perhaps indeed for Hallam himself) the greater problem is that the 'distressful realities' sound like early Coleridge on a bad day:

> Ay me! I fear
> All may not doubt, but every where
> Some must clasp Idols. Yet, my God,
> Whom call I Idol? let thy dove
> Shadow me over . . .                    (p. 41)

*Sea fairies*, by contrast (though Hallam can hardly have been wrong in again disliking the title), is among the most beautiful poems in the volume, fully in keeping with the pursuit of the ideal. It is also very harshly cut by Tennyson, losing in its later forms nearly all the exquisite opening section of the sirens' song:

> Whither away, whither away, whither away? Fly no more:
> Whither away wi' the singing sail? whither away wi' the oar?
> Whither away from the high green field, and the happy
> blossoming shore?
>> Weary mariners, hither away,
>>     One and all, one and all,
>> Weary mariners come and play;
>> We will sing to you all the day;
>>     Furl the sail and the foam will fall
>>     From the prow! One and all
>>     Furl the sail! drop the oar!
>>         Leap ashore!
>> Know danger and trouble and toil no more.
>> Whither away wi' the sail and the oar?
>>         Drop the oar,
>>         Leap ashore,
>>         Fly no more!
> Whither away wi' the sail? whither away wi' the oar?
> (p. 149)

'The features of original genius', as Hallam remarks, 'are clearly and strongly marked' in *Poems, chiefly lyrical*. More surprising is the claim that follows: 'The author imitates nobody; we recognize the spirit of his age, but not the individual form of this or that writer.' The words are carefully chosen. Small borrowings from the Romantics are common in the volume; imitation is not. *Mariana* patently owes something to *The thorn* (as well as to *Measure for measure* and Crabbe), but the poem is as distinctively Tennyson as *The thorn* is distinctively Wordsworth. Only *A spirit haunts the year's last hours* can be said to keep its eye throughout upon a specific source, and there Tennyson powerfully asserts his difference.

From the opening line, with its allusion to Keats's figure of Autumn, at the cider press, watching 'the last oozings hours by hours', we are asked to make comparisons. The season, we note, has moved on since the Ode, changing ripeness to decay. The spirit, among the 'mouldering flowers', is no delicate personification of drowsiness; he haunts, talks, and has work to do. Thoughts of death, merely touched in by the swallows of Keats's final line, are dominant now. The poet, present in *Autumn* only as the questioner ('Where are the songs of Spring? Ay, where are they?'), is found at the centre of this fetid landscape: 'my whole soul grieves / At the moist rich smell of the rotting leaves':

> A spirit haunts the year's last hours
>   Dwelling amid these yellowing bowers:
>     To himself he talks;
>   For at eventide, listening earnestly,
>   At his work you may hear him sob and sigh
>     In the walks;
>     Earthward he boweth the heavy stalks
>   Of the mouldering flowers:
>     Heavily hangs the broad sunflower
>       Over its grave i' the earth so chilly;
>     Heavily hangs the hollyhock,
>       Heavily hangs the tigerlily . . .
>
> (p. 67)

The boding refrain of the last four lines offers a perfect example of Keats modulating into Tennyson, Romanticism merging into the later period. That the *Song* should stand comparison at all with Keats at his greatest is the more remarkable when we remember that the Tennyson of *Poems, chiefly lyrical* is twenty-one – Keats's age when he published the promising, but far less accomplished, *Poems* 1817.

# 40

# THOMAS DE QUINCEY

## Klosterheim
*or, the masque*
1832

Though among the most active periodical-writers of his age, De Quincey published just two books, *Confessions of an English opium-eater* (1822) and *Klosterheim* (1832), and one hodge-podge, *Walladmor* (free translation of a German forgery of Scott, 1824). Hazlitt made volume after volume out of his essays and lectures (six in the years 1817–19 alone, including *The round table* and *Political essays*); even Lamb published his *Works* in 1818; De Quincey waited till the end of his life, then permitted an American editor to bring his writings together (24 vols, Boston, 1851–9), before himself arranging *Selections grave and gay* (14 vols, Edinburgh, 1853–60). In the circumstances one might expect that *Klosterheim*, with *Confessions*, would be thrown into relief. Instead, it has been neglected by publishers and disparaged by critics as a gothic novel written for money in the dated style of Ann Radcliffe. This despite Coleridge's often quoted letter to Blackwood of 26 May 1832, comparing De Quincey's novel favourably to Scott:

> I have read nothing since the *Quentin Durward* which would compare in interest with *Klosterheim*; and in purity of style and idiom, in which the scholar is ever implied, and the scholarly never obtrudes itself, it reaches an excellence to which Sir W. Scott . . . appears never to have aspired, rather than to have fallen short of.

Coleridge, though referring in his letter to 'my old friend, De Quincey', was not being merely loyal. *Klosterheim*, as its date implies, should be seen as a half-way stage between the broadly autobiographical *Confessions* and the myth-making *Suspiria de profundis* of the 1840s. Nobody was better placed than Coleridge to recognize in the intensity of its prose, the terrors and interweavings of its plot, a refraction of the

# Thomas De Quincey

opium-eater's experience. 'Many years ago', De Quincey writes in *Confessions*,

> when I was looking over Piranesi's *Antiquities of Rome*, Mr Coleridge, who was standing by, described to me a set of plates by that artist, called his *Dreams*, and which record the scenery of his own visions during the delirium of a fever. Some of them (I describe only from memory of Mr Coleridge's account) represented vast Gothic halls: on the floor of which stood all sorts of engines and machinery, wheels, cables, pulleys, levers, catapults, &c, &c, expressive of enormous power put forth, and resistance overcome. Creeping along the sides of the walls, you perceived a staircase; and upon it, groping his way upwards, was Piranesi himself . . .

The *Carceri* series is brilliantly evoked (almost certainly in its blacker, more impressive, second state of 1760), but which opium-eater created this final detail? 'Follow the stairs a little further', De Quincey continues,

> and you perceive it come to a sudden abrupt termination, without any balustrade, and allowing no step onwards to him who had reached the extremity, except into the depths below. Whatever is to become of poor Piranesi . . . raise your eyes, and behold a second flight of stairs still higher: on which again Piranesi is perceived, by this time standing on the very brink of the abyss. Again elevate your eye, and a still more aerial flight of stairs is beheld: and again is poor Piranesi busy on his aspiring labours: and so on, until the unfinished stairs and Piranesi both are lost in the upper gloom of the hall. With the same power of endless growth and self-reproduction did my architecture proceed in dreams. (*Confessions*, 163–4)

Such is the vividness of De Quincey's prose that one never again looks at the *Carceri* prints without seeking Piranesi on those upper stairs. He is not there. Nor do the stairs creep 'along the sides of the walls', or rise in ever-diminishing flights. For that matter, the halls are far from Gothic, if one understands by that term an architectural style, or anything related to the middle ages. The opium dream, or the opium eye, is at work.

De Quincey is fascinated by recession. Hidden in the upper gloom of the hall, and the imagination, Piranesi appears again and again, smaller each time and nearer the abyss. The *Theory of Greek tragedy* of 1840 discusses the Greeks in relation to *Hamlet*, *Hamlet* in relation to the play within a play, and the play within a play by analogy with the picture in a picture:

> We see a chamber . . . exhibited by the artist, on the walls of which (as a customary piece of furniture) hangs a picture. And, as this picture again might

represent a room furnished with pictures, in the mere logical possibility of the case we might imagine this descent of a life below a life going on *ad infinitum.*

It is a thought that might occur to anyone, but De Quincey's ingenuity carries him a further stage:

> The original picture is a mimic, an unreal life. But this unreal life is itself a real life with respect to the secondary picture; which again must be supposed realized [made real] with relation to the tertiary picture, if such a thing were attempted. (Masson, x, 344)

*Klosterheim* offers no such complexities. The story is told by a narrator who keeps his distance. De Quincey is in no obvious way present, and certainly enters into no discussion of alternating illusion and reality. We have, on the face of it, a gothic novel about the Thirty Years' War – or perhaps an historical novel with gothic trappings. Either way, it is tautly written, but the plot is make-believe. Nor is there any characterization to speak of. Character-portrayal, however, does not have to be seen as a virtue. The Greeks, De Quincey believed, sited their plays in the past precisely to avoid it:

> Antiquity availed powerfully for their purposes, because of necessity it abstracted all petty details of individuality and local notoriety – all that would have composed a *character*. It acted as twilight acts (which removes day's 'mutable distinctions'), and reduced the historic person to that sublime state of monotonous gloom which suited the views of a poet who wanted only the *situation*, but would have repelled a poet who sought also for the complex features of a character. (Masson, x, 351)

Dimmed by a twilight illusion of the past, the picture De Quincey offers of an early seventeenth-century German princedom declares itself to be unreal. Klosterheim, a month's journey from Vienna, is shrouded in forests, honeycombed with secret passages, and insulated from the war. Unreal as it is, however, the town assumes a kind of normality as we descend into the 'life below a life', the world of the masked 'ruler of the night'. Sublime in his 'monotonous gloom' (one recalls Wordsworth's 'visionary dreariness' and Burke's 'a clear idea is another name for a little idea'), the Masque joins the midnight masquerades designed to entrap him. For a moment the Landgrave, ruler of the day, seems to have him in his power. Suspense is brilliantly contrived. Finally the Masque unmasks. But not before we have passed into another, more theatrical, realm of illusion. Fiction clearly intrigued De Quincey. It was not his natural mode, but it offered scope for the heightened oppositions and vivid descriptive passages in which he delighted:

Again, therefore, the masques prepared to mingle in the dance; again the signal was given; again the obedient orchestra preluded to the coming strains. In a moment more, the full tide of harmony swept along. The vast saloon, and its echoing roof, rang with the storm of music. The masques, with their floating plumes and jewelled caps, glided through the fine mazes of the Hungarian dances. All was one magnificent and tempestuous confusion, overflowing with the luxury of sound and sight . . . (p. 184)

Twelve hundred have been invited to the Landgrave's ball, twelve hundred-and-one are known to be present. Twelve hundred have invitation-cards, one has not:

All had now been told off, within a score. These were clustered together in a group; and in that group undoubtedly was The Masque. Every eye was converged upon this small knot of cavaliers . . . Not a word was uttered, not a whisper; hardly a robe was heard to rustle, or a feather to wave.

The twenty were rapidly reduced to twelve, these to six, the six to four – three – two; the tale of the invited was complete, and one man remained behind. That was, past doubting, The Masque! (pp. 191–2)

*Suspiria de profundis*, ten years later, was to bring to such passages the larger dimension of myth, turning the 'storm of music' into 'the passion of the mighty fugue' (*English mail-coach*), replacing Klosterheim and its masked dances with the dream city of Savannah-la-mar, subsisting beneath the waves of time:

This city . . . like a mighty galleon with all her apparel mounted, streamers flying, and tackling perfect, seems floating along the noiseless depths of ocean . . . Thither, lured by the loveliness of cerulean depths, by the peace of human dwellings privileged from molestation, by the gleam of marble altars sleeping in everlasting sanctity, oftentimes in dreams did I and the Dark Interpreter cleave the watery veil that divided us from her streets. (Ward 198)

Though it is the architecture of his dreams for which De Quincey claims the 'power of endless growth and self-reproduction', in the case of Piranesi and the staircases the artist clearly has it too. The ever-present climber towards the abyss is also the engraver, 'busy on his aspiring labours'. Like the Shelley of *Mont Blanc*, gazing down into the Ravine of Arve at his 'own separate phantasy', Piranesi (in the Coleridge-De Quincey version of events) creates an external self, or an external state of mind. The Dark Interpreter of *Suspiria* shows 'self-reproduction' at its most sophisticated. 'Who is he?' De Quincey asks, half mocking, half mysterious: 'He is a shadow, reader, but a shadow with whom you must suffer me to make you acquainted' (*Dark interpreter*, Ward 187). The Dark Interpreter is, and is not, the writer's imagination, having, we learn, the power to swerve out of his orbit and 'mix a little with alien natures' (*Spectre of the Brocken*, Ward 182).

How then are we to know fact from fiction, truth from illusion? What is there behind the mask? Does the gothic become reality as we pass through the picture within a picture? Is the consciousness within our consciousness to be trusted? Opium, for many years the ruler of De Quincey's night, holds and withholds the answers, associated (like the Masque) with terrors and uncertainty, yet 'just, subtle and mighty' too:

O just, subtle and mighty opium! that to the hearts of poor and rich alike, for the wounds that will never heal, and for 'the pangs that tempt the spirit to rebel', bringest an assuaging balm; eloquent opium! . . . thou buildest upon the bosom of darkness, out of the fantastic imagery of the brain, cities and temples, beyond the art of Phidias and Praxiteles – beyond the splendour of Babylon and Hekatómpylos . . . (*Confessions*, 114)

Though cruder in its workings, the gothic is akin to myth, and akin to dream, providing on the level of fiction an entry to the opium world of illusion and equivocal truth. In its twilight realm of the distant past, the town of Klosterheim is a 'picture within a picture' of human life, into which writer and reader descend, just as De Quincey and the Interpreter 'cleave the watery veil' that separates them from the dream-city of Savannah-la-mar. In each case there is a sense of the mind descending into its own inner depths, questing for the 'organizing principles which fuse into harmony' the 'heterogeneous elements of life' (*Palimpsest of the human brain*, Ward 169). Klosterheim indeed strangely resembles the mind of the opium-eater, isolated from its surroundings, controlled in its waking consciousness, yet taking on by night an anarchic aspect at once threatening and creative.

As a follower of Wordsworth, and reader of the unpublished *Prelude*, De Quincey had valued opium in *Confessions* as an entry into reverie, a losing of self-consciousness in the world of Romantic imagination. 'At that time', he writes of the Oxford period (when he spent his Long Vacations at Everton, near Liverpool),

I often fell into these reveries upon taking opium; and more than once it has happened to me, on a summer night, when I have been at an open window, in a room from which I could overlook the sea at a mile below me and could command a view of the great town of L[iverpool], at about the same distance, that I have sat, from sun-set to sun-rise, motionless, and without wishing to move. (*Confessions* 113; Ward 70)

Affinities with Wordsworth, no doubt present in the original experience, are heightened by awareness of the *Prelude* as De Quincey comes twenty years later to write the *Confessions*. Clearer still are the links as he turns, with the Ascent of Snowdon (1805 *Prelude*, xiii, 10–75) in mind, to comment on the scene described:

it has often struck me that the scene itself was somewhat typical of what took place in such a reverie. The town of L[iverpool] represented the earth, with its sorrows and its graves left behind, yet not out of sight, nor wholly forgotten. The ocean, in everlasting but gentle agitation, and brooded over by a dovelike calm, might not unfitly typify the mind and the mood which then swayed it. (*Confessions*, 113–14)

'A meditation rose in me that night', Wordsworth had written, standing back from the sea of mist that covered Mount Snowdon,

> and it appeared to me
> The perfect image of a mighty mind,
> Of one that feeds upon infinity,
> That is exalted by an under-presence,
> The sense of God, or whatso'er is dim
> Or vast in its own being . . .
> (1805 *Prelude*, xiii, 66–73)

De Quincey too is concerned with the mind's feeding upon infinity (in literature, not least, where power is said to consist in the 'exercise and expansion' of the reader's 'latent capacity of sympathy with the infinite'; Masson, xi, 56), but his allegorization and Wordsworth's are as revealing in their difference as in what they have in common. Wordsworth offers an intuition, confident of its rightness. He may indeed present alternatives – 'the sense of God', *or* the dim and vast in one's own being – but that is because thinking can go no further. There cannot be a resolution. De Quincey, by contrast, asks an explanation, demands it of the God who ought to care. Why the suffering, why the graves?

The questions have the poignancy of unassuaged personal grief. We can name the occupants of those graves: De Quincey's sisters, Jane and (more especially) Elizabeth, Catharine Wordsworth, by now possibly

Klosterheim

Ann of Oxford Street as well. All loved, and loving, and dead –
unreasonably, unwarrantably dead. Why? Within the mythic framework of *Savannah-la-mar*, the Interpreter will provide his strange and
terrible answer:

'This is sad, this is piteous; but less would not . . . suffice for the agriculture of
God. Upon a night of earthquake he builds a thousand years of pleasant
habitations for man. Upon the sorrow of an infant he raises oftentimes from
human intellects glorious vintages that could not else have been. Less than these
fierce ploughshares would not have stirred the stubborn soil.' (Ward 198–9)

Limited by its gothic form, *Klosterheim* does not confront the
unassuaged grief, or see in human suffering an 'agency in the hands of
nature . . . a Demiurgus creating the intellect' (*Dark interpreter*, Ward
187). De Quincey has yet to conceive of 'the agriculture of God'. Yet the
novel is part of a movement beyond the autobiographical and
Wordsworthian into what is felt to be the deeper understanding of loss in
*Suspiria*. Passing from the room of experience into the picture that is
memory, from memory into dream, from dream into myth, De
Quincey views his grief at greater and greater depth, in larger and
stranger perspectives. *Klosterheim* has, as Coleridge says, a 'purity of
style and idiom'; it is a making of experience into fiction, a distancing of
the self, that leads on to the abstraction of story-telling in the fragments
of *Suspiria*. Significantly, De Quincey himself in the Dream Fugue
turned to music in an attempt to define the new mode. Images of the
picture within the picture, of layers in a palimpsest, were too static to
catch the fluid recurrence of theme and allusion of this writing at its
greatest:

Sweet funeral bells from some incalculable distance, wailing over the dead that
die before the dawn, awakened me as I slept in a boat moored to some familiar
shore. The morning twilight even then was breaking; and, by the dusky
revelations which it spread, I saw a girl, adorned as with a garland of white roses
about her head for some great festival, running along the solitary strand in
extremity of haste . . . vainly I shouted to her of quicksands that lay ahead . . .
only the fair young head and the diadem of white roses around it were still visible
to the pitying heavens; and, last of all, was visible one white marble arm. I saw by
the early twilight this fair young head, as it was sinking down to darkness – saw
this marble arm, as it rose above her head and her treacherous grave, tossing,
faltering, rising, clutching, as at some false deceiving hand stretched out from the
clouds . . . (*English mail-coach*, Ward 269–701)

235

# Index

# Index

Darwin, Erasmus, 2, 29–33, 81–82, 170;
  *Botanic garden*, 29, 81; *Economy of
  vegetation*, 29, 82; *Loves of the plants*, 2,
  29–33, 81–82; *Phytologia*, 29; *Plan for
  the conduct of female education*, 29;
  *Temple of nature*, 29; *Zoonomia*, 29, 81
David, king, 136–7
Davies, Scrope, 176
*Declaration of the rights of man*, 41
De Quincey, Jane and Elizabeth, 234
De Quincey, Thomas, 2, 51, 59, 198,
  201, 214, 229–35; *Confessions of an
  English opium-eater*, 123, 206, 229,
  230, 233–5; *Dark interpreter*, 232–3,
  235; *English mail-coach*, 232, 235;
  *Klosterheim*, 2, 229–35; *Palimpsest of
  the human brain*, 233; *Savannah-la-
  mar*, 232, 235; *Selections grave and
  gay*, 229; *Spectre of the Brocken*, 233;
  *Suspiria de profundis*, 229, 232–3, 235;
  *Theory of Greek tragedy*, 230–1;
  *Walladmor*, 229
Deism, 81, 132
Donne, John, 108; *The canonization*,
  108; *A valediction: forbidding mourning*,
  31–32
Drury Lane theatre, 124, 125, 127
Dryden, John, 156, 176
Dyer, George, 63, 66–67, 131, 202;
  *Complaints of the poor people of
  England*, 66

*Eclectic review*, 121
*Edinburgh magazine*, 2, 15, 210
*Edinburgh monthly review*, 163
*Edinburgh review*, 83, 112, 120, 179, 210
Education, 54
Eliot, George, 111
Ellis, George, 78; *Specimens of English
  poets*, 78
Encyclopedists, 81
*Englishman's magazine*, 223
Evans, Mary, 25, 66
*Examiner*, 112, 121, 129, 135, 136, 147,
  166, 172, 181, 203, 208

Fielding, Henry, 141, 177
Forteguerri, 156
Fox, Charles James, 47, 68
France, French revolution, 35, 37–43,
  54–55, 60–64, 65–71, 112, 114, 129;
  Directory, 82; fall of the Bastille, 34,
  35; invasion of Switzerland, 82;
  National Assembly, 37, 40, 52;
  National Convention, 61; September
  massacres and reign of Terror, 48, 57
Franklin, Benjamin, 34, 35, 39
Frend, William: *Peace and union*, 2, 47–
  50
Frere, John Hookham, 1, 2, 77–78, 81–82,
  154–61, 176; *Poetry of the Anti-jacobin*,
  2; *Whistlecraft*, 1, 154–61
Fricker daughters (Mary, Edith, Sara,
  Martha), 61; *see also* Sara Coleridge
Fuseli, Henry, 205; *Nightmare*, 32

Galignani, 211
George III, 5, 49
George IV (as Prince of Wales), 5
Gifford, William, 78, 113, 138
Gilpin, William, 1, 5–9, 27, 193, 195;
  *Mountains and lakes of Cumberland and
  Westmoreland (Lakes tour)*, 5, 6;
  *Observations on the river Wye (Wye
  tour)*, 1, 5–9,
Girondins, 22, 64, 65, 68, 114
Gisborne, John, 187
Glorious revolution of 1688, 35–36;
  Society for Commemorating the
  Revolution in Great Britain, 36–37
Godwin, William, 1, 44, 65, 70, 80, 81–
  82, 130, 132, 133, 140; *Caleb Williams*,
  57, 80; *Enquirer*, 81; *An enquiry
  concerning political justice*, 1, 51–59, 60,
  65, 80, 129
Goethe, Johann Wolfgang von, 2, 16–
  20; *Faust*, 128; *Sorrows of Werter*, 2,
  16–20, 140, 141, 204–5; *Stella*, 78,
  141, 143
Goldsmith, Oliver, 17, 24, 26; *Deserted
  village*, 26

238

# Index

# Index